THE HOUSE THAT JACK BUILT

THE HOUSE
THAT JACK BUILT

The Collected Lectures
of Jack Spicer

Edited and with an Afterword by

Peter Gizzi

Published by

WESLEYAN UNIVERSITY PRESS

Middletown, Connecticut

Published by Wesleyan University Press, Middletown, CT 06459

www.wesleyan.edu/wespress

Printed in the United States of America   5 4 3

CIP data appear at the end of the book

Acknowledgment of Copyrighted Material

"Two Presentations," by Robert Duncan, from *Roots and Branches*. Copyright © 1964 by Robert Duncan. Reprinted by permission of New Directions Publishing Corp.

Excerpts are reprinted from *The Collected Poetry of Robinson Jeffers*, Volume Three, 1939–1962, edited by Tim Hunt, with the permission of the publishers, Stanford University Press. Copyright © 1995 by the Board of Trustees of the Leland Stanford Junior University.

"O Taste and See," by Denise Levertov, from *Poems 1960–1967*. Copyright © 1964 by Denise Levertov. Reprinted by permission of New Directions Publishing Corp.

Excerpts from *The Collected Books of Jack Spicer*, edited by Robin Blaser, copyright © 1975 by the Estate of Jack Spicer, are reprinted with the permission of Black Sparrow Press.

Excerpts from *One Night Stand & Other Poems*, copyright © 1980 by the Estate of Jack Spicer, are reprinted by permission of Grey Fox Press.

Uncollected and unpublished materials by Jack Spicer are printed with the permission of Robin Blaser, literary executor of the Estate of Jack Spicer.

Grateful acknowledgment is made to *The American Poetry Review* and *Boxkite*, in which parts of this book first appeared.

Frontispiece photo of Jack Spicer courtesy of the Helen Adam Collection, State University of New York at Buffalo.

This is the melancholy Dane
That built all the houses that lived in the lane
Across from the house that Jack built.
This is the maiden all forlorn, a
    crumpled cow and a crumpled horn
Who lived in the house that Jack built.
This is the crab-god shiny and bright
    who sunned by day and wrote by night
    And lived in the house that Jack built.
This is the end of it, very dear friend, this
    is the end of us.

                —JACK SPICER

for Robin Blaser

CONTENTS

PREFACE

Acknowledgments

A special thanks to Robin Blaser for his generous support and advice, for preserving and opening Spicer's archive, and for his permission to bring this edition into print; to Donald Allen for discovering a generation and for his permission to reprint from Spicer's early poems *One Night Stand*; to Warren Tallman (in memoriam), without whom these lectures would never have happened; and to John Martin for keeping *The Collected Books of Jack Spicer* in print these past twenty-three years.

I'd like to thank my dissertation committee: Charles Bernstein, Robert Creeley, and Susan Howe of the Poetics Program at the State University of New York at Buffalo.

Because I've been working simultaneously on two Spicer projects (the lectures and the letters), the following acknowledgments reflect support for both projects. I'd like to thank the following agencies: The Graduate Student Association of SUNY Buffalo for a Mark Diamond research grant, the English department at Brown University for the appointment of Visiting Scholar (1994–1995), the Humanities division of the University of California, Santa Cruz, for a COR travel grant, and, last but not least, Robert Hunter of the Rex Foundation. I would also like to thank the following librarians and collections: Charles Watts of the Special Collections of the Bennett Library at Simon Fraser University, Robert J. Bertholf and Michael Basinski of the Poetry/Rare Books Room at SUNY Buffalo, Bonnie Hardwick of the Bancroft Library at UC Berkeley, and Emily Wolff of the California Historical Society.

Thanks to Kevin Killian for sharing early drafts of his work on Spicer's biography, for ongoing discussion, and for reading over six hundred pages of both the lectures and letters manuscripts.

Of the many who have contributed information, advice, citations, interviews, discussion, and genuine interest, I would like to thank: Bruce Boone,

Angela Bowering, George Bowering, David Bromige, Julie H. Brower, Lori Chamberlain, Joseph Conte, Clark Coolidge, Stephen Cope, Michael Davidson, Tim Davis, Steve Dickison, Ulla Dydo, Lew Ellingham, Steve Evans, Larry Fagin, Ed Foster, Raymond Foye, Alan Gilbert, Michael Gizzi, the late John Halverson, Gladys Hindmarch, Lisa Jarnot, Ricky Jay, Stephanie Judy, Joanne Kyger, Nathaniel Mackey, Graham Mackintosh, Tom Marshall, Andrew Maxwell, Eileen McWilliam, Andrew Mossin, A. L. Nielson, Linda Norton, Loisa Nygaard, Michael Palmer, Bob Perelman, Marjorie Perloff, Stan Persky, Kristin Prevallet, Jamie Reid, Aaron Shurin, Juliana Spahr, Holt Spicer, George Stanley, Catriona Strang, Ellen Tallman, Karen Tallman, Suzanna Tamminen, James Taylor, Joe Torra, Arthur Vogelsang, Tom Vogler, Keith Waldrop, Rosmarie Waldrop, Barrett Watten, Charles Watts, and John Wieners.

I'd like to thank the individuals in my classes at Brown University and UCSC who read, discussed, and "got" with Spicer's poetry. In particular I'd like to mention Chris Brignetti, MacGregor Card, Bill Gregoire, Mike Grinthal, Stephanie Hindley, Kelly Holt, Eleana Kim, Jon McCoy, Karen Pittelman, Bianca Pulitzer, Sam Truitt, and Magdalena Zurawski.

And finally, a personal thanks to Elizabeth Willis for allowing a ghost into our house, for two years of generative conversation and unconditional support, and for her assistance in preparing the final manuscript.

A Note on the Text

For such a noncanonical figure, Spicer has elicited a significant number of remarkable essays, many of which refer to the lectures. But often the text that has been cited is the abridged version of the first lecture, which was published in *Caterpillar* 12, or the excerpts printed in *The Poetics of the New American Poetry*, and a more complete edition of the entire series of talks has been long overdue. In the notes and Afterword to the lectures I have tried to illuminate various traditions and countertraditions that informed Spicer's period and to share some of the "correspondences" that occurred when researching specific facts, restricting myself primarily to books and information that would have been available to Spicer in his lifetime. The notes and commentary are by no means exhaustive, as Spicer's field of reference continues to resonate in further ways.

The difficulty of both transcribing and editing an oral or performative text into print media has been discussed by Dennis Tedlock, Jerome McGann, and others. Spicer's lectures are authentic oral texts—that is, he was not reading from notes—but they are texts in which the performative aspects of the text (the room tone, hesitations in speech, audience laughter, etc.) are of only peripheral interest. It was clear to the audience that Spicer's purpose in the lectures was literally to "tell the truth." In my interviews with them, many of the audience members expressed the sense that Spicer felt he was offering something akin to his "dying words." Given this air of finality and the importance of accurately conveying the "sense" of the lectures, I have seen my role as that of facilitating the reading and comprehension of the text as much as possible while retaining an authentic text (refraining from any extensive editing based on my own interests) and including extraneous information such as laughter only when it illuminates the degree of audience comprehension and when it displays Spicer's quick, off-the-cuff humor.

Textual editing of Spicer's words has been kept to a minimum. I have limited my involvement to the following: (1) trimming a substantial number of the text's "speech whiskers," those ticks of speech that have lost meaning by their repetition, such as umms, you knows, wells, and yeahs; (2) rearranging the few passages that contain multiple interruptions and as a result are almost impossible to follow as a written text; (3) omitting the passages of audience chatter that are blatantly off the track or are obscured to the point of being indistinguishable because of simultaneous talk; (4) making minor modifications, as when Spicer misspeaks and then corrects himself; (5) correcting, when Spicer misquotes the title of a book, for instance; and (6) making minor additions for the sake of clarity when a sentence trails off inaudibly because the conclusion is assumed.

In this project I have several predecessors. An abridged version of Lecture 1 was edited for *Caterpillar* 12, by Colin Stuart and Stan Persky. Stephanie Judy made a transcription of the Vancouver lectures for Robin Blaser which Blaser subsequently passed on to Michael Davidson, who took on the project for a time along with Lori Chamberlain. The project was passed on to me in late 1991. Stephanie Judy's transcription proved instrumental in supplying some of the names of the audience members.

Since I wanted to see the collection into print, I decided to begin by re-transcribing all four lectures, then using the other various versions for assistance when a passage was unclear to me. I made another draft inserting paragraph breaks, trimming speech whiskers, and listening again for possible errors. I then edited the entire text, making minor adjustments for clarity and grammatical correctness. Finally I listened to the tapes again, restoring a few of the "whiskers" that mark Spicer's speech, cutting back a few of the more intrusive cul-de-sacs in the passages of group discussion, and attributing names to those voices identified by others attending the lectures.

Pauses are marked in the text with sentence and/or paragraph breaks in order to preserve as much of Spicer's phrasing and emphasis as possible — except where it seems to be a pause for deliberation where there is no break or shift in content.

I have used brackets sparingly to mark a break in the tape recording of the lecture (which may constitute a break in continuity) and to insert information for purposes of clarification where the emphasis is clearer in spoken form or where the references would be unclear to someone outside of Spicer's circle.

The Appendix to this volume is made up of miscellaneous prose from Spicer's archive. It includes two pieces from UC Berkeley's *Occident* magazine: a short, humorous review of Henry Miller's *Remember to Remember* and "The Poet and Poetry — a Symposium," Spicer's first public talk, delivered in 1949. Also reprinted here are three essays by "John L. Spicer," the name Spicer used for this small opus of literary scholarship and for his one published article in linguistics. While working in the Rare Book Room of the Boston Public Library, Spicer was asked to review and assess volumes purchased by the collection. Included are his reviews of Thomas Johnson's three-volume edition of *The Poems of Emily Dickinson*, with a "Correction," Wimpfeling's *Adolescentia*, and a sixteenth-century German edition of *The Legend of St. Meinrad*, all published in the *Boston Public Library Quarterly* in 1956 and 1957 and later collected by Spicer as a pamplet. All footnotes in the Appendix are Spicer's. The Appendix concludes with an interview conducted by Tove Neville within the last month of Spicer's life and published in the *San Francisco Chronicle*.

KEY

ONS	*One Night Stand & Other Poems*
CB	*The Collected Books of Jack Spicer*

From *The Collected Books of Jack Spicer**:

AL	*After Lorca*
A	*Admonitions*
FFG	*Fifteen False Propositions Against God*
ASSNR	*Apollo Sends Seven Nursery Rhymes to James Alexander*
LM	*Lament for the Makers*
HC	"Homage to Creeley"
TP	"A Textbook of Poetry"
HG	*The Holy Grail*
L	*Language*
BMV	*Book of Magazine Verse*

From the Lectures:

I	Vancouver Lecture 1: Dictation and "A Textbook of Poetry"
II	Vancouver Lecture 2: The Serial Poem and *The Holy Grail*
III	Vancouver Lecture 3: Poetry in Process and *Book of Magazine Verse*
IV	California Lecture: Poetry and Politics

* Page references in the text reflect the pagination of *The Collected Books*.

INTRODUCTION

Although the American poet Jack Spicer was born in 1925 in Los Angeles, California, he claimed his birth year to be 1946, when he met the poets Robert Duncan and Robin Blaser at the University of California, Berkeley. Out of the intense fraternity of these three eccentric young men, dubbed the "museum poets" for their bookishness, was born the "Berkeley Renaissance." Spicer would spend the rest of his life in the San Francisco Bay Area, with only a few brief departures. Most notably his excursion to New York and Boston in 1955–56 would prove to be a defining moment in the development of his poetic vision, as it further solidified his allegiance to the American West and his identity as a California poet. He lived in San Francisco and worked as a researcher in linguistics at UC Berkeley until shortly before his death by alcohol poisoning in 1965 at the age of forty. He is survived by roughly four hundred pages of poetry, some still unpublished; a detective novel; a handful of essays; some two hundred letters; at least three plays; four lectures, which were given shortly before he died; and a legacy of poets and readers to whom these lectures were and are delivered.

The four lectures took place within a thirty-day period from June 13 to July 14, 1965. The casual seriousness of these talks is typical of Spicer's public style and should not be interpreted as offhand; they are the only authoritative account of his poetics outside of his poems and letters. Although Spicer was noticeably intoxicated and disheveled, he took these events seriously and made sure that they were being taped. As transcriptions of oral texts recorded at the end of the poet's life, the lectures gain a certain oracular power and finality: Spicer's statements are not prophetic but contrary, allusive, and purposeful. His humor or "wicked wit," as Warren Tallman put it, is charismatic. He has that particular gift of being both irreverent and to the point. As a public speaker he is not the "roman candle" type, as he disarmingly claims in the second lecture; instead, he says, he simply wants to be honest, and this struggle sometimes ties his sentences in knots. He writes to Graham Mackintosh before giving a lecture in 1954: "There's a big difference between talking as a teacher, which is easy, and talking as a poet, which is heartbreakingly difficult if you want to talk honestly." Because of the difficult honesty of their pitch, these talks are also riddled with disappointment and uncertainty about the future of the poet — that is, the poet as a cultural figure in general and the poet as Jack Spicer in particular, a highly intelligent, lonely, middle-aged, gay, baseball-loving alcoholic, one of the great poets of his time, recently unemployed, dying, and at the height of his poetic powers.

The first three of these talks, which have come to be known as Spicer's lectures, were announced in Vancouver as "semi-public readings with commentary," and formally they retain the quality of talking marginalia on Spicer's own poetry as he attempts to discuss his poetic practice and life experience with his audiences. While Spicer foregrounds the practice of writing poetry, there is an avuncular tone throughout that shows Spicer's deep concern with the business of being a poet, particularly a young poet, who must learn how to manage the destructive force of the poem.

At times the surface of the talks seems resistant to both newcomers and initiates. Because they are offered as "readings," some familiarity with Spicer's work — particularly the poems he reads — is necessary to grasp the extensive network of references he enacts within the course of the talks. As he says in Lecture 1, the poems are right where the commentary is wrong. It becomes clear by the final Vancouver talk that he is at times less interested in delivering an exposé of his practice than in getting some feedback about his poetry from the audience. As a good teacher he wants to see whether or not they've "got" it, and as a poet he wants to begin to establish a vocabulary through which to discuss it.

The spirit of the talks is essentially that of Spicer's "letters to a young poet." He is sympathetic to the concerns of the young and is aware of their struggle for reality. In *Fifteen False Propositions Against God*, he writes from an abiding concern for the community of youth:

> Trees in their youth look younger
> Than almost anything
> I mean
> In the spring
> When they put forth green leaves and try
> To look like real trees
> Honest to God my heart aches when I see them trying.
>   (FFG, 90)

It is well documented that Spicer spent much of his last decade with younger poets; he held court by day at Aquatic Park and by night at the various local bars in North Beach. He was not overly encouraging to young people who wanted to be poets. One of the repeated statements in Lecture 3 is his line from *Book of Magazine Verse*: "kid, don't enter here," echoing Dante's inscription over the gates of Hell. The statement functions as a warning to the young about the practical dangers and uncertainties of choosing a life in poetry—a life that, Spicer admits, can never live up to the expectations of popular legend or Romance and like a Grail quest is bound to end in failure or in a success so limited that it amounts to failure.

The struggle for meaning and identity is, of course, not limited to the young, nor is the difficulty of bringing order and openness to the experience of writing. In his talks, Spicer tries to outline in a general way a method he considers useful for his audience members, a machinery that is available for each of them to engage with their own material. As he says in Lecture 3: "I don't expect anyone to trust me on this thing, but I would like to see people experiment and see what they can do in terms of their own lives."

Spicer himself is, in part, a product of the 1950s white, masculinist, postwar America, with all its "honor" and disappointment. On the surface he is sometimes xenophobic and recalcitrant, and in certain ways he is an unattractive figure of cultural production. But the turbulent humanity that is everywhere manifest in his poetry makes the achievement of his work all the more remarkable—even a triumph.

In the context of his times, Spicer was not beatnik but bohemian, a mixture of California "funk" or "junk" assemblage and high aesthetic practice. Like the compositions of the visual artists Wallace Berman, Bruce Conner, and George Herms, his poetry dissembles and rearranges rather than declaims. Spicer wasn't easily assimilable even within the counterculture of the period, represented at the 1965 Berkeley Conference by Allen Ginsberg on one hand and Charles Olson on the other. What John Ashbery says of Frank O'Hara can be applied to Spicer in his time: he was "too hip for the squares and too square for the hips . . . a category of oblivion which increasingly threatens any artist who dares to take his own way, regardless of mass public and journalistic approval" (6). This condition is not new: in 1852 Baudelaire describes Poe as being of that *genus irritable*, suffering from a "tyranny more cruel and more inexorable than that of a monarchy, namely public opinion" (Baudelaire, 40, 136). Like Poe, Spicer is of that genus of American artists who are only marginally understood in their own period but whose work appears increasingly contemporary and increasingly necessary as time goes on.

In fact, Spicer has all the curious attractions one needs to become a cult figure: minor status in his life, alien to most middle class conventions, unhygienic, singular to a fault, and absolute. Though cult status is a highly esteemed position in American mass culture, it is an unfair label to give any artist, as it disregards the enormous effort and patience that go into art-making in favor of a perceived authenticity. It is also a highly impractical status to negotiate—a fate Spicer would have wished upon no one, least of all himself.

What is interesting about these documents is the fact that in spite of his almost annihilating contrariness, Spicer presents himself as more of a traditionalist than an innovator. He discusses some of his own sources and suggests that poets should not only read poetry but bring new information to poetry, all the while following his practice of dictation (outlined in Lecture 1), composing serially (Lecture 2), creating a community through poetry (Lecture 3), and not "selling out" (Lecture 4). Though these talks remain imperfect utterances, they are the work of an original poet inadequately trying to shed light on an extremely private and ancient practice—one that borders on the devotional, the hermetic, the populist, and the absurd.

By maintaining the question-and-answer format within the lectures, Spicer shows how difficult it is to talk about poems in a public forum and how little it has to do with the actual writing of good poetry. It does have something to do with the culture of poets, though, a society both imaginary and real, of which Spicer was an outspoken citizen. Speaking to audiences composed mostly of young poets and students, he expresses his suspicion of poetic professionalism and the certain loneliness and doubt that attend poetic composition.

The first three lectures were delivered as a series ($2 each or $5 for the series) at 2527 West 37th Avenue, the house of Warren and Ellen Tallman in Vancouver, British Columbia, in June of 1965. The room the lectures were given in was a large living room, perhaps twenty by fifteen feet. Spicer stood in the corner and spoke to the people seated in the room and on the adjoining staircase. There were somewhere between fifteen and twenty-five people attending on any given evening.

Warren Tallman, who organized the event, was a professor at the University of British Columbia. In 1963 Tallman, along with Robert Creeley, then in Vancouver as a visiting lecturer, had put together a poetry festival that included Creeley, Charles Olson, Robert Duncan, Allen Ginsberg, Denise Levertov, Philip Whalen, and the Canadian poet Margaret Avison. It was a defining moment. Young American and Canadian poets came from all over the continent to check out the news.

In January of 1965, Spicer was invited to Vancouver to read with Lew Welch at UBC's annual Vancouver Festival. Gladys Hindmarch recalls Spicer's reading as magical, with students sitting silently through their lunch period to listen to him read from his book *Language*. When Spicer expressed how much he liked Vancouver, Warren Tallman invited him to return that spring and stay with them. In mid-May of 1965, Spicer, Robin Blaser, and Stan Persky read their poetry at the New Design Gallery.[1] Spicer stayed on with the Tallmans, delivering the first three lectures in Vancouver in mid-June. The audience at the Tallman house was made up of Warren and Ellen Tallman; their daughter Karen; the established poet Dorothy Livesay; the violinist Harry Adaskin; UBC professor Elliott Gose; a lively group of young poets and students, many of whom were connected with UBC, *Prism*, or the poetry newsletter *Tish*, including poets Peter Auxier, George Bowering, Judith Copithorne, and Jamie Reid; fiction writers Angela Bowering and Gladys Hindmarch; filmmakers Sam Perry and Dennis Wheeler; and the anthropologist Neep Hoover and his wife Leni.

The fourth and final lecture was given a month later to a larger audience in an auditorium at the Berkeley Poetry Conference put together by Richard Baker, Thomas Parkinson, Donald Allen, and Robert Duncan in July of 1965. The '65 Berkeley Poetry Conference was in part a response in the United States to the success of the previous Vancouver event. Included along with the American participants from the 1963 Vancouver Conference were Ted Berrigan, Robin Blaser, David Bromige, Ed Dorn, Ken Irby, Joanne Kyger, Ron Loewinsohn, Ed Sanders, Gary Snyder, Jack Spicer, George Stanley, Lew Welch, and John Wieners.

---

1. For more on the New Design Gallery reading see Lecture 2, note 3. Robin Blaser and Stan Persky would ultimately move to Vancouver, as would George Stanley, another poet of the Spicer circle. In 1975 Blaser was responsible for editing *The Collected Books of Jack Spicer*, which includes all of Spicer's mature work from *After Lorca* (1957) to *Book of Magazine Verse* (1965). It also provides one of the most substantial extrapoetic documents of the New American Poets: Blaser's essay "The Practice of Outside."

Thinking and writing about Jack Spicer is not unlike a Grail search. His statements are mercurial, and his lines refuse to be pinned down into a stable system of meaning. His poems repeatedly disrupt even their own procedures by jamming the frequencies of meaning they set up. All these conditions make their discovery and placement in critical terms not impossible but beside the point. Like the Grail, what Spicer's work accomplishes is not any declared goal but the assembling of a community of peers for a specific and unified purpose. Introducing Spicer's last public reading at the Berkeley Conference, Thomas Parkinson characterized Spicer's effect in a way that befits his legacy:

I was trying to think of what it was that Jack does for people who've known him long and rather deeply. I think that one of the things that he always does for us is to ask that we do our better work. In this sense, I suppose that Jack has been a conscience for many of us at points when we might not have done our better work and we might have settled for something less. And I think this is a very important thing that he does for all of us. And seeing his own work, which is always his better work, and which becomes, to my sense at least, better as he goes on, is a constant rebuke to those of us who are likely to do less than we should.

The exacting demands of Spicer's "better work" are, in part, the product of his ability to embrace paradox and his willingness to listen. In fact, the clearest message that emerges from these lectures is the importance of the poet's listening—to a community, a culture, a crisis, a human condition, the commotion of the imagination—past personality, personal gain, or even authorial intention, in order to apprehend the "uncomfortable music" of the poem. Spicer is not merely a satirist critiquing metaphysical belief systems, nor is he a zealot investing in tropes of the sacred to bolster up evidence of an invisible world. He has made a synthetic world in which the immanent and empirical coexist. Where the two polarities intersect, Spicer composes his Real.

By being purposefully inexact and giving a paucity of detail and slightly bizarre examples of poetic composition ("Martians," etc.) within the lectures, Spicer allows for a meaning that is much more unwieldy than a more systematic thesis would allow. Instead he defines many of his terms negatively and even defines his own practice by how it differs from that of his peers. He allows contradictions to arise—particularly the contradictions that his poems themselves manifest. In so doing, he creates an emptiness, a center, which no one can own. Like the city square of Paul and Percival Goodman's *Communitas*, this center is available to everyone, providing a structure to which we are *all* marginal.

THE HOUSE THAT JACK BUILT

Dictation and "A Textbook of Poetry"

JUNE 13, 1965

🐌 Given on the hundredth anniversary of William Butler Yeats's birth, the first of the Vancouver lectures begins with a mixture of humor, tension, and seance-like charm. The structural correlation of Yeats's being visited by spooks and Spicer's being visited by Yeats takes on a magical significance in the context of a lecture about poetic sources, voices, and ghosts: Spicer introduces Yeats as his poetic precursor—his ghost father—and his poetics perform a kind of serious play (like *Hamlet*) in which the living are responsible for carrying out the desires of the dead. Spicer presents his poetic practice as an act of "dictation" that engages the dead in the economy of the living. He describes it as both a "dance" and a "game," but the dance is a *danse macabre* and the game is a ball game in which you play for more than your life.

In the course of the lecture, Spicer places himself in opposition to both Romantic and symbolist poetics by disavowing the notion of the poet as a "beautiful machine . . . almost a perpetual motion machine of emotion until the poet's heart broke or it was burned on the beach like Shelley's" (I, 5). Spicer insists that the poet does not drive the poem; the poem drives the poet. Instead of becoming a master of words, the poet is mastered by words, which "turn mysteriously against those who use them" (HC, 125).

The lecture also provides a useful account of Spicer's sense of his own immediate context and perhaps for this reason it has been the most quoted of the four lectures, thanks to the printing of an earlier version in *Caterpillar* 12 (July 1970). Instead of focusing on poetic invention, Spicer introduces an idiosyncratic genealogy of poetic reception beginning with Yeats's automatic writing on a train ride through California in 1918; backtracking to Blake; whistlestopping with Pound, Williams, and Eliot; moving on to Spicer's contemporaries Charles Olson, Robert Duncan, Robert

Creeley, and Robin Blaser; and arriving at Spicer's reading from his own "A Textbook of Poetry."

But the genealogy of poetry presented in the lecture is not simple, and Spicer uses the work of his peers to further define his own practice by negation. The only poet who escapes Spicer's thorough critique is Robin Blaser, with whom he seems to be in such agreement that at times he speaks for both of them. It is important to note, however, that when Spicer spars with his contemporaries it is not to denigrate the work of his peers. His poetry and letters repeatedly make it clear that an exchange of poetic judgment is also a way of expressing respect and reciprocity.

In this light, one of the interesting moves in this lecture is Spicer's identification of Olson as someone whose practice is closer to his own than Creeley's or Duncan's—an unusual assertion since in Lecture 4 he identifies Olson as one of the "bosses" of poetry, corresponding to President Lyndon Johnson. Likewise, while Spicer expresses dissatisfaction with Denise Levertov's writing of poems around a "great metaphor," he says so within the context of seeing her as a "good poet." And his sparring with Creeley comes in the context of their common ground: they both use the same term—"dictation"—to describe their writing experience in different ways.

In discussing the poetics of his contemporaries, Spicer reveals the differences and affinities within their practices but keeps his own model of composition open and even contradictory. According to Spicer's motley procession of metaphors, the poet is a host being invaded by the parasite of the dictating source of the poem; this source is "Martian"; the poem is the product of a dance between the poet and his "Martian" source; the poet is like a radio receiving transmissions; poets exist within a city of the dead; "spooks" visit poets with messages from hell; and the poem itself becomes a hell of possible meanings.

Within this agglomerate of multiple figures, Spicer opens the discourse of poetic composition by placing dictation outside of any fixed taxonomy and by refusing to claim his practice as an incontrovertible or absolute good. What distinguishes Spicer's model from the "English department" version of poetic composition is in part its disruption of the hierarchy of inspiration. For Spicer, the dictating sources or "spooks" come across to the poet rather than coming down from an inspired and orderly Heaven. They are disruptive on every level—meaning, syntax, diction, narrative form—and are not easily dominated by theory. In fact, the game he has created is so good that not only poets are subject to the strange reversals of language; words turn against everyone who uses them.

In this war of meaning, the critic gets drawn out of safe hiding and into the Open or Outer Space of Spicer's vocabulary. By insisting on a "low" vocabulary to discuss his poetics, Spicer draws the critic outside the safe clinical territory of authorized critical discourses and into the language of baseball games, popular movies, TV, and bar talk. The purposeful absurdity of his terms of poetic composition are a kind of "no trespassing" sign, a Crowley-like warning to the uninitiated, or a Cerberus to the underworld of the poem.

Since the poet's dictating source is neither god nor muse, there is no way of knowing if the intruding figure (the radio broadcast, the parasite from outer space, the "Martian") is any better or smarter than the poet caught in this outrageous entanglement. This game between the material and invisible worlds places the poet in the embarrassing position of merely following orders from a beyond. But, Spicer assures his young audience, the best condition for the poem is one of not-knowing, and the poet has a better chance of that with dictation than with self-expression. The better the poem, the less responsible the poet is for it. So Spicer wages battle with the creative ego in terms that remain provocative in an age still searching for poetic authenticity and identity.

In spite of his futuristic language, Spicer proposes an extremely traditional (*not* to say conventional) view of poetry, emphasizing the guild-like aspects of the art, and even using antique metaphors like mountain climbing throughout the lectures. He foregrounds the endurance it takes to wait for lines and to be generally available for the poem. Because the ground of poetic composition and community is difficult and unstable, Spicer's proclaimed goal in this and other lectures is to prepare younger poets for the hardships of poetry, to help them manage themselves to become more durable and less afraid to fail against the absurd demands of the poem.

JACK SPICER: Well, I really ought to explain the structure of the three lecture/readings, more than is on the flyer that some of you saw. Essentially what's going to happen is that each evening I'm going to read some of my work. In each reading there's going to be a discussion of the problems that have to do with poets as far as I see what the problems are with poets. And they're pretty much in order of importance. I think the problem of poetic dictation is perhaps the first problem a poet has. The second problem—one you can't really "get" too well without understanding what poetic dictation is or isn't—is a serial poem. And the third lecture on Thursday night will be a sort of an autopsy or a looking at the growth of a poem I'm writing now—the problems of a person in the middle of a poem, what comes up to make things different. In other words, I'm rather assuming that all of you are interested directly as poets in the writing of poetry, and I'm not going to talk about aesthetic theory except where I think it has something to do with the problems of anyone writing poetry.

Now, tonight is rather an interesting time to discuss poetic dictation. It's Yeats's birthday. He'd be a hundred today if he weren't up there with the big skywriters in the sky. And Yeats is probably the first modern who took the idea of dictation seriously. And he might be a good person to start out from, seeing as how—although I don't know why a birthday should be so important—it still is his birthday.

He was on a train back in, I guess it was 1918. The train was, oddly enough, going through San Bernardino to Los Angeles when his wife Georgie suddenly began to have trances, and spooks came to her.[1] He'd married at the age of forty-five, something like that, a rather rich woman who everyone thought he married just because she was a rich woman and Lady Gregory was getting old and wasn't about to will him money.[2] Georgie was in the tradition of the Psychic Research Society and all of that, and so naturally they would come in the form that the Psychic Research Society would think spooks would come in.[3] And she started automatic writing as they were going through the orange groves between San Berdoo and Los Angeles.

And Yeats didn't know what to make of it for a while, but it was a slow train and he started getting interested, and these spooks were talking to

him. He still, I'm sure, thought that Georgie w
him. He probably was in a nasty mood after ha
try on the Southern Pacific, which I imagine in
than it is now. But he finally decided he'd asl
spooks as Georgie was in her trance. And he ask
He asked, "What are you here for?" And the sp
to give metaphors for your poetry."

That's something which is in all English depe
it was the first thing since Blake on the business
ing from the outside rather than from the inside. ...... words, instead
of the poet being a beautiful machine which manufactured the current
for itself, did everything for itself—almost a perpetual motion machine of
emotion until the poet's heart broke or it was burned on the beach like
Shelley's—instead there was something from the Outside coming in.

Now, the difference between "We have come to bring metaphors for
your poetry" and what I think most poets who I consider good poets today
believe—and this would include people as opposite in their own ways as,
say, Eliot on one hand and Duncan on the other—is essentially that there
is an Outside to the poet. Now what the Outside is like is described differently by different poets. And some of them believe that there's a welling up
of the subconscious or of the racial memory or the this or the that, and they
try to put it inside the poet. Others take it from the Outside. Olson's idea of
energy and projective verse is something that comes from the Outside.

I think the source is unimportant. But I think that for a poet writing poetry, the idea of just exactly what the poet is in relationship to this Outside, whether it's an id down in the cortex which you can't reach anyway,
which is just as far outside as Mars, or whether it is as far away as those
galaxies which seem to be sending radio messages to us with the whole of
the galaxy blowing up just to say something to us, which are in the papers
all the time now. Quasads, or . . .

Q: Quasi-stars.[5]

JS: Something like that. At any rate, the first step is reached, I think, with
Yeats. But the way that it works—"We have come to bring metaphors for
your poetry"—this is like "we have come to bring fertilizer for your
fields," that kind of thing. You know, "well, you have such nice poetry,
Mr. Yeats, and we spooks have come down from above to give you
metaphors to hang it on to."

is not really what happens in my own experience, and I'll be about my own experience most of the time. But I think I can also for the experience that others I know have had in dictated poetry. I think the first kind of hint that one has as a poet—and I must confess I was, as Karen [Tallman][6] would say, a retard in this respect—is after you've written poems for a while and struggled with them and everything else, a poem comes through in just about one-eighth of the time that a poem normally does. That's the first experience. And you say, "oh well gee, it's going to be much easier if I can just have this happen very often."

So then you write seventeen or eighteen different things which are just what you're thinking about at that particular moment and are lousy. It isn't simply the matter of being able to get a fast take. It's something else. But the fast take is a good sign that you're hooked up with some source of power, some source of energy.

Then the next thing is you suddenly figure out, well gee, when I've been wanting something, say I'm in love and I want to sleep with this person and, you know, the normal thing is, with a fast take, you write all these things down with an idea of, essentially, a way of selling a used car. [Laughter]

And this doesn't work.

So one day, after you've had this first experience, which just was something you couldn't imagine, and the poems haven't come this clean, this fast—and they don't usually, in dictated poetry anyway. Again, suddenly, there comes a poem that you just hate and would like to get rid of, that says exactly the opposite of what you mean, what you have to say, to use Olson's thing in one of its two meanings.

Olson says the poet is a poet when he says what he has to say. Now, you can read that two ways: what he "has" to say, namely "I want to sleep with you honey," or "I think that the Vietnam crisis is terrible," or "some of my best friends are dying in loony bins," or whatever you want to say that you think is a particular message. That's the bad thing.

But what you want to say—the business of the wanting coming from Outside, like it wants five dollars being ten dollars, that kind of want—is the real thing, the thing that you didn't *want* to say in terms of your own ego, in terms of your image, in terms of your life, in terms of everything.

And I think the second step for a poet who's going on to the poetry of dictation is when he finds out that these poems say just exactly the opposite of what he wants himself, *per se* poet, to say. Like if you want to say something about your beloved's eyebrows and the poem says the eyes should fall out, and you don't really want the eyes to fall out or have even any vague connection. Or you're trying to write a poem on Vietnam and you write a poem about skating in Vermont.[7] These things, again, begin to show you just exactly where the road of dictation leads. Just like when you wrote the first poem which came easily and yet was a good poem, a poem beyond you. In the second stage you then say, oh, well, then I'll just write this thing and I'll take a line from someplace or another, or use a dada or a surrealist technique (in a different way than I'm going to use the word "surrealism" tonight, but the French surrealist way of placing things together, taking the arbitrary and all of that) and that won't be what I want to say, and so that'll be great. That'll be hunky dory.

Unfortunately, that doesn't work terribly well either. You have to not really want not what you don't want to say. It's a very complicated kind of thing. You can't play tricks on it. That's the second stage.

The third stage I think comes when you get some idea that there is a difference between you and the Outside of you which is writing poetry, where you feel less proud of the poem that you've written and know damn well it belongs to somebody else, that your wife had the child by another father, and the wife being inside you, which makes the metaphor rather bad.

But then you start seeing whether you can clear your mind away from the things which are you, the things that you want, and everything else. Sometimes it's a twelve-hour struggle to get a ten-line poem, not changing a single word of it as you're writing, but just as it goes along, trying to distinguish between you and the poem. The absolute distinction between the Outside and the inside.

And here the analogy of the medium comes in, which Yeats started out, and which Cocteau in his *Orphée*, both the play and the picture, used a car radio for, but which is essentially the same thing. That essentially you are something which is being transmitted into, and the more that you clear your mind away from yourself, and the more also that you do some censoring—because there will be all sorts of things coming from your mind, from the depths of your mind, from things that you want, which will foul up the poem.

For example, mediums always have to have the accents that they were born with. There's a medium who's supposed to have been in contact with Oscar Wilde, and she—I think mediums are almost always, if not always fake, but just pretend that mediums were real because some of them may be, particularly in primitive tribes—she got all sorts of epigrams and they came out in Cockney because she only spoke Cockney.[8]

Now, if you have a cleft palate and are trying to speak with the tongues of men and angels, you're going to still speak through a cleft palate. And the poem comes distorted through the things which are in you. Your tongue is exactly the kind of tongue that you're born with, and the source of energy, whatever it is, can take advantage of your tongue, can make it do things that you didn't think it could, but your tongue will want to return to the same normal position of the ordinary cleft-palate speech of your own dialect.

And this is the kind of thing that you have to avoid. There are a great many things you can't avoid. It's impossible for the source of energy to come to you in Martian or North Korean or Tamil or any language you don't know. It's impossible for the source of energy to use images you don't have, or at least don't have something of. It's as if a Martian comes into a room with children's blocks with A, B, C, D, E which are in English and he tries to convey a message. This is the way the source of energy goes. But the blocks, on the other hand, are always resisting it.

The third step in dictated poetry is to try to keep as much of yourself as possible out of the poem. And whenever there's a line that you like particularly well, which expresses just how you're feeling this particular moment, which seems just lovely, then be so goddamn suspicious of it that you wait for two or three hours before you put it down on paper. This is practical advice and also advice that makes you stay up all night, unfortunately.

But even if you're not interested in poems as dictation, you will find, two or three years later, that the lines you liked best when you wrote them were the ones that screwed up the poem. The poem was going one way, and you had this beautiful line. Gee, it was a lovely line, and just expressed how you felt at the particular moment—and oh lord, how lovely!

But at the same time, you are stuck with language, and you are stuck with words, and you are stuck with the things that you know. It's a very nice thing, and a very difficult thing. The more you know, the more languages you know, the more building blocks the Martians have to play with. It's harder, too, because an uneducated person often can write a better poem than an educated person, simply because there are only so many building blocks, so many ways of arranging them, and after that, you're through. I mean, the thing behind you is through. And it can make for simplicity, as in good ballads, American and English. In the long run, it can make for really just good poetry. And sometimes for great poetry, an infinitely small vocabulary is what you want. Perhaps that would be the ideal, except for the fact that it's pretty hard to write a poem that way.

But the more building blocks, the more you have to arrange your building blocks and say to the Martian, "Oh no, Mr. Martian, it doesn't go this way. That spelling p-r-y-d-x-l doesn't make any sense in English at all. We'll change it around." And then you make an anagram of it, and you spell what the Martian was trying to say. The more building blocks you have, the more temptation. The more you know, in a university sense, the more temptation there is to say, oh yes—yes, yes, yes—I remember this has to do with the Trojan War, or this has to do with this, this has to do with that, and so forth.

But on the other hand, given a source of energy which you can direct, you can direct yourself out of the picture. Then given the cooperation between the host poet and the visitor—the thing from Outside—the more things you have in the room the better if you can handle them in such a way that you don't impose your will on what is coming through.

And that's the whole problem you have in modern poetry—the fact that most poets from, say, nineteen to twenty-seven that I know, who are good in San Francisco, are really against education because they know that education is essentially going to fuck them up because they can't resist, if they have all of these benches and chairs in the room, not to arrange them themselves instead of letting them be arranged by whatever is the source of the poem.

Now, Creeley talks about poems following the dictation of language.[9] It seems to me that's nonsense. Language is part of the furniture in the room. Language isn't anything of itself. It's something which is in the mind of the host that the parasite (the poem) is invading.[10] Five languages just makes the room structure more difficult, and also, possibly, more usable, but it certainly doesn't have to do with any mystique of English or anything else.

Duncan's business of words and their shadows and sounds and their shadows seems to me again taking the things which are in the room rather than the things which are coming into the room. And it seems to me that, essentially, you arrange. When you get a beautiful thing which uses the words and the shadows of the words—the fact that "silly" once meant "blessed" instead of "silly" as it now does, something like that—you ought to be very distrustful, although at the same time the thing which invades you from the Outside can use it.[11]

Now the other kind of thing, other than Olson's energy, which to him is not something from a great galactic distance out there but something you plug in the wall, and it's really the machine which is the converter of the electricity which makes another machine work, and so forth. And I don't agree with that either, but I go nearer to that.[12]

Then there's finally Williams, who sees in objects essentially a kind of energy which radiates from them. The fact that this chair has a chairness, a nimbus around it, a kind of an electrical thing which gives energy enough so that it can be transformed almost directly—*it*, the thing that the chair in its chairness radiates—into poetry.[13]

And all of these things I think are perfectly useful explanations of it. I prefer more the unknown.

Well, now this is in introduction to the whole problem. Now I would like to see whether I can get some questions from you people before I start out on "A Textbook of Poetry," which in some ways contradicts some of the things I've said. But it is right where I'm wrong.

Q: If a poet were listening to what you had said, and he said no, this is all wrong, I do it myself, is he not writing poetry then?

JS: Well, now which is all wrong?

Q: The whole idea, this whole sense of a medium, of the poet as host to the visitor. He'd say no, I'm the visitor myself as well as the host. I control everything, and nothing outside of me controls it.

JS: Do you really feel that, completely, in your poetry, that . . .

Q: No. No, this is a hypothetical situation.

JS: Well, I just have never met a poet who's gone beyond just, you know, the first couple of years of poetry, who would say that. Really. Including academic poets. I mean, even academic poets I think would have some high-faluting thing and they'd quote Coleridge and all of that, but essentially, I don't think that anyone who's a practicing poet, even a practicing bad poet, who's done it for a long enough time, would disagree with the fact that there *is* something from the Outside. I mean, you get this in Longinus for christ's sake, all of these pretty square people going all the way back. Saint Thomas Aquinas says it, and you can't have anyone who's farther away from poetry than him. But I do think that an awful lot of poets feel at the back of their minds that they would really rather express themselves. "This poem is me. I am this poem," you know, and so forth.

Q: Yeah. Maybe that's more what I meant, that it's behind you, yet you write a poem that you know damn well is you, and you're not letting it come in. Is it a poem then? Maybe what I mean is, is that the only possible source that one can accept?

JS: Well, can you think of a poet who would demonstrate that? I mean, I'm a real practical person, and you know these "iffy questions," as President Roosevelt used to say. You know, if your aunt had balls she'd be your uncle, but . . . [Laughter]

Say Pope, for example, he would seem to be a person who kept his own identity all the way through. You take the great things of Pope's, *The Rape of the Lock*, for example. There are some things which come through that you just would swear that this little hunchback who was interested in politics could not have written, and that must have scared the hell out of him. And this is the kind of wit that only a ghost could make. "Why has man not a microscopic eye? / For this good reason / Man is not a fly."[14]

I really do think that it's probably true for all the arts, but I think it is true for poetry, that anyone who's doing anything more than just dabbling on the surface, trying to write diaries essentially, and so forth, has this feeling, and even if he tries to resist it, it's pretty hard.

WARREN TALLMAN:[15] Well, Jack, in Duncan's poem "Two Presentations," he mentions the Hindu girl on the bus. Can this come from other people? Or does it come from out of the blue?[16]

JS: Well now, that's another thing which probably should be mentioned here. I think Robin Blaser's poetry is an example of this. I don't know how many of you people were at the New Design Gallery when he read. I think, from what I've seen, that there's no question that objective events *can* be caused in order for poems to be written. In *The Moth Poem*, Robin had moths just coming in the wildest places, where the odds would be about a million to one of the moths being just exactly in the place that he wanted the poems written. But I was there a couple of times when it happened.[17]

And I think that it is certainly possible that the objective universe can be affected by the poet. I mean, you recall Orpheus made the trees and the stones dance and so forth, and this is something which is in almost all primitive cultures. I think it has some definite basis to it. I'm not sure what. It's like telekinesis, which I know very well on a pinball machine is perfectly possible. And the Duke experiments have not shown it impossible at all.[18]

As for the physical world reacting, you don't know really. But, yes, I think that you do have things happen simply because the poem wants them to happen. No question about it. And how this operates, I haven't the vaguest notion. You could probably figure it out scientifically if you knew enough about the science of chance, combination, permutation, all of that. I don't know. But I know that it has happened. It's happened less to me than it has to other people, and I think it's happened more to Robin than to Duncan, who tends to fake up a few things like any good medium does. [Laughter]

Q: What happens if the poem wants you to happen?

JS: I think both you and the poem explode. [Laughter] No, really, it's like saying what happens if a farmer wants a cow to happen, you know. The farmer wants to milk the cow. The cow is to be milked. And I suppose there could be a kooky farmer that wanted the cow simply to remain in its cowness. But I don't really know what would happen except the cow would get awfully sick after a few days of not being milked.

I just don't think that whatever the source of energy is gives really very much of a damn about you. It wants to keep you in good condition, just like the farmer wants to keep the cow in good condition. Or the butcher, or the rancher, and then the butcher wants to keep the steer in good condition until it's butchered.

GEORGE BOWERING:[19] You said that the visitor is limited by the tongue of the host. I'm thinking of the Pentecostal church where people go into a state and start speaking with the tongue of God and something that they don't recognize themselves. And this has been taped, in an experiment in Seattle a couple of years ago.

JS: Yeah, I'd have more respect for that except that a few years ago at North Beach John Ryan and I decided to start talking in Martian, just to bug the tourists.[20] And after a while we could actually converse in Martian to each other, with no recognizable linguistic things or anything else. But right now I could speak in tongues and it wouldn't be anything but some kind of a switch that you can pull. It's perfectly possible for me to fake an unknown language. So I don't know. On the other hand, the experience of Tzara and others may mean that there's some way there.[21] I just don't really believe in it too much because— *hyem beggedy skreet um ik schudt merdit tek umpolsya. Ishne betronya temp? Gah. Kushnee pad ta* [Martian].

GB: But I can look at you, you know.

JS: *Daschnye bootl pont.*

GB: You've got another language going at the same time too, you know, with gestures . . .

JS: *Gol sidneye pudya padya. Spa!*

GB: But these people are . . . [Laughter]

GLADYS HINDMARCH:[22] Jack, I was going to ask you if you've ever had the experience of having a line that you're satisfied with at the time that then you did like later, and that wasn't going in the other direction—a direction other than what the poem was. I think you're so definite about, if you're pleased with it, then it is wrong.

JS: Well, everybody as a host to this parasite has a different reaction. But my thing is that I write it down too fast to be pleased with it. If it's really a good line that I liked, then I'd see that I liked it after the whole thing was through. In other words, if there's no resistance, if the thing saying the thing is exactly what the host wants to say, the host just doesn't have any feeling that he's said anything. It goes through like a dose of salts.

Q: That could sound as if you were so busy writing it that you had no time to stand back and make a judgment on it.

JS: Yes, but on the other hand, there are plenty of times when you're so busy writing it and you have to wait for two hours because the thing is coming through in a way that seems to you wrong. It may be that you hate the thing that's coming through so much, and you're resisting it as a medium. Or it may be that the thing which is invading you is saying, "yeah, well that's very nice but that hasn't anything to do with what this is all about." And you have to figure that out, and sometimes it takes a number of cigarettes, and occasionally a number of drinks, to figure out which is which. And it's a dance in some way, between the two. And you often fall on your ass—hit the wrong one.

GH: What you're saying is that you shouldn't interfere with it?

JS: No. You have to interfere with yourself. You have to, as much as possible, empty yourself for this. And that's not noninterference. I mean, it's
almost an athletic thing. It takes a huge amount of practice to be able to
avoid blocking a person when you're not supposed to block the person on
the play, when you're supposed to let him in to be mousetrapped. It takes
a huge amount because you have this natural impulse. You know. Anyone's coming by, you block him. And the business of being able *not* to do
something, especially things which are so important to you, are you, takes
a tremendous amount of patience. And it doesn't take humility, since I've
never seen a humble poet.

Q: Jack, where do ideas fit in this discussion? I have the feeling that you're
talking about writing a poem starting with virtually nothing and letting it
come as you start to write it, and this is when you talk about the thoughts
coming straight through. What happens if you have an idea to begin
with? How would that fit into the discussion here? If you have an idea that
you want to develop and individual lines wouldn't count as much as the
overall effect?

JS: Well, what I'm trying to say is if you have an idea that you want to develop, don't write a poem about it because it's almost bound to be a bad
poem. You can have an idea that you want to develop, and the poem develops an idea which is a little bit different. Say, like Pope's "Essay on
Man" which was supposed to please Bolingbroke enormously and didn't,
and didn't please Pope. I'm using just about the so-called most disciplined
poet there.[23]

   I mean, you can really start out with an idea that you want to write
about how terrible it is that President Johnson is an asshole, and you can
come up with a good poem. But it will be just by chance and will undoubtedly not simply say that President Johnson is an asshole. And it will
really have a meaning entirely different from what you started out with
the idea of.

   I mean, if you want to write a letter to the editor, then the thing to do is
to write a letter to the editor as far as I can see. And it doesn't seem to me
that's what poetry is for.[24]

DOROTHY LIVESAY:[25] You said this thing was like a dance. Then it really is
the rhythm, more than anything else, that's coming through, not words,
not ideas.

js: Well, it's the rhythm between you and the source of the poetry. You have to dodge here, it has to dodge there, and all of that. And you're going to make some missteps. And maybe the source is just as bad as you are. I've never been able to figure that one out. I mean, this Martian, this ghost, this whatever the hell it is, may be just as dumb in its own way as you are and may misstep too. But since, when you're dancing you worry about where you misstep, not how your partner does, you try to adjust your step to your partner's. So it is in this sometimes horrible interlocking of you and the poem. And the you just has to—well, it doesn't lead.

Q: Then would the poet not be a creator? But the poem itself would exist outside the poet in sort of a spiritual existence, wouldn't it?

js: You mean can we take credit for our poems? Well, is a radio set a creator of the radio program?

Q: No. Well, that's what I mean.

js: Yeah. But at the same time you don't get the radio program if the radio set has static in it.

Q: Oh no, no. But the poet is an agent then, or . . .

js: Well yeah, like a mother is, yeah. But you know, it's pretty hard for a father to have a baby. I mean, good agents are kind of hard to find these days. I don't really see that it's anything less to be proud of to be a good agent.

Q: Oh no.

js: No. I really honestly don't feel that I own my poems, and I don't feel proud of them.

Q: Well, you start saying, well, I'm going to write a poem, you know, and sit down to accomplish that, and you're just letting yourself interfere completely.

js: Not necessarily. It depends. I'm usually suspicious if I want to write a poem, if I figure, oh this would be just a great time. I've had a lousy time at the bar. I'm frustrated, everything else. I'd feel great in the morning if I had a poem.

Well, I know very well that this is a lousy, lousy time to write a poem. But occasionally, after an hour or so of me trying to write the poem for the poem, a poem nudges me on the back and starts coming through. And by that time it's sunup and I'm real pissed off at the whole thing because, really, if I'd known it would be that late that I'd have to work, I'd rather have gone to sleep instead, and not have the glory of it, you know.

But it depends, I think, on the person. Everyone's a different kind of host, and I can just tell you about my own experiences and no one else's. And I think that the general things I've outlined are true about dictated poetry.

Q: Is it the great poem that scares the poet?

JS: Yeah. It says something that the poet not only didn't mean to say but doesn't quite understand, or draws back from and says, "oh yeah? But this isn't right." Or the poem, when you're trying to seduce somebody, will make the person run five miles away screaming.

Q: Where does this put the audience? You know, like if it scares the poet, how does the audience fit around this?

JS: To begin with, I don't think that messages are for the poet any more than the radio program is for the radio set. And I think that the radio set doesn't really worry about whether anyone's listening to it or not, and neither does the poet. The poem may have some Nielsen ratings of its own. It carries on in the middle distance somewhere. But I don't really think the poet ought to worry about that.

On the other hand, I think the poet ought always to bring the poems, read the poems, to an audience, simply because often he can find things from the audience's reaction that he didn't understand the poem said, which tell him something about it. I mean, it's just as important to be able to understand your own poetry as someone else's. And most poets I know, including some that I admire, don't read their own poems. I mean, they read them out loud to audiences, but they very seldom read them back to see what the things are that would scare them about them. They just, you know, put them in orphan asylums. Grove Press and that kind of thing. Just leave them there and get fifty bucks for 'em and you know—a baby farm.

Q: I don't see where this theory would allow for individual abilities though.

JS: Well, I think the individual abilities are the same as the individual abilities in sainthood.

Q: I wasn't thinking of, say, individual ability with the radio. If you have a number of radios tuned into a source, then the same material would come through from each radio.

JS: No, it wouldn't.

Q: Good hi-fi sets or bad hi-fi sets.

Q: Well, okay, you're talking about a source now. Are you talking about a source for you and a different source for him and a different source for him, or are you talking about a universal source?

JS: That's what I don't know. I would guess so offhand. Spirit mediums get five or six different programs playing almost simultaneously, and there are some which are definitely against the spirit medium—the little Eva voice and the so forth and so on.[26] I would guess that there are a number of sources, but I have no idea what they are, and frankly I don't think it's profitable to try to find out.

But as far as the radio sets are concerned, it's not a good analogy now because even the worst transistor is built pretty good. But if you take the first days of radio, I imagine the difference in transmission of signals and static and so forth would have been enormous. And I would think that we probably always will be crystal sets, at best.

WT: Jack, in the 1940s in Berkeley, did you and Duncan share this process you are talking about now, or is this something that's occurred much later as a way of writing poetry, or a kind of poetry?

JS: I don't think that either of us had intellectualized it or come to grips with it, no. I think that the more you write poetry and the more you see what poetry has to do and doesn't have to do with your own life, the more you get to that. And we both got to it at an earlier age than Willy Yeats did. Still, I don't think that any intellectualization of the thing really matters too much, but I do think that if you keep your ideas closed and your mind open, you have a better chance by and large.

DL: What about the dream? Do you dream poems, wake up with them?

JS: No. I dream that I'm writing poems sometimes. But I've never woken up with any lines from them.

DL: This does happen. How would you relate that to what you are saying?

JS: I don't know. I mean, there are all sorts of physiological mechanisms in the human being that are pretty difficult to understand. Dreams are certainly one of them.

The only experiences I've had with dreams is dreaming about what happened the next day in just as idiotic a way as if it had happened the day before. You know, if somebody loses a pencil and you can dream it either the day before they lost a pencil or the day afterwards, and in both cases it doesn't have anything to do with anything. I mean, it's just because they lost a pencil. So, what do you get from that? At least that's my experience with dreams. But I guess other people have had different experiences. It's perfectly possible. Drugs, the same thing. I've never been able to get anything out of drugs, but some people have.

Well, let me now read if we can get this light on. Because essentially some of this will deny what I've said, because it's only my intellectualization of what I know myself, well, not as one that's being dictated to at the moment.

This "Textbook of Poetry" is the third part of *Heads of the Town Up to the Aether*, which is a complicated book. It's all one book. I'm going to break it up into three sections because I want to simply take the message of it rather than the serial nature of it. Next Tuesday, this coming Tuesday, I'll talk about the serial poem in terms of *The Holy Grail*, another book, and how things all connect.

The three books in *Heads of the Town Up to the Aether*—the "Homage to Creeley," the "Fake Novel About the Life of Arthur Rimbaud," and finally, "A Textbook of Poetry"—all connect in very important ways. But I think the only thing that I have to tell you is that, in a sense, the first book, the "Homage to Creeley," was on the analogy of Dante's *Inferno*; the second book, the "Fake Novel About the Life of Arthur Rimbaud," is analogous to the *Purgatorio*; and "A Textbook of Poetry" is analogous to the *Paradiso*.

And there are images that come through here that have been reinforced. The "Homage to Creeley" is based almost entirely on Cocteau's *Orphée*, the second book on the biography of Rimbaud, and the third book on sort of the wisdom of the thing. Throughout the whole book runs the business of the pathway down into Hell and the methods of communication — the radio, the dead letter office, and the fake novel. And finally, this "Textbook" which is printed as if it were prose and has to be read more or less as if it were prose.

Okay, now, this is arbitrarily going to be broken into three parts. I'd like you people to listen to the first part and not listen to it as poetry, which you can't really get unless you read the whole book. But listen to it for what it says and what we've been talking about and for differences between what it says and what I say. And there are some differences. This, I think, is as near to dictation, without interference from me, as I've written.

[Reads from "A Textbook of Poetry," 1–10 (TP, 169–73)]

What does that say that I didn't say? I think quite a bit. Curious your reactions.

Q: I'd say it's mystical for a California climate.

JS: Oh. Yeah. Well. We get many climates in California. [Laughter]

Q: Before you started reading, you said that these were dictated thoughts, that they weren't your own.

JS: No. They were not dictated thoughts. They were dictated poems.

Q: Dictated poems. But they weren't your own. I mean, you didn't organize these thoughts or consider them before you went to write the poem?

JS: No.

DL: Well then how do you relate it to the film?

JS: Oh, *Heads of the Town* consists of three parts, and this is the third part. So far, there's one mention of the previous parts to come in, the Eurydice thing. But no, this has nothing to do with the film whatsoever.

DL: Then you don't know how Eurydice got in there.

JS: Well, she's been there for three thousand years. Yes.
    Was it because you can't take poems as messages, or that you can't . . .

DL: I can't take it as being something not a part of yourself.

GB: The main trouble I have is that there's an awful lot of abstraction in this part of the book, more than there is in the other part.

JS: Yes. Yes.

GB: And I have a hard time with the abstractions if they're coming at me in a lineal fashion as they have to come when you're reading aloud. That is, I can make it better on the page if I'm allowed to go back and forth, and go from here to there. The best part that I can catch when you're reading is the business about the rope trick because then I have an object and recognizable people that come to me as image so that, you know, it gets into my head a lot faster.[27]

Q: The same with the circle.

WT: Jack, I don't know the Dante well enough. You call this "A Textbook of Poetry."

JS: Mm hmm.

WT: Are these instructions? Or are they cantos? Or are they stages?

JS: Well, you're asking things in terms of the serial quality of the poem, which I'd rather answer next time. The point is, what I was hoping was that you'd see contradictions between what I was saying and what the poem was saying.
    You're right, George, that it goes too fast really, when reading, to do it. But the kinds of things which are picked up are of interest to the poet. The things where the mind stops and the contradictions develop.

GB: I think it's also because I have a hell of a time with abstract words. I have a hard time with abstract things, you know, like an imagined dog instead of a real dog, or a dog I see, a saw-with-my-eye dog. And then I have a further difficulty with abstract words.

JS: Yes. This is a poem essentially about the abstract Word, the Logos, in the beginning was the . . .

Q: Maybe I really missed it, but the low ghost—I'm not sure whether that's the medium that's trying to get through or whether it's the poet who's screwing up, like the medium who's the high ghost.

JS: Have you read this poem before?

Q: No. First time I've heard it.

JS: Well, you just made one of the puns that this poem makes a little bit later, which is remarkable. And George's dog—there's an imaginary dog in the poem, too, which frightens the hell out of me. [Laughter] Maybe we'd better turn on the lights and take a second take. I don't know. There've been three comments that anticipated the poem. Your California one too. You won't get all of them in the second part.
   [Reads "A Textbook of Poetry," 11–19 (TP, 174–78)]
   That's the second part. You can turn the light off again.

Q: The thing about soul and flesh—I think you said you have to be soulless? You have to get rid of the soul or something. But then you said that it's important to brush up against the flesh. Your flesh?

JS: Well, yeah.

Q: That's a contradiction.

JS: No. No, in the first place, these poems are largely using the incarnation of Jesus as a metaphor for poetry. Metaphor means, you know, bearing across, which is a nice pun in itself. And the soul and the body are two things which both have to be incarnated in the kind of poem which goes through. It's not necessarily the same soul. In other words, the soul of the poet is not the soul rubbing up against.[28]
   I've been trying deliberately to break the poem tonight so that you would listen to the part of the poem which has to do with what poems are about, rather than to the poem itself. Doesn't seem to be too much response to this kind of thing.

PETER AUXIER:[29] Well, you were talking about the city. And then cities became a metaphor. It sounded like real cities, like San Francisco, Vancouver, and then this was a place where there were, what, cities of poets?

JS: Cities of anything.

PA: Yeah.

JS: "Chittering human beings." Yes. Communities. Like this is a city at the moment.

PA: And I got a funny, strong sense that you felt that—or that the dictation said that—poems and poets were very much a communal thing and it wasn't a soul battling with the dead.

JS: The sole worshipper, yes.

PA: Or that is part of the communal thing. And that's where the dead come in.

JS: Yes. There is the City of God, the *civitas dei* of Saint Augustine, which all of the cities, including the glass palace, in some way mirror and are imitations of. And the City of God is a metaphor just like Christ is a metaphor, borne across. It's the ideal city as compared to the real city.

This group here, which is just an arbitrary division of the full twenty-nine parts into threes, is essentially, I would say, about the relation of the poem to the audience, and the poets to the audience. You will notice that the ghosts also inhabit the cities, and the cities develop ghosts after they develop slums.

PA: That's where I got confused about Heaven, which is what I plugged in for city at one point.

JS: It *is* plugged in for it. Just like "the word" is sometimes capitalized and sometimes lower case. There is confusion between the City of God and the city; the *communitas* and the *civitas dei*.

WT: Borne across as a metaphor.

JS: Yes. Transfer in Latin.

WT: But does it also have to do with birth? Born, to bear?

JS: No. No, no, no. Neither the Greek nor the Latin used it that way.

WT: Well, something's been dictating to you. No, I don't mean this seriously, but your speech is interspersed with birth and . . .

JS: Could be. I don't know.

WT: I mean your conversational speech.

JS: Oh, I see.

WT: Not the poems, but just when you lay back, give birth . . .

JS: Well, I can't *bear* the thought of that. [Laughter]

WT: Okay. [Laughter]

DL: Could I ask how this concept of the City of God—the various definite metaphors that are there—how you came to see them? Did you see them as the poem was being written?

JS: I tried not to. When I'm writing a poem, I always try not to see the connections. If you remember in the previous part I read, one of the poems ended with "Teach." And the next poem had "Taught. As a wire. . . ." The pun did not occur to me while the poem was going on.

DL: Coming back to look at it you saw it?

JS: Yeah, you have to kill your animal before you stuff it, and looking at it is the stuffing of it.

DL: That section about the puzzle of your grandmother's is so extraordinarily personal, as if it's a recollection.

JS: It was.

DL: Then how do you say you want to put yourself out entirely?

JS: No. What I'm saying is—just like I said the Martians could take these alphabet blocks and arrange them in your room—you have the alphabet blocks in your room: your memories, your language, all of these other things which are yours which they rearrange to try to say something they want to say. They are using my memories. In the dictated poems of any poets I know, their memories are used, naturally, because that's all there is to it.

I mean, when I say Martians, it's just to be funny. But just to make it even funnier, suppose Martians were trying to communicate. They couldn't really say "*pnixlz* on the *prazl*" and so forth and so on. They would have to use your own memories of what your things were rather than theirs.

And so, the nearest relationship I can see—or that the Martian can see is, that if my grandmother chewed up the jigsaw puzzle, which was in her bedroom when she died in the living room, it could mean, in different people's memories, different people's terms, almost anything. Which is why poetry is hard to translate.

Q: These messages are coming in code, really. You're not getting the precise terms of the source. You're getting the terms that you're forced to work within.

JS: Right. Right. Right. Right. Right.

Q: So it comes in a kind of code. But in a couple of poems I heard a couple of distinct voices. Or a sense that there was somebody, something who said one thing and then something else said, "Screw you."

JS: Yes, that's printed as a separate voice. Wasn't it odd that you people predicted three of the metaphors in the poem?

DL: The low ghost.

JS: The Lowghost, the invented dog, and the California thing.

Q: The high ghost.

JS: Yes, the high ghost as well.

GB: I read the book about three years ago, but I didn't remember the dog. I remembered the lamp image and the Indian rope, but I didn't remember the dog. Maybe I did without knowing it.

JS: Yeah. That takes you out of the thing. Still, the Lowghost.

Q: How do you know which voice is which?

JS: Oh you don't, except that there are two voices, the one being against human love and the other being against divine love. And so it's rather simple to keep them apart, on account of the fact that . . .

Q: You know, it might be the same voice just putting on masks.

JS: Yes. All I mean is that in the poem they're divided by a big dash, you know, starting out one voice, starting out the other. That's all. And the "Imagine this as lyric poetry" at the end of that is sort of the clash of one voice against the other, using, I suppose, the dichotomy of the human and divine love that's in my poetry generally, and is particularly in the earlier sections of this book.

Well, we might as well go to the last part.

GB: Jack, at the end of that part when it says that the Lowghost is reduced to using words—that really sounds to me carefully said by yourself. That portion. When did you become conscious of Logos as Lowghost?

JS: Well, I was very unhappy with it, because it sounded so funny. That was one of the lines that I waited for two or three hours. I can see it now fairly well.

You see, the Word, the Logos is—and this is impossible to read out loud, just like the whole personification thing is—the word is half the time with capital W, uppercase, and half the time with the lowercase w, you see. And so Lowghost then becomes Word. In other words, the words which are being used are simply a reflection of the Word, with the capital. And the pun doesn't get as funny when you have him pinned to the cross, and the business of the shadow—which was written, incidentally, on Good Friday, for some obvious reason.

Let's try the last section now. (These are not sections in the book. They're just sections of selection.)

[Reads " A Textbook of Poetry," 20–29 (TP, 178–83)]
That's the end.

Q: What happens when the sources disappear?

JS: You either write bad poetry or you stop writing. Until they come back.

Q: And you would say that there isn't much hope in chasing them because you might find them or the people in there just might run away
harder. Is that it?

JS: You have to keep a kind of lookout for them. You can't catch them like
canaries by putting salt on their tails, but you sort of give them an even
chance. I mean, show them there's a good dinner of blood like in the
Odyssey where they dug the trench and slit the throats of the sacrificial
animals. And all of that is likely to summon them.

Q: Well, you have to be available and vulnerable, in that case.

JS: Yeah. That's one of the problems.

Q: Well, what I was directing the question at simply was your tension
about finding out what the sources are. You say you don't ask questions.
Why don't you ask questions? It seems to me if you could name the
sources you might be able to get closer to them.

JS: Well, I think the answer to that is this. I think it's a fairly good answer.
You'd have to read some of the things I've read. E. M. Butler's *Myth of the
Magus* is a good example of those people who wanted to understand what
the sources were and summon them down—like Faust is a good example—and generally got messed up by them.[30] You have to be much more
gentle. Otherwise they destroy you. And I suppose there's nothing wrong
with that because time destroys you anyway. In the meantime, though,
you do get some poems when you have a nonaggression pact with whatever it is.

Q: Jack, somebody said that the problem with Faust, though, was that he
should have gone through with it, that he shouldn't have been afraid of
being damned, that that was all right too—to be damned.

Q: You have to be able to take the consequences of practically anything.

JS: Take what you want and pay for it, says God. But there are some things that you can buy that cost you a hell of a lot more than you think they cost. I don't know. I just have never seen anyone who messed with finding things out. I mean, philosophy about it is fine. Making lovely statements, writing essays doesn't hurt anybody. But the closer you get to it the worse off you get, and the more it eats into you.

It's like the ring in Tolkien. It's a pretty powerful juju. Better not mess with it too long, and better stay away when you've used it.

Q: Getting back to this idea of the creative insights being isolated from the medium. Are you saying that all poetry has to be written this way, or that some poetry is written this way, or what?

JS: Well, I certainly don't know. If you mean it as a recipe for baking a cake, obviously no. If you mean believing in all of this, obviously no. But it's my firm conviction that all poetry, good poetry, is written this way, in spite of the poet.

Q: The reason why I mentioned that is—this isn't meant as a criticism, but—in these poems, I think part of the reason why there was silence after the first reading that you gave is that in a lot of your poems one line will convey a powerful lot of information, and the next line conveys very little. And it works sort of back and forth, that you've got bits of insight coming through here and then, it seems to me that, unless the line would take an awful lot of study, it doesn't seem to say very much that directly connects to anything. And my thinking on this is that if someone took the idea and sat down and labored it and labored it, and worked it over until he solidi-fied it, then, first of all, he's not writing mediumistically, and secondly, he has an idea that he begins with and works it into the poem, which is the exact opposite of what you're saying. And yet, it would seem to me that's one way of writing a poem.

JS: Well, it's one way a lot of people write poems, including good poets. However, I think that when they do write good poems, the other thing sneaks in.

Q: Yeah?

JS: Ron Loewinsohn is a typical example in San Francisco.[31] He's written some very good poems. He would tell me the plots of poems he was writing: I'm going to write a poem about Willie McCovey and there'll be this and this and this, and there'll be this sequence, without having written the poem.[32]

Jeez Ron, I mean, why don't you write a short story or a letter to the editor? And usually it doesn't work out. Occasionally it does. And occasionally the thing gets through and the poem about Willie McCovey doesn't turn out to be about Willie McCovey at all and doesn't have the same point he wanted.

It just seems to me a bass-ackwards way of doing things, to try to get your ideas in first and then let the ghost knock 'em down. But I haven't the vaguest notion whether that's the only way of writing poetry. I think that for Duncan, Creeley, Olson, me, and Ginsberg when he was writing poetry, that was a way. And Williams too, in his own funny sense, where he thought of the objects as the source of energy, the magickers, rather than anything else. Especially in *Desert Music*, where the objects were taken over by something else.

I don't think there's one formula, but I do think that the simplest thing for a poet is not to try to say I have a great metaphor, and I'm going to put it down on paper and expand it. Well, the only good poet who I think does it to some extent is Denise Levertov, and the poems I like of hers are all poems that scared her and that she didn't really want to have written.[33]

Q: I still want to talk some more about the sources, the ways they have of making themselves known, and the way they have of coming out in the world. Now, like poetry isn't everything. There must be other ways, equally, where the spirits or the Martians can become active, or can code their activities, or code whatever messages they're trying to get out in this world. I mean, they can code it into the way that you're walking down the street just as well as they code it into a poem. And then something about Gertrude Stein fits here too, where she said that all writing except that which will describe objects in motion will be poetry some time in the future. Very soon, she felt. And what describes objects in motion will be prose. There seems to be a connection there somewhere.[34]

JS: Well, I don't know. I'd have to think about that Stein.

WT: Jack, earlier you were talking about the way language figures in this process, and you were voicing some criticism of Creeley's notion of how language figures. I'm still not clear on this since language so clearly figures so powerfully as your medium.

JS: Well look, Warren, let's just take it simply first, with words. Let's just do it that way. And then we can go to language because language is a complex system which involves word, gesture, and all of that sort of thing, and it's a higher abstraction than words.

WT: All right.

JS: The point is that words are not something which in themselves are anything but Lowghosts, instead of the Logos. Words are things which just happen to be in your head instead of someone else's head, just like memories are, various other pieces of furniture in this room that this Martian has to put the clues in.

Now language is a more complicated thing, but at the same time, it is a structure. It hasn't yet been scientifically described, and it's doubtful if any two people have the same language. I'm now speaking as a professional linguist and not as a poet. And it seems to me that it simply is another layer of stuff that the Martians have to penetrate and have to work with.

Please don't get me wrong. Martian is just a word for X, you know. I am not saying that little green men are coming in saucers and going into my bedroom and helping me write poetry. And they ain't.

But I think that it's just a higher level of abstraction than the one that Duncan uses and is less usable because Duncan's at least includes Pound's way of getting to this thing, where Pound simply uses history in its ultimate sense. Not history the way it was in that discussion we've heard, but history in the sense of everything connecting to everything else. When Duncan talks about words, he does it the same way: that you follow back the word and so forth. That you can follow back a word to its source. You can't, unfortunately. But even assuming you could, you'd get something which was, well, some nice furniture to work with, but no more than furniture, as history is.

The second book of this thing, the "Fake Novel About the Life of Arthur Rimbaud," is essentially about history, which Duncan—I said "Duncan" instead of "Dante," goodness—which Dante's *Purgatorio* is also essentially about. And the business of history is an important thing, but essentially it's furniture.

wt: That's what I still don't understand.

js: Well, I think essentially that it's an accident that I have this history in my skull instead of some other history which is absolutely alien to me.[35] But the poem could be written through just as easily. And if I were an Uzbek poet of the ninth century, I would have a history which would be just as usable in poetry and everything else.[36] And if I knew that the Uzbek word went back to the Tocharian, which came from Indo-European invaders and all of that, it really wouldn't matter terribly too much. It's just one of those things.

The words are counters, and the whole structure of language is essentially a counter. It's an obstruction to what the poem wants to do, and the more you understand about the words and understand about the structure of language, the easier it is for you to see where the obstructions are and prevent them if possible from interfering with the message of the poem. But that's about all I think you can do with it.

And you have someone like Eliot who was really just hung up by this and wasn't able to write any poetry after *The Waste Land* on account of it because he thought he didn't know enough history. He'd gotten a few historical things and so he thought, well gee, I'd better write plays because I don't know enough about what my Muse is.

Obviously all these things are important for human beings and since I'm a human being, some of my best friends are too. But I don't think that ultimately that's as important as just cleaning things up so that the invaders, the things which are parasitical on you and create poems, can come in.

wt: Well, let me push this just a little bit further. For instance, among this word furniture, you have a kind of quote wicked wit, just in the words—just, you know, knocking around in the furniture. Does this interfere with the messages?

js: Yeah. I'm always suspicious when my wit comes in. Those are the places where I pause the longest, and undoubtedly sometimes it does come in. I don't think it did in the Lowghost thing, although I would say that was one of the places where I paused the longest.

You're talking about a glass, and you have an inkwell and the two things they have in common are they can be filled with a liquid and spilled. And there's kind of an incongruity about it because you would never drink out of an inkwell and you would never dip your pen into a glass. And if you put an inkwell and a glass and fill them both up with something, you show in some ways how things are related even though they don't seem to be.

And this is the kind of a thing which the pun does. It gives interconnections between things which do have interconnections but you don't really know about them until you've had them given to you that way, and generally in an absurd way. I think that the pun not only has to do with the magic of words, which we still have as relatives of the ape, but also it has to do with our recognition that things are like other things and words can sound alike and it can be something which brings you closer to the nature of reality as well as being quite funny.

I mean, let's take a typical pun. The guy who jumps off the twentieth story window and the guy on the fifteenth story looks at him and he yells, "You got vertigo?" And the guy who's falling yells back, "No, only about fourteen more stories."

Well, now, this is incongruous. It causes great pain and everything else. But it connects the two kinds of things—the observer from the window who wondered why the guy fell out of the window, and also the guy falling out of the window. They're both part of an existential moment, and "vertigo" and "far to go" bring them together somehow. And it has something to do with the experience of witnessing death.

WT: Also, since it was fourteen stories it was obviously a writer. [Laughter]

JS: Yes.

Q: What happens when the poem is concerned with the poet?

JS: Well, it all depends. I think that in good poems where the poem's concern seems to be with the poet as poet, say—like Marianne Moore's "imaginary garden with real toads in it"—the poem ain't. It's about a lot more things than that. It's about the whole business of being able to go by the imagination into whatever other worlds there are, where the real toads can't eat the flies of the imaginary garden, and the imaginary garden doesn't even feel the step of the real toad.[37]

Do you have an example of what you mean?

Q: What I mean is if the medium is saying something about the poet, I feel that the poet may be caught in a paradoxical situation.

JS: He is, yeah. Except for the fact that the poet is not exactly the person who's there the next day, you know, going to his job or talking to friends or getting drunk in the bar. The poet that the poem is talking to is something rather different. I can't remember any good advice that I've gotten from one of my poems, that helped me be any happier or any better or sleep with any more people or get any more money or anything else. Poems are pretty useless for anything like that. The advice that they give is just not interested. It's like somebody treating you fairly abstractly. At least I've never had any experience with a poem that I wrote that was really interested in my welfare, namely what I want, my happiness, or anything else. It's usually been the opposite way. They've kicked me in the teeth a few times, but they never really helped me much.

Q: Does that include your audience too?

JS: Does what?

Q: Well, I've always thought the audience can grow from the poem, and you're saying that a kicking in the teeth may be a kind of growing?

JS: I'm not really getting you. You mean people who read your poems— what effect they have on you?

Q: No. What effect your poems have on me, for example.

JS: Oh!

Q: They should help me, shouldn't they?

JS: Well, they don't help me. They might help you as a poet or something like that. I don't really know what they're for. I can't imagine why these dumb Martians are doing all of this. It's probably some funny game they play.
    But in some sense, they do, actually. There's, I guess, a deep place where the poems do have instructions for the poet that do matter, even if the poem ultimately says, "jump off the Golden Gate Bridge."
    In that sense, I was really thinking of, you know, the day-to-day things that one does. It's the day-to-day things. I'd reply the way that Jimmy Walker who was mayor of New York replied when there was an anti-vice

investigation on dirty books in the twenties. He said to the committee that was considering censorship regulation, "I never saw a girl who was made pregnant by a book."[38]

And, on the other hand, there have undoubtedly been girls who, by the effect of a book, in the long run, have been made pregnant. But it's kind of a real secondary sort of thing.

Q: I mean, when you write a poem and it scares you, and it's a good poem, therefore it's going to affect your thinking or your actions or something. And also your audience, like when you read a poem and all of a sudden the poem scares you. It's got to do something to you because if it doesn't do something to you, what's the sense in its existence?

JS: I'm not sure that there is any sense for a poem's existence. I wish I could tell you the opposite. I would say that I'm sort of an agnostic in this thing one way or the other. I'm not sure. I simply know that I have to write it like that.

It's a very funny thing. It probably has to do, again, with the pieces of furniture in the room. But it seems to have shaped the last twenty years of thinking. I remember when I was a kid I used to like to climb mountains with a guy who was in the Sierra Club who climbed mountains, and he had heard about Mallory and Irvine and all of this business of climbing up Mount Everest and disappearing and Mallory, I guess, saying "Because it's there." This struck me as one of the wildest, most far-out things in the world. Now kids nine years old use it. It's become a part of our way of thinking of things.[39]

But in a sense, I think it's one of the few things that we, spanning the couple of generations there are between you and me, have in common. The answer to the question of the poem is the same answer that Mallory answered to "Why do you climb Everest?" Not to get to the top, or to make an important scientific discovery but "because it's there."

WT: But your Everest is the spirit world. That is, evidence of that is there.

JS: Yeah. Yeah. But I doubt if . . .

Q: It's the ghost. No, it's the Heaven that sounds like it's there, not the city, that always comes through like a goal or a distant place to be reached. But the immediate presence is the ghosts always, who are much more earthly sounding in your poems, like they're there.

JS: Yeah. Well, they're there. Yeah. You connect.

Q: . . . Or it's one of the things you're faced with, it seems like.

JS: Unfortunately. But after all, they had abominable snowmen up on Everest.

Q: Is it the ghosts that scare you?

JS: No. They're sort of no more scary than an audience. [Laughter]

DL: What do you expect of an audience?

JS: What I expect from an audience is that I learn something about what parts of the room I have to clear out that I haven't cleared out already.

DL: That's to say it's a feedback to you?

JS: Well, yeah. I suppose that if a good poet made money like, say, a good drummer or a good singer or a good real estate man or a good used car dealer, he might feel more guilty that he uses an audience for his own purposes, although I haven't seen used car dealers feel particularly guilty.

But, no, I think that one of the better things about a poet being in the kind of economic state that he is in—and has been in for about a thousand years—is the fact that really he personally doesn't give a damn about the audience except how the audience can, in turn, help him clear away the lumber that's stuck in the room. They can make things clearer simply by reactions here and there. You know, where the reactions themselves don't mean anything, and no one else in the audience would get it.

In other words, the poet may try, like "our favorite Martian," to communicate the poem like the Martian communicates the poem to the poet.[40] And there's of course a loss in intensity and amplification and all of the other things, where you have a relay station. But he does it. I don't know why the Martian does it, but he does it for pretty damn selfish reasons and reasons which don't have too much to do with the audience, although I've noticed that when there aren't people around who are interested in my poetry that it hurts my poetry. But interested would mean attacking it as well. The thing that I get the least out of is someone saying, "oh, Mr. Spicer, that was a beautiful poem." I cringe up like that because that is one thing I don't give a damn about.

WT: Jack, could you go back? Blake evidently was a solid sender, or receiver.

JS: Yeah, except when he decided that he was a solid receiver, then he started writing those damn prophetic books which I have gone through two, three times, and I can't make any poetry out of them whatsoever. I mean, I can make poetry every once in a while, see it happening. But when Blake really was sure that the angels were speaking to him, they stopped speaking. It just may be my blank on Blake, but God knows I've tried. You get up and then you start these damn things that the angel gobbledygook and the angel so-and-so and so-and-so, and it is the river of light, and the something is shining in the something or other. I'm sure I could compose a Blake prophetic book on a computer with a very little bit of programming for the tape.

WT: What do you think he was doing? Just hallucinating or something?

JS: Well, no. I think he got the idea that he was writing prophetic books all right. And so he started writing prophetic books. I think the angels had already left him. Take *Songs of Innocence and Experience*, or take the kinds of thing that he jotted down in the flyleaves and the margins of the books he was reading while he was writing this what seems to me ghastly stuff. He wrote some just marvelous things. I remember, there's one thing which I don't think is included in Blake's Random House *Collected Works*. He put it in, I think, Johnson's *Lives of the Poets*, just on the margin. He put "The eighteenth century, the bat on leathern wings, winking and blinking, winking and blinking, winking and blinking like Dr. Johnson."[41]

All this time he had the angels going on in big lines and, you know, snakes and all that kind of thing. I don't know. There have been plenty of things I've rejected before which I finally found something in, and Blake may be one of them.

DL: Well, what about Blake's language in the poems that probably are really sent? The language fits into meter and rhyme.

JS: Sure.

DL: Yours don't, but in certain places you have rhyme. What I'm trying to get at is how conscious or unconscious, how from the outside it is.

JS: Well, if you were to take a rhymed poem versus an unrhymed poem of

Blake's, there'd be more likelihood the rhymed poem would be good, than the unrhymed poem, although there are some great unrhymed poems. Still if you just selected by odds . . .

WT: All the *Songs of Innocence and Experience* are terribly, heavily, conventional rhyme.

DL: I'm just asking where do you believe this rhyme comes from?

JS: Well, if you recall the business of the "Screw you" thing—it rhymed to show us the sense of time as a kind of thing which goes on and on, and it's part of the furniture. It's part of what I as a linguist would call language, just like sentence structures which change century by century are, or anything else. It's a kind of a linguistic convention which they can use. It's the kind of furniture in the room. And the furniture in the room a hundred years ago is different than it is today.

Rhyme was a radical thing when it came in, in the eighth century, terribly radical. All of the really cultured poets thought it was just awful and attributed it rightly to Gothic influence and these dirty Oakies from the hills, the Germanic tribes who didn't use rhyme themselves. Rhyme is one of the things which is used linguistically by poets, and poets now use rhyme pretty damned functionally. They use rhyme the way you'd use italics or caps or some other sort of thing.

DL: Or a pun.

JS: I do think there's a difference in puns because I do think that puns connect things up more than rhymes do, or rhymes tended to do. That was one of the troubles with rhyme. I prefer, as a convention, Old English alliterative verse to rhymed verse though I wouldn't like to have to write in either of them. Rhymes, for my ears, don't work terribly well. I've written plenty of rhymed poems, but . . .

DL: No, I was just trying to see how you felt about a Martian using this.

JS: I think you have to get your house prepared for him. And the thing that you're most comfortable with. It doesn't really matter terribly. That sort of formalism is just a question of where you have the most freedom and where you don't.

DL: But a sonnet is a very conscious form. Now is this conscious form done by the Martian? Or is it done by the poet after the Martians leave?

JS: The Martian says, look, I have to get into this goddamn box, which is fourteen lines tall, and I have to rhyme here, there, the other place. I have to screw my body up this way and that way and so forth. One of the nice things about it, the Martian says, is that the poet, on account of the fact that he's forced by these rhymes, won't be able to put in too much of what he wants to put in himself. [Laughter]

If he wants to have the word "orange" ending the line because he's seen a girl in an orange dress, he's then going to have to invent a rhyme for orange, which there ain't in this particular language of this critter and so this will keep him from putting some of the personal in.

I think that's one of the advantages of rhyme—that it restricts the personal of the poet. But it seems to me that it's like wearing a straitjacket in order to restrict you from scratching your nose.

Q: I don't think the poem would exist as a sonnet outside, like in the Martian's language. But when it comes through the poet, when the poet gives it physicality, then it is a sonnet.

JS: Sure.

Q: But, then, the poet is doing a conscious thing by writing it, isn't he?

JS: The point is that you have to clear out all of the junk from your mind which is going to interfere with the poem coming through, and there are a number of techniques of doing it. One of the techniques is to have something very arbitrary, like standing on your head and whistling "Dixie." And the rhyme thing, particularly these complicated rhymes, are very arbitrary. If the Martian can't get through, you're even less likely to get through than the Martian, and this great message that you want to tell is even less likely to get through than the great message the Martian wants to tell.

That's one of the advantages of the tight rhyme structure—that it keeps you out of it. But, on the other hand, you don't put on a straitjacket in order not to pick your nose.

WT: Jack, you said metaphor is to bear across or carry across or bear over or something. I don't see that that's any different than rhyme. Since rhyme carries, bears across from whatever the clue is to the recipient of the clue. I don't see that rhyme is different from metaphor.

JS: You mean that rhyme is a kind of punctuation?

WT: No. Rhyme in terms of sound is a carrying across or a bearing over from some sound to a similar sound. And I can't see that that's different than a metaphor is, which also is a bearing across, or a carrying over. Like puns. Aren't puns metaphors? Aren't they carrying across?

JS: Look Warren, I have to sound like a damned linguist again, but essentially it's just like in chemistry or physics. You have the most simple particles, more complicated particles, and all of that, and you can do a hell of a lot more with a molecule. A molecule is much more like a human thing. It can be much more personified—namely calling it a virus when it is a virus—than can, say, an electron or a proton.

And sounds are pretty goddamned simple things. Furthermore, as far as rhyme goes and sounds go, the tone-leading of vowels and all of that, if you took the vowels which are in the dialects of people here, who mostly come from the same area, some of them have nine, some of them ten separate phonemic vowels. And when you have a hundred years' difference, you have "tea" and "say" rhymed in Pope, for example, which was a perfectly proper rhyme in Pope's time. It's still a rhyme in Irish, where it's "tay," or at least in provincial Irish. These things change faster and change more in terms of geography than things like puns, which essentially have to do with the morphemics of words, the roots of the words, which is a higher degree of abstraction. I have nothing against rhyme. Christ, I think that in some ways it's a very nice thing, and everyone uses it.

But I do think that the eighteenth and nineteenth centuries at least made a mistake of using it without great success, except maybe for Rimbaud in French and Lewis Carroll in English. There was very little use of rhymes that let the imagination free, and in both their cases they would use nonsense words occasionally, and this forced them to nonsense, which was great.

But we don't exactly have to be forced to nonsense today. It's just a way of doing things. It's a way of discipline. I'm sure that for some people it's a very good way. I've nothing against it. It just seems to me that you swim against all sorts of tides if you exclusively use rhyme.

Now Helen Adam, who's a very good poet in San Francisco, not only uses rhyme but ballad metric, and does it very well.[42] She lets the rhyme and the metric lead her into some of the strangest places you can imagine. And that's very good, and it may be the right thing for a person. As long as it frees your mind of what you *want* to say instead of what you *need* to say, what the poem needs you to say, anything which takes out the trap of the personal is all to the good. Palindromes too. Anything, if it works. But that's furniture.

Q: I don't quite follow your answer because Warren, as I understand it, said that the rhyme carries over, as the metaphor does. And your reply to that seems to me that in the eighteenth century Pope took a word which we pronounce as "tea" and pronounced it "tay" and thus got a rhyme.

JS: No, he didn't "thus" get a rhyme. It was in the English of the time.

Q: Quite. Therefore rhyme is not a valid mechanism because there is one word which has changed in the whole of the enormous corpus of the English language from Chaucer to the present day, when rhymes all work still, except for these one or two exceptions, or a dozen, or twenty or thirty.

JS: Well, you're certainly not going to say that a student of yours who's trying to read Chaucer will be able to get the sounds of the rhymes looking at Chaucer, without some instruction in what it sounded like in Chaucer's time. You remember how barbarous Chaucer's metric was supposed to be until they discovered the fact that *e* was sometimes pronounced and sometimes not.

Q: Well, the rhymes wouldn't be affected like the meter would.

JS: Rhymes certainly would if you have them add on it or not. Couth and sooth for example. The thing is that rhymes are a small, rather unstable unit. I have nothing against them, but they're less stable than puns are, although certainly puns aren't terribly stable. But if they're informed into the poem . . . Shakespeare's puns in his comedies are very seldom informed because they're temporary, but Shakespeare's puns in his tragedies are usually ones that are recognizable even though they don't seem like puns anymore.

WT: Jack, moving back to dictation—the fact that a good part of Yeats's dictation was by way of his wife—how do you parse or construe that? Does that make perfect sense to you?

JS: No. It doesn't a bit.

WT: But it worked. He wrote great poems.

JS: He did. I haven't the vaguest notion how. Tom Parkinson, as you know, talked to Yeats's wife Georgie, who's still alive, and tried to get her to admit that she was faking the whole thing out, and that Yeats was just using this as a business for getting the thing, and Georgie wouldn't admit it.[43] But she certainly seemed to be a dumb woman. I really don't know. This kind of thing only happened once, and I really don't know what happened. Maybe if I had met someone like Georgie, I could find out, but right now I haven't the vaguest notion, except that I'd say the verdict on it was at best not proven.

WT: I get the sense from some of his poems that he also wrote them from either visual dreams or hallucinations.

JS: The horrible green birds poem?

WT: Well, the "Byzantium" one.

JS: No. There are, I think, something like twenty-four revisions of that one, and the images change and everything else. This is arguing against myself because I don't believe in revisions. But there are revisions on that one. It's not a "Kubla Khan" in any sense of the word.

Q: The Hindu girl that Warren mentioned in Duncan's poem. Is that part of the furniture too?

JS: It's part of the furniture in the sense that anything in the poet's memory is part of the furniture. Like my grandmother's jigsaw puzzle is part of the furniture. But the difference is that my grandmother occurred in the past, and the Hindu girl occurred while Duncan was writing the poem, which is, you know, making things happen—the poem making things happen. And that's the difference.

In the long run, the past and the present and the future are pretty much the same kind of furniture in the room. Just because a thing happens tomorrow that is in the poem today doesn't really mean that there's anything more mysterious than something that happened yesterday being in the poem today. I mean the future, the past, and the present are in some ways entangled. I don't know how, but they are, and so I just don't think it's terribly important. I mean, you can't really produce a Hindu girl at the snap of your fingers if you want her in the poem.

Q: I sort of get the feeling that when this happened in the present, Duncan probably felt, now that's just what I want. If he felt that way, he'd have to be suspicious or reject it, wouldn't he?

JS: Yes. Although you generally tend to see the thing as something more mysterious than that. It really doesn't matter, as long as it isn't anything that you're really involved with. The Hindu girl could be an airplane as far as the purpose of the poem goes, if it happened the right way in the poem.
  I mean, things that you ought to be suspicious of are things that you can use for your own personal interests rather than anything else. I wouldn't worry about if something appears. It's like an epiphany. Well then, use the epiphany, but just realize that there could be about twenty-seven other epiphanies which would be just as good, if they'd happened.

Q: What happens to the poem if you find that you have interfered with it, entered into it? Do you scrap it?

JS: What I generally do is work by building up a number of poems into a long poem, and I find often that where it seems I've interfered, or where I have interfered, the poem comes back and just like the oyster, when it gets a grain of sand in its belly, coats it over and makes a pearl. The things that write the poems just incorporate that without too much trouble. But then if the poem just stops, the progress of the poem just stops, then I throw everything away, including the good stuff.
  You see, my writing since I was a mature poet has always been in terms of short takes, very seldom a poem—I mean a section—of over forty lines, but almost always a poem which is built up from these sections which I'll talk about on Tuesday in the serial poem discussion. And so, my tendency is, if I really get to a place where the goofing I did with the poem doesn't

allow a pearl to be made of the sand grain, I just throw the good parts of the poem away as well as the bad because, you know, there are plenty of poems.

Q: That could be a form of revision, though, if the poem came back again.

JS: No, it wouldn't be a question of that. It would be a question that I would keep the poem which I knew I'd interfered with, and go on. And if I couldn't go on, if I came to the edge of the mountainside, and just couldn't get up the goddamn cliff, then I'd throw away all of my path up to the mountainside, including all of the good climbs I did as well as the mistake I made in the wrong turning.

Notes

1. See Yeats's account in *A Vision* (8–9). Yeats recalls the incident as occurring on "the afternoon of October 24th 1917, four days after my marriage." While the precise date is open to debate (Harper, Vol. 1, 1–49), placing this event on a train between Los Angeles and San Bernardino is evidently Spicer's innovation. In his Introduction to *A Vision* Yeats places his visit to California in early 1919, but his papers indicate the trip took place in 1920.

2. Augusta, Lady Gregory (1852–1932), the Irish playwright, codirected with Yeats and J. M. Synge the Abbey Theatre in Dublin. Her patronage of Yeats seems to have begun shortly after they met, around 1896 (Yeats, *Memoirs*, 99 ff.).

3. The Society for Psychical Research was formally established in London in 1882, but it developed out of a group of Cambridge intellectuals including Henry Sidgwick, Henry Jackson, F. W. Myers, and Edmund Gurney during the 1870s. Its members and proponents in England included Ruskin, Tennyson, Lewis Carroll, and William Gladstone. William James was at the forefront of the SPR in America. The early SPR tended to investigate the physical phenomena of rappings, table tiltings, and slate writing, but after a number of hoaxes and sleights of hand were exposed, its focus shifted to the manifestations of "mental mediums": visions, automatic speaking, and automatic writing. One of its declared long-term goals was to establish a kind of rational groundwork for religious belief (Gauld, 353, etc.). The SPR provides an interesting intersection of religion, science, literature, pragmatism, and the history of magic and charlatanism. Some of the "physical mediums" that generated the initial interest in psychic phenomena were amateur and professional "conjurers" who were able to distract audiences long enough to accomplish a sleight of hand without their realizing it. The medium's supposed authenticity was contingent entirely upon effect—the ability to make physical magic pass for psychical experience, which on one level, of course, it was. A point of correspondence in Spicer's poetic practice would be the legerdemain in the time and timing of his lines, invoking one narrative, quickly switching to another, then another, so that the reader is thrown off by the poem's repeated foiling of readerly expectation. Contrast this to the more Romantic surface of Duncan's

poems or the formal invocation that authenticates the blur between past and present in H.D.'s *Helen in Egypt*, or the authenticity of place that "speaks" in Olson's *Maximus*. Not only does Spicer take on the lowest popular-culture version of "dictation" by talking about composition in terms of "Martians" but he debunks the very notion of authenticity since the process is unknowable—it cannot be authenticated—no matter how you represent it. In many ways Spicer's talk is in keeping with the the goal of the SPR, which is to attempt to explain materially a phenomenological experience.

4. Blake's poetics of visitation are recorded in both his poems and his letters. "Europe: A Prophecy" and "Jerusalem" both begin with announcements that they are "dictated" poems (Blake, 60, 146).

But Blake's letters give more detail. He writes, for instance, to William Hayley: "Thirteen years ago. I lost a brother & with his spirit I converse daily & hourly in the Spirit. . . . I hear his advice & even now write from his Dictate—" (Blake, 705). To John Flaxman, he writes: "Milton lovd me in childhood & shewd me his face" (707). To Thomas Butts (great-grandfather of poet Mary Butts), he writes in detail about the composition of two different poems: "my Abstract folly hurries me often away while I am at work, carrying me over Mountains & Valleys which are not Real in a Land of Abstraction where Spectres of the Dead wander," and "I have written this Poem from immediate Dictation twelve or sometimes twenty or thirty lines at a time without Premeditation & even against my Will" (716, 729).

5. Quasars were discovered in 1963. Also known as "quasi-stellar radio sources," they are objects emitting significant amounts of radio energy several billion light years from earth.

6. Karen Tallman is the daughter of Ellen and Warren Tallman. She befriended Spicer when he was staying at their house during the month of the lectures. She was twelve at the time.

7. I offer the following correspondence as an unlikely but interesting possibility: Spicer may be referring here to John Ashbery's long poem "The Skaters" published in the magazine *Art and Literature* in the previous year. The title, "The Skaters," obliquely picks up on the last line of Stevens's "Of Modern Poetry" which rehearses what poetry must be in the present. Most notably, "it must speak about war" and can be about "a man skating, a woman combing (239)."

8. A surprisingly large number of mediums in both England and America claimed beyond-the-grave contact with Oscar Wilde, and a number of them were published. See, for instance, Smith, who ends her account by promising that Wilde "has suggested that he is in a position to resume some of his literary work again; but, knowing as I do the difficulties and uncertainty of automatism, I dare not promise anything definite" (164).

9. See Creeley's letter to the editor printed in *Contact* in 1953, reprinted in *A Quick Graph*, where he discusses the problem of imagining a printed poem as simply a transcription of speech: "This is why *line* is a problem, an immense one. We let it dictate to us—bend us into a formal structure not at all our own, as words would otherwise find their relations. We let it block the actual impulse" (27).

10. This sentiment is reminiscent of William Burroughs's dictum, "Language is a virus from outer space."

11. See, for instance, Duncan's "Passages 15: Spelling" as an example of the concept of words and their sources or shadows (*Bending the Bow*, 48–50). See also his discussion of chiaroscuro in "Ideas of the Meaning of Form" (*Fictive Certainties*, 91).

12. For Olson on "energy" and "kinetics" see his essay "Human Universe": "There is only one thing you can do about kinetic, re-enact it. . . . Art does not seek to describe

but to enact. And if man is once more to possess intent in his life . . . he has to comprehend his own process as intact, from outside, by way of his skin, in, and by his own powers of conversion, out again" (*Collected Prose*, 162). In "Projective Verse," he writes that "a poem is energy transferred from where the poet got it . . . by way of the poem itself to, all the way over to, the reader. Okay. Then the poem itself must, at all points, be a high energy construct and, at all points, an energy-discharge" (240).

In a letter to Charles Olson that accompanied his first book, *After Lorca*, Spicer writes: "I've discovered what I owe to you and hate owing it." In 1946 Olson writes a Poundian radio broadcast as William Butler Yeats speaking from the grave, called "This is Yeats Speaking," which corresponds with Spicer's use of Yeats in Lecture 1 and his "Introduction" from a posthumous Lorca in *After Lorca*.

In San Francisco in 1957 Olson presented a version of his lecture, "The Special View of History," in which he makes a nod to Yeats's practice of dictation: "The messengers which came to Yeats through his wife's voice as a medium, and through whose instructions he wrote the Vision—a spiritualistic Spenglerism of time—Yeats was honest enough to quote in these words, 'We come to bring you images for your verse.' It may turn out in the end that this dogmatic system of mine is no more" (*Special View*, 35–36).

Of further correspondence: in 1953 Olson wrote a book review about *The Saga of Billy the Kid* by Walter Noble Burns, which at times even sounds Spicerian: "All we got is what the best men have kept their eye on. No figures, no forms, no known largenesses whatsoever. Zero. Not even a digit, no string tie. Perfect. . . . The time hasn't come when we are that sure, that we can ask a question, and live. We are still more masters of the outside, still (like heroes of the woods, and these gunmen) we don't break a twig." (*Collected Prose*, 312–13). Spicer's serial poem "Billy the Kid" was published in 1959.

13. Williams's "objectness" is famously embodied throughout his work, from the "Red Wheelbarrow" poem to his epic *Paterson*: "No ideas but in things—" (8).

As an example of Spicer's own take on "thingness," see one of his most often quoted works, the first poem from "Thing Language" (L, 217). Of the many discussions of this poem, see especially Conte, McGann, and Silliman. See also Spicer's serial poem *A Red Wheelbarrow* (103–105).

14. "Why has man not a microscopic eye? / For this plain reason / Man is not a fly." (The quotation comes from Pope's "Essay on Man.")

15. Warren Tallman (1921–1994) was a professor in the English department at UBC. He was instrumental in establishing the Vancouver literary scene of the 1960s. He organized the Vancouver poetry conference in 1963 and was responsible for bringing to town a steady stream of American and Canadian poets. With Ellen Tallman, he hosted Spicer's three Vancouver lectures in his home. He coedited *The Poetics of the New American Poetry* (1973). His collections of prose are *Godawful Streets of Man* (1976) and *In the Midst: Writings 1962–92* (1992).

16.   Caught in the swirl of waters,
        bobbing heads of the young girls, pubescent,
             descending from the bus,
        pass on or out, into the street beyond
             —one dark Hindu face among them passes
             out of my ken.
                    (*Roots and Branches*, 76)

17. *The Moth Poem* is dated 1962–64.

18. The Duke experiments—conducted at Duke University in the 1930s—were a

scientific investigation into the existence, nature, and predictability of extrasensory perception. The experiments were in many ways connected with the work of the Society for Psychical Research in both England and America (see note 3), including the fact that the head of the psychology department at Duke, William McDougall, was a prominent member of the Society in England and ultimately became the leader of the American branch of the Society. Essentially the experiments proved the existence of ESP and other telepathic experiences but were unable to demonstrate their scientific use value (see Rhine). In terms of Spicer's poetics, though, their interest is primarily their use of a radio-wave model for telepathic transmission.

19. George Bowering (b. 1935) was a founding coeditor of *Tish* (1961–63) and went on to edit *Imago* (1964–74). His many books of poetry include *Sticks and Stones* (1963), *Rocky Mountain Foot* (1968), *The Gangs of Kosmos* (1969), *Kerrisdale Elegies* (1984), and *Delayed Mercy* (1986). He won the Governor-General's Award for poetry in 1969. His prose collections include *A Way with Words* (1982) and *Imaginary Hand* (1988). He reviewed Spicer's *Heads of the Town Up to the Aether* in *Tish* 16.

20. John Ryan (1928–1994) was a friend of Spicer's in the North Beach bar scene in the 1950s. (See Ellingham and Killian.)

21. Tristan Tzara, a key figure in both the dadaist and surrealist groups, was an adamant proponent of cut-up techniques and automatic writing, which he felt offered a literary counter to the senseless brutality of World War I. His recipe "To Write a Dada Poem" was: "Take a newspaper. Take some scissors. Pick out an article which is as long as you wish your poem to be. Cut out the article. Then cut out carefully each of the words in the article and put them in a bag. Shake gently. Then take out each piece one after the other. Copy them down conscientiously in the order in which they left the bag. The poem will resemble you and you will find yourself to be an infinitely original writer with a charming sensitivity even though you will not be understood by the vulgar" (quoted in Peterson, 35–36).

As for Martian activity and influence, Tzara's peer André Breton discussed composition explicitly as "dictation" and was fascinated by the mechanistic qualities of writing as they were investigated by the Society for Psychical Research, particularly the mediumship of Catherine Elise Muller (1861–1929), whose experiences could be classified into verbal-auditory, vocal, verbal-visual, and graphic phenomena (resembling Spicer's divisions of *Language* into phonemics, graphemics, and so on). She recorded conversations that came to her from elsewhere, spoke in unknown languages—including those she claimed were received from Mars, Ultra-Mars, Uranus, and the Moon—and was taken over by "Martian" characters (Breton, 140, 142, n. 154).

22. Gladys (Maria) Hindmarch (b. 1940) is a fiction writer who lives in Vancouver. Her publications include *The Peter Stories* (1976), *A Birth Account* (1976), and *The Watery Part of the World* (1988).

23. Alexander Pope dedicated his "Essay on Man" to Bolingbroke, claiming that he was developing Bolingbroke's ideas, though Bolingbroke didn't agree.

24. Spicer's comment is not entirely offhand since he himself wrote letters to the editor on several occasions. The following letter to the *San Francisco Chronicle* was probably never published, for obvious reasons:

[n.d.—late 1964/ early 1965]

The Editor, Sir:

The Chronicle has done very well for an American newspaper in covering our latest adventures in and around South Viet Nam. When it is not an election year, the Chronicle can almost be called courageous.

Nevertheless your reporting (or rather your rehash of wire-reporting) shows definite signs of what was known in several wars affectionately as "the gook-complex." A typical example, more common in radio and television than your newspaper, would be, "Three Americans were killed today in an ambush around Ng Zing Air base. (Two or three paragraphs in between.) There were also five thousand loyal Vietnamese soldiers injured or killed." Separating the sheep from the gooks. Maybe some of the South Vietnamese gook-soldiers that got killed believed in their cause (which we are technical experts in) more than the three Americans who died. I think they were idiots if they did, but even gook-soldiers can be idiots.

If we play with their lives, we might as well print their names.

Sincerely yours,
Jack Spicer

(Do not print this letter if you decide to cut it.)

25. Dorothy Livesay (1909–1996) was a prominent Canadian poet and political activist. Her collections of poetry include *Day and Night* (1944), *Poems for People* (1947), *Plainsongs* (1969), and *Collected Poems: The Two Seasons* (1972), among many others. Her 1967 collection *The Unquiet Bed* was influenced by Spicer. Her autobiographical prose has been published in three volumes: *Beginnings: A Winnipeg Childhood* (1973), *The Raw Edges: Voice from our Time* (1983), and *Journey with My Selves* (1991). In 1972 she edited the anthology *Forty Women Poets of Canada*. She received two Governor-General's Awards and was an Officer of the Order of Canada.

26. "Little Eva" (from *Uncle Tom's Cabin*) is a voice from Spicer's first dictated section of "The Imaginary Elegies" (CB, 333).

27. Marco Polo describes an "Indian rope trick," some version of which was popular in men's clubs in London at the turn of the century. It is described in English books of the thirties and forties: A man throws a rope into the air, and one end of it stays up behind the edge of the upper curtain, beyond the view of the spectators. The magician climbs the rope until he is out of sight. His assistant climbs the rope after him and is cut into pieces that fall onto the stage. Blavatsky also mentions the "trick" in *Isis Unveiled*. Also see Norman Finkelstein's reading of the Indian rope trick in the context of Spicer's critique of the academy (Finkelstein, 96).

28. N.B.: Spicer uses the homonym "sole"/"soul" in the poem, so it is impossible to know how to transcribe the word here.

29. Peter Auxier (b. 1941) became one of the primary editors of *Tish* issues 20 through 40. His poems appeared in *Tish* 18, 19, and subsequent issues.

30. *The Myth of the Magus* traces the Faust legend within a general history of magic, referencing the Zoroaster, Moses and Solomon, Pythagoras, Christ, Merlin, Joan of Arc, Helen of Troy, and others. Butler's introduction to the text also provides another possible reading of Spicer's own construction of himself as a poet-magician. That is, coming from a "mysterious origin" (some of Spicer's fake claims to ancestry are Mary Baker Eddy and the Blackfoot Indians); being "initiated" into a cult or brotherhood of peers (the Berkeley days); proving himself through the "magical contest" of his Magic Workshop; being tried and "vanquished," "persecuted," or excluded by his peers, which brings about his doom and provokes a "last scene" that embodies a "solemn and prophetic farewell" (2–3).

31. Loewinsohn's (b. 1937) early books include *Watermelons* (1959) and *The World of the Lie* (1963) which includes the poem "Mrs. McCovey."

32. Willie McCovey (nicknamed "Stretch") was a first baseman for San Francisco most of his career, 1959–1980.

33. It is well documented that in 1957 Spicer read his poem "For Joe" from *Admo-*

nitions, at a post-reading party for Levertov. (See Davidson, 172–73; see Ellingham and Killian, 124–27.) While the poem was dedicated to Joe Dunn, a straight man with whom Spicer was in love, the sentiment of the poem's opening lines—"People who don't like the smell of faggot vomit / Will never understand why men don't like women / Won't see why those never to be forgotten thighs / Of Helen (say) will move us into screams of laughter"—echoed later in the poem by the more direct line "The female genital organ is hideous"—was provocative enough for Levertov to eventually respond with her own poem, which voices a similar sentiment, with the regret that she didn't have the nerve to agree at the time:

> Hypocrite women, how seldom we speak
> of our own doubts, while dubiously
> we mother man in his doubt!
>
> And if at Mill Valley perched in the trees
> the sweet rain drifting through western air
> a white sweating bull of a poet told us
>
> our cunts are ugly—why didn't we
> admit we have thought so too? (And
> what shame? They are not for the eye!)
>   (Levertov, 70)

In the poem "Who Is at My Window," also in *O Taste and See* (1964), Levertov uses the refrain *"timor mortis conturbat me,"* from the William Dunbar poem whose title Spicer uses for his 1961 book, *Lament for the Makers.*

34. The passage is cited from Stein's lecture "Poetry and Grammar": "I decided and *Lucy Church Amiably* has been an attempt to do it, I decided that if one definitely completely replaced the noun by the thing in itself, it was eventually to be poetry and not prose which would have to deal with everything that was not movement in space" (245).

35. Spicer discusses this sense of tradition (what I would call lyric history) as "generations of different poets in different countries patiently telling the same story, writing the same poem, gaining and losing something with each transformation—but of course, never really losing anything. This has nothing to do with calmness, classicism, temperament, or anything else. Invention is merely the enemy of poetry" (AL, 15).

36. The choice of Uzbek and Tocharian seems intentionally offhand and arbitrary enough to impress his audience with his facility as a linguist, but Spicer's references often also construct an additional layer of information or informed reading, through punning for the pleasure and edification of those who share his reading affinities. The Uzbek as a people were also characterized by settling in agricultural communities rather than being nomadic, so this may be an inside reference to his commitment to living and publishing only within the San Francisco Bay Area while other Bay Area poets headed east and being "on the road" became the beat thing to do, with Ginsberg acting as the ultimate poetry nomad. In his essay "The New American Poets" for *Harper's* (which would have appeared on the stands only a few weeks before these lectures), Rexroth uses the term "Uzbek" to refer to "localist" poetics, which he seems to view as ultimately more universal than the conscious imitators of the "latest Bloomsbury fads," whose Eliotic verse remains provincial. While Rexroth does not list Spicer as a "localist," Spicer would surely have placed himself there. But it is also possible that Rexroth is using Uzbek in its agricultural sense to refer to the southern agrarians.

37. See the version of Moore's poem "Poetry" in her 1935 *Selected Poems* and 1951 *Collected Poems.* The poem appears only in truncated form in *The Complete Poems* (1981).

38. James J. Walker (1881–1946) was mayor of New York from 1925 to 1932. He started out as a songwriter. Walker was famous for making Babe Ruth cry when he scolded him publicly for his wild lifestyle, although he too was known for his own wild ways. Walker was a friend of Franklin Roosevelt, and both were members of the Tammany political club. At one time he was considered for the appointment of Commissioner of Baseball, but lost out to a Californian, Judge Landis.

39. Spicer is referring to the quest for Everest of George Herbert Leigh-Mallory (1886–1924) and Andrew Irvine (1902–1924). Given his love of puns and his discussion of seriality (II, 54) as a kind of getting lost in the woods which involves giving up one's own sense of direction in order to follow the path's sense of direction, Spicer may be having fun with the auditory puns of Mallory's Everest and Malory's Grail quest. As a young man, George Mallory was nicknamed "Galahad" by his close friend Geoffrey Young. According to Mallory's biographer, the two shared "an appreciation of poetry and discourse, and a love of the manipulation of words." Mallory intended to become a writer; at one point he was the teacher and poetic mentor of Robert Graves (Holzel and Salkeld, 16–17, 23–24, 38).

Spicer uses mountain climbing as a metaphor for poetic composition throughout the lectures. A recent study of the Mallory-Irvine expedition suggests Mallory made it to the top, knowing that he was using too much oxygen to make it back. Figurally, Spicer is much like Mallory in the sense that the achievement of his practice reaches an apex, but he dies in spite (or because) of it.

40. "My Favorite Martian" was a popular TV show on CBS from 1963 to 1966. In the show, the "Martian" was called "Uncle Martin," and a theremin-like electronic instrument would play every time his antennae went up or when he exercised his powers of levitation. Other popular shows of the time about extraterrestrials were *Twilight Zone* (1959–1964, CBS), *Alfred Hitchcock Presents* (1962–1965, CBS and NBC), *The Outer Limits* (1963–1965, ABC), and *Alcoa Presents: One Step Beyond* (1951–1961, ABC).

41. The passage also appears as an "anthem" in Blake's early work, "An Island in the Moon," a novelistic fragment in which three characters—Suction the Epicurean, Quid the Cynic, and Sipsop the Pythagorean—discuss literary history on an island that "seems to have some affinity to England":

Lo the Bat with Leathern wing
Winking & blinking
Winking & blinking
Winking & blinking
Like Doctor Johnson
(Blake, 458)

42. Helen Adam (1909–1993) was a Scottish-born poet known primarily for her ballads. She lived in San Francisco during the fifties and sixties and was an integral part of the San Francisco scene. She attended Spicer's "Poetry as Magic" workshop.

43. Thomas Parkinson (1920–1992), a Yeats scholar who taught at UC Berkeley, was a longtime friend of Spicer's. Parkinson was also deeply involved with issues of the Free Speech Movement Spicer discusses in Lecture 4. He is the author of *W. B. Yeats, Self Critic* (1951) and *W. B. Yeats: The Later Poetry* (1964).

VANCOUVER LECTURE 2

The Serial Poem and The Holy Grail

JUNE 15, 1965

🦂 In Lecture 2, Spicer continues his discussion of poetic dictation, proposing that the larger scaffolding of books can also be dictated. Spicer uses the term "book" in this lecture to mean a measure of composition, as opposed to a "collection" of poems. *The Holy Grail* is an intricate assemblage of seven "books" (chapters) of seven poems each.[1] For Spicer, the order of the poems is crucial since the overall structure of the book is dictated just as the lines of individual poems are dictated, and according to Spicer it should not be read out of sequence. *The Holy Grail* is an assemblage of narrative fragments from Grail legend, popular culture, folk song, etc., composed in such a way that what it narrates is not just a "legend" but also the process of poem-making out of multiple sources.

This discussion of seriality is the most lecture-like of Spicer's presentations, with the last third of the lecture taken up in a debate with Elliott Gose,[2] an English professor at UBC, who pushes Spicer on to a further discussion of other poets who are significant to his practice, particularly Hart Crane, T. S. Eliot, and Wallace Stevens. Spicer is also drawn into a comparison between poetry and other arts like music, and he clarifies his view that poetry is neither for entertainment nor for individual betterment, ultimately agreeing with Gose that composition by dictation is a form of spiritual exercise or a meditative discipline.

The confusion among the audience members during the lecture makes apparent how unusual Spicer's insistence on dictation—the literally de-authored status of the dictated poem and its necessary waiting for alien intervention—must have been within the world of sixties self-expression, confessional poetry, and the emergence of identity politics. In contrast to the freedom discourses that were particularly intense and determining on the Berkeley campus (as evidenced in Lecture 4), Spicer's poetry reveals a distrust of all liberation narratives as merely replacing one form of tyranny with another.

In fact, part of what makes Spicer's work move so compellingly against the grain of his time is its resistance to issues of personality and identity and its placement of the poet in the frankly clerical position of a fatigued copyist or, at most, a translator. One of the signatures of Spicer's work is its disruption of self-driven narratives and rhetorical structures even in a seemingly narrative poem like *The Holy Grail*, in which the tendency toward dramatic monologue is overturned through an overall aesthetic of assemblage and a character's self-expression is disrupted through the linguistic manipulation of puns. More than any other art form, poetry "riddles" us. We are intellectually stumped and physically shot through, to quote just one of the puns that run haywire through Spicer's poems.

As a serial poem, *The Holy Grail* is unlike other serial projects like Pound's *Cantos* in the sense that it does not arise out of a planned system. Spicer explains that a true serial poem moves forward without looking back. Although Spicer implies that *The Holy Grail* might be read as a "novel" (II, 73), the individual "books" are not organized according to a narrative progression, and all its books are contemporaneous. Seriality, then, is not just a manifestation of temporal sequence, and it does not serve any overarching narrative or rhetorical concern. For Spicer, serial composition is the practice of writing in units that are somehow related without creating a totalizing structure for them. Their connection is purely poetic. That is, the poet must ignore the poem's progress in order not to unify its content into a message she or he can control. Like Orpheus, the poet is instructed not to look back.

But the rules of the serial poem—and of poetry generally—are not in themselves absolute. Being human, the poet does look back, and the rules only generate more imaginative forms of evasion. Spicer's terminology of the "boojum" and of aliens, radio, and Martians, is in itself an evasion or substitution. Such terms are like the device of the "McGuffin" in the films of Alfred Hitchcock, in which the action turns on the chasing of a clue that has nothing to do with the "real" story but serves to bring the action forward. It is both indispensable and beside the point, like Poe's purloined letter, which one looks for endlessly, yet, finding it, is "no better for the letter" (HG, 208).

Spicer claims seriality as a necessary element of poetic practice by arguing that poems "cannot live alone anymore than we can" (A, 61). In fact, his insistence on the community-making function of serial poems leads him to disown his earlier non-serial work as "one night stands." Spicer seems to be proposing that not only should his poems be read in relation to each other but that his own work, or any poet's work, should also be considered within the context of his poetic peers, living and dead—the community created through shared texts—since messages often come from other poets and his work often echoes that of poets he admires. It is a way in which one can textually place oneself within a community that transcends geography and even time.

But, not unlike Malory's community of knights, this community is also a comparative universe of argumentation and gaming, and this lecture foregrounds the essentially oppositional structure of Spicer's poetic thinking. Through the course of the lectures, he insists on argument as a means of drawing people out into an engaged group discourse, a community that talks one out of one's armor. In the lectures this insistence sometimes appears as a plea, echoing the fourth Percival poem in *The Holy Grail*: "If someone doesn't fight me, I'll have to wear this armor all of my life" (HG, 192).

JACK SPICER: Tonight I'll say a few words about the serial poem, read an example of the serial poem, we'll talk about it for a while, and then if you want particular sections repeated we can do it, but I'm going to try to do this thing straight through.

The whole business about the serial poem was sort of a joke to begin with. Not the fact of what I think it is but the name of it. Essentially it came from when I was talking with Robin Blaser. If you went to the New Design Gallery reading you heard three of his poems, all serial poems, what I would call that.[3] And we were saying that, in spite of the fact we had absolutely different poetics in almost every way, that Duncan, he, and I had a kind of a similarity, and what was it? And it occurred to me that it was a serial poem. Now with Duncan this isn't entirely true, but what I consider Duncan's two best poems—*Medieval Scenes*, which was published separately and is in Duncan's *Selected Poems*, and *The Opening of the Field*—are both pure honest-to-God serial poems.

I'll try to get to what a serial poem is in a minute. Robin kept asking me all the way, when we went to the radio station. I talked about serial poems. He kept looking sort of at me and said, "But you promised to tell me what a serial poem was." And I said I didn't really know. But I think I do now. I think in a way you have to get exactly what a serial poem isn't first, and then you get some idea of it.

A serial poem, in the first place, has the book as its unit—as an individual poem (a dictated poem, say, as we were talking about on Sunday night) has a poem as its unit, the actual poem that you write at the actual time, the single poem. And there is a dictation of form as well as a dictation of the individual form of an individual poem.

And you have to go into a serial poem not knowing what the hell you're doing. That's the first thing. You have to be tricked into it. It has to be some path that you've never seen on a map before and so forth. You can't say—now to give examples of what it isn't—you can't say to yourself, as Lawrence did in *Birds, Beasts, and Flowers*, which is a beautiful book, but is not a serial poem, "I am going to write poems about birds, beasts, and flowers," or else say, "Well, gee, I've been writing poems about birds, beasts, and flowers, and so let's put it in a book and call it *Birds, Beasts, and*

Flowers, and separate the poems out by way of birds, beasts, and flowers."

A serial poem, in its essence, has to be chronological. In other words, the book, which is a unit like a poem is, has to be absolutely chronological. It has to be chronological in the writing of the poems. You can't just say, "well, I wrote a lot about birds and I wrote a lot about animals and I wrote a lot about flowers, so all my poems for the last five years which I'd like to get published, some of which have been published in magazines, I'll distinguish in three parts." That's not the kind of thing.

Or not like Wallace Stevens's *Harmonium*, which is closer to the serial poem on one side. Stevens has always had a very good editorial intelligence. He took a large number of the poems he liked that he'd written in about a four-year period, and which do connect in a way and do make it almost seem like it's a poem which proceeded under its own laws, not the poet's laws. But at the same time, he didn't.

Now this is the other thing that the serial poem is not, and Olson and Pound are good examples of that, although with both of them, the planned poem, the non-serial poem, can, if you get caught up in it, become a serial poem. Pound thought that the *Cantos* would end at Canto 100. He had said it many times to many college professors and really believed it. It had something to do with Dante. He was very, very unhappy and surprised, I'm sure, when there was Canto 101, 102, and so forth.

With Charles Olson, the same thing happened with *The Maximus Poems*. He had an idea of what *The Maximus Poems* were when he started writing, and it's changed as he's been going on. There will probably be Maximus poems for a long time. Now this is a kind of dictation that is a little bit different from the kind of dictation I was talking about last week. Of course, it's dictation of form, you realize. It's not the same thing as dictation of lines, but it follows more or less the same laws. Olson started out with the idea, I guess, of a man facing human history and facing it from his own direction, which was Gloucester. The poems have gone by accretion to something more than that and I'm sure have scared him many times by the way that they go.

Or take Williams's *Paterson*. He thought "Paterson One," when he'd written "Paterson One," it was the end of *Paterson*. It's another thing.

But it's not quite the same thing as letting the poem have its head. In Olson's books of Maximus poems, there is an ending where you can see damn well the poet said, "Well, we're finished with that, thank God. Let's go to something else."

It's a slightly different thing than the poem which is really a serial poem where you just say, well, I'm going into the woods on a path that I have no idea about. I'm not going to look backwards on the path at all or make Indian signs on the trees to see where I am. I think for the ideal serial poem you don't really reread the poems before it. In other words, if you've gone, say, five poems and you're beginning to have a suspicion that there's a section. You don't know how long a section is, but say the sections have been in terms of seven poems for two parts already. There's a great temptation to look back and see what material you have to connect together. That is the one thing which I think *The Opening of the Field*, the poems that Robin read, and I think all of my books as far as they're successful, have done. Not looking backwards. Letting the poem look forward. Just following the bloody path to see where it goes. And sometimes it doesn't go anywhere.

What I'm saying is you have a unit: one unit, the poem, which is taken by dictation; and another unit, the book, which is a more structured thing, but it should be structured by dictation and not by the poet. When the poet gets some idea this is going to amount to this or it's going to amount to that and he starts steering the poem himself, then he's lost. He's lost in the woods. He's in the brambles and all of that. Or else he pulls out a Boy Scout compass and goes back to the nearest bar. And he trusts his own sense of direction rather than the path's sense of direction.

That essentially is what I've meant by the serial poem. And what I'm going to read tonight is an example of one that I wrote, being completely unsuspicious that the thing was even starting out to be a book of poems. And then when the first book — the first part — was completed there was a surprise in the kind of form that took place within it. They're called books in this because it's the Holy Grail and it does seem to follow Malory's path in a way that I never thought it would.[4] I hadn't any idea until I got about halfway through the book that the voices in the poem were the voices of the people who were looking for the Grail, or else involved in the hunt for the Grail.

I'd started out with a couple of poems which were obviously about Gawain, who sort of interested me as a character, mainly from *Gawain and the Green Knight*, nothing else. And then they started growing, and finally there was a poem which seemed to stop everything, and I thought, "oh gee, good, I got a Gawain poem." Fine. You know, mazel tov.[5] Unfortunately, the night after that there came a new poem which was obviously about Percival. This annoyed me terribly. And this also ended up on a seven. It turned out all the poems did. But always without my even letting myself know how many poems there were, which is the important thing —the poet keeping himself ignorant of the way that the form is going.

Robin once said, in talking about a serial poem, that it's as if you go into a room, a dark room. A light is turned on for a minute. Then it's turned off again and you go into a different room where a light is turned on and turned off.

And I suspect one of the reasons that makes people write serial poems—I'm sure this was true at least of Duncan's *Medieval Scenes* and most of the poems of Robin Blaser's and my poems—is the business that if you can get the focus on the individual part enough, you have a better chance of dictation.[6] You have a better chance of being an empty vessel, of being filled up by whatever's Outside. You don't when you are writing a long poem because when you are writing a long poem—not composed of separate parts but a long poem, say, a five- or ten-page poem—naturally, you can't write a five- or ten-page poem, if you're a good poet at least, within a humanly recognizable period, in one sitting.

It's possible, although it's sometimes awkward, to write these parts and be completely divorced from these parts, in one sitting. And it does seem to me that it's much easier to write a dictated poem if you can write it in one sitting because the next morning you have great ideas of what the poem means, and it's you, not the poem, that's talking. It's possible to go back to the poem, and you've got twenty lines, and you add another twenty. It certainly is possible. But it's more difficult. And I think this business of the take from one room to another, from one frame to another, is partly—not because that's a particularly attractive aesthetic form, or anything else, but simply—because it's easier on the poet.

Q: In the meantime, are other poems happening to you?

JS: At first they did. I'd say this was also true for both Robin and Duncan, so yes, I think I can say this is true.

Incidentally, I am never going to give you brilliant answers. I'm going to try to find an honest answer for things. I've been hearing the tapes of various of these poetry things, and questions usually are for someone to go out and sparkle like a roman candle.[7] I'd like to, you know, just say what I think is true.

Pretty much you can't do it, for a very simple reason: you get something which just seems to be completely out in left field, has nothing whatsoever to do with the poem, and unfortunately, it *is* in the poem if you just go on and trust it. The temptation is to say, "oh, well, no, this isn't going in the right direction." And there you're dictating the path to the poem instead of the poem dictating the path to you. I'm sure that somebody who is very conscious of his art and everything else could do it. But I don't think that I've been able to.

Duncan has a funny thing. Inside of serial poems like in *The Opening of the Field*, he has "The Structure of Rime" which starts before and goes afterwards, sort of like a thread through all of his poems. It's kind of a super-serial poem, which can enter any book at any time and is sort of a counterpoint, a formal stiffening, like using a sonnet right in the middle of something which is completely almost prosaic.[8]

There are all sorts of variations you can make on this thing. But it does seem to me a much more fruitful way of writing poetry—naturally, because that's the way I write it—than some of the others, where you just write a lot of pretty good poems, and then you put 'em into a book, and you call the book something, and people read the poems and see no connections between them whatsoever.[9]

On the other hand, writing a narrative poem, like say the best narrative poem in the language, "The Hunting of the Snark," in some ways resembles a serial poem.[10] But at the same time you know that Carroll had from the beginning to the end the snark as a boojum, and it's rather like writing a detective story, rather than having the murder being committed in front of you, as happens in a serial poem.

Are there any other general questions before I start up this poem?

Q: You say you can't interfere with the pathway or you can't look back at the signs that you left.

JS: I think the myth about Orpheus and Eurydice is doing exactly that kind of thing for Greek poetry. If you look back, Eurydice doesn't come up with you out of Hell.

Q: So when do you know when you're on another path?

JS: When you're on the wrong path?

Q: Well, you know, like *The Moth Poem*. He thought it ended, didn't he? And then at the reading he read another poem. So when does it stop without your messing things up, without looking into things too far?

JS: Well, Robin has a very complicated thing. Robin's *Moth Poem* is a separate publication [that's part of a larger book].

You remember two days ago I read the "Textbook of Poetry." It was from the bigger book *The Heads of the Town Up to the Aether*. The first book I wrote of it was the "Homage to Creeley" and I thought that was the end of it, and I actually had it mimeographed and sent to a few people because I was sure it was the end of it. Only it turned out not to be. But the unit was still the unit, and all three units in *The Heads of the Town* can be read separately.

I think Robin has a grand unit which includes all three of the poems that he read [including *The Moth Poem*] and some more, each one of them existing as a sort of a semi-book. This was certainly true of Yeats, who came nearer to the serial poem in his later works than most people did.

There's plenty of fudging that's allowed in this kind of thing. René Char said that a poet should have a sign on his wall saying "Cheat at this game."[11] And this is true enough if you know the right time to cheat, and if you don't you get clobbered. Somebody pulls out a gun from his boot and shoots you with all of the five aces you have in your hand.

Well, let's start out. I don't know how many of you know anything about the Grail and what the Grail meant. If you've read Tennyson's *Idylls of the King*, it will rather hurt you a bit. If you've read Malory, it will help you. If you don't know what happened in the search for the Grail and all of that, presumably if the poem's good enough, it won't matter. And if you've read Jessie Weston, you might as well leave the room.[12]

[Reads *The Holy Grail*, Books of Gawain, Percival, and Lancelot (HG, 187–97)]

Warren, would you get me a drink? I'm going to go straight through, so I need something. "The Book of Gwenivere" needs a drink. She's a bitch in this book, a real bitch. [Pause] We resume.

[Reads Book of Gwenivere (HG, 198–201)]

Told you she was a bitch.

[Reads Books of Merlin, Galahad, and The Death of Arthur (HG, 202–13)]

Some of you light a cigarette and just relax for a minute. I think maybe first would be not to talk about the serial poem, think of it, or ask questions about it, but ask questions about things you don't understand in the poem, which is a fairly simple poem, actually. Except for the damn people in it.

Q: Jack, did the medium just stop, you know, dictating at the end of the Book of Arthur? He stopped then, after he ran out?

JS: Well, he stopped. He wrote the end of the Book of Arthur and that was it—"The Book of the Death of Arthur," you know, *Morte d'Arthur*. If you've been writing poems which are sections which are seven poems long, and you're finishing the seventh section, and the seventh section is about the death of Arthur, and the dictation is about the death of Arthur, then it certainly sounds like the poem's over. If it had gone on, I'd have gone on with it, but I was quite relieved when he finally gave his last testament.

Q: The Tonys—who were the Tonys?[13]

JS: The proper names in the thing are simply a kind of disturbance which I often use. I guess it's "I" rather than the poems because it's sort of the insistence of the absolutely immediate which has nothing to do with anything, and you put that in and then you get all of the immediate out of the poem and you can go back to the poem. I've always found it's a very good thing to put in these immediate things which are in your mind and then just ignore them. It's like the "tap tap tap" the branches make in *Finnegans Wake*.[14]

Q: I know. You get right away from both of them as soon as you start.

JS: Yeah, well this is true throughout the poem. And it's true in Duncan and it's true in Robin, too, although proper names are used differently. Though very few poets use live people, people's names and so forth, if they mean them.

Q: The fact that there's no ocean in the Grail legend, and that you come back to the ocean in "The Book of Lancelot" and in Tarawa.[15] What's happening?

JS: What's happening is the business of the Irish versus the non-Irish. There is an ocean on the coast of Ireland and certainly Tristan, for example, does sail the ocean. The Grail legend itself doesn't have it, but the ocean is always at the outside of this thing. And the real Grail thing is happening on the inside, within inland seas.

Q: Who was "the old flash"?

JS: Oh, that's Frankie Frisch.[16] It's a literal quotation from him. He was on second base and he'd just barely gotten off of second base before the runner that'd just made a clean hit had gotten to second base, and he said "Climbing up the back of the old flash."

Q: In the seventh poem of "The Book of Lancelot" I'm at a loss.

JS: Why?

Q: First of all the horse strikes me as a difficulty, and the fact that the horse is called "Dada."

JS: Well, Lancelot is the figure of the poet as a fool, sort of, in this. "The Book of Lancelot" I find the least dictated and the most labored, the one that I'm the least happy with, the one I got into the most.

But one of the things, stories about how the word "dada" was formed was they stabbed in the dictionary and the word "dada" meant hobby horse.

But I would agree that there are things that are radically wrong in most of "The Book of Lancelot" because it was the poet being conscious of himself during the poem. However, I think Gwenivere rescues it by talking about Lance in a different kind of way.

Q: Gwenivere's about the clearest book of them all.

JS: It's the easiest, yes.

Q: Yeah.

JS: She's a bitch.

ELLEN TALLMAN:[17] I don't know why you keep saying that.

Q: She's kind of seductive.

JS: Well, I . . . yeah.

ET: No, I mean in terms of the poem.

DOROTHY LIVESAY: I don't think that's in the poem. I agree with you. She isn't a bitch in the poem.

JS: Well, she doesn't want to find the Grail. She'd rather sleep with Lancelot, which is reasonable enough.

ET: That doesn't seem bitchy.

JS: She certainly doesn't like the adventures very much. I think it's the eternal war there.

GEORGE BOWERING: She's not respectful anyway.

JS: She certainly isn't, and she is a witch.

Q: How long did the book take to write?

JS: About nine months.

GB: A gestation period.

JS: Books generally take anywhere from, I think, seven months to a year and a half. I'd say that's about the bit with me. All mammals have different gestation periods, and all books do too. But with me it's generally that the thing has gone up to an end, a sheer cliff face like I was talking about last time, and stays that way where it feels half done and you get some idea about the length of the thing, although you're often surprised by it. But you get some idea of how far you've gone into the forest. And if it's taken seven months to get a certain amount of distance on the path, then you say, "well, what the hell, I'll go back to Go and not collect the two hundred dollars," and so forth. Yes?

Q: Who was the fool-killer? I don't know anything about the Grail legend.

JS: The fool-killer ain't in the Grail legend, it's something that western Americans know as the kind of thing which your grandmother frightens you with. When you do something very stupid they say, "Fool-killer's gonna getcha."

Q: It's coming out in a movie with Tony Perkins.

JS: What's coming out?

Q: *The Fool Killer.*[18]

JS: Oh, that's right. There was a novel called *The Fool Killer*, wasn't there? I never read it.

Q: The movie's coming out pretty soon.

JS: Oh, God. Well, that's all right. They're gonna sell Percival. Percival was sort of the kid of the Grail thing. He left home when his mother died on account of it, and everyone died on account of it. He was sort of the vice-president of the Grail. He didn't go off for the Grail but he got to be served from the Grail and he was sort of the innocent. He sounds much better than Galahad to me, who left everybody just sitting there and everything just as bad as it was and went off with the Grail into the big distance up there.

No, the fool-killer is something that I think any westerner, especially from the Southwest, would know about. I don't know if they have him in New England, but "the fool-killer's gonna getcha." Did you have any as far north as Berkeley?

Q: Yeah.

Q: Are Percival and Lancelot both fools then?

JS: In different ways. Lancelot's an old fool. Percival's a young kid. He was going to take the Grail. He doesn't quite make the Grail, according to Malory, on account of the fact that once he sleeps with a woman who seduces him in some very complicated way, he can't ever really do the same thing as Galahad, who was completely pure. But he's sort of the best person in the whole Grail story as far as I can see.

DL: Why were you annoyed when you said then Percival came along?

JS: I was annoyed because I'm always lazy and when something is finished, you know, if you suddenly see that instead of being finished, this thing is going to go on and on and on, and you don't know for how long, it's a sort of an annoying thing.

Q: The distinction in "The Book of Galahad" between foolish and fool-ish?

JS: The fool is a kind of a holy thing as well as something which is just stupid, and that's the distinction. Percival has confused with his shadow and as his shadow, the fool-killer. But fool-killer in a sense is a pretty powerful juju to have working for you, if you accept it and just say well, yes the fool-killer's coming along with me. You remember the first of the greater trumps of the tarot deck is the fool who is dancing with some dogs off a cliff and obviously is never going to fall. And he has the number zero.

Q: And in-vented?

JS: Well, there's the "in" thing which has to do with the holes in things — the outside and the inside. There are, I think, three breaks where the "ins" are separated. I don't know that there are any "outs" separated, but I think that's what that is.

Any questions from people who haven't got the text with them? In a way, it's more interesting. Although I enjoy answering questions on the text, it's even more enjoyable to see what questions come up just from hearing the thing go by once like a big rapid express train.

WARREN TALLMAN: What role do the recurring things play in your own thought as you go along, like the forest, and the boat, and the Grail of course, and the fool, and the ocean?

JS: I try not to think about them, and if I remember, I just say "oh Jesus, here this comes again; what does it mean?" And then trying to get my mind away from being, talking, thinking about that, and so forth.

Now the boat is an essential thing. The Grail maiden takes both Percival and Galahad in the boat. The boats are always sailing up and down the river. Elaine sails down the river; her corpse does. And it's sort of river country. As a matter of fact, the heart of the Grail legend isn't too different from the geography of Vancouver. It's that kind of a thing. From what I hear the Grail stuff actually took place on the coast of Wales. But if it was in Glastonbury, it's an inland sea, where the ocean's thirty, forty miles away and you can't really get to it. Not at all unlike Vancouver. And that's why the difference between the ocean and the non-ocean, and why the Lady of the Lakes is . . .

WT: I'm interested in the particular mental action by which you remain, in a sense, ignorant of that which is in your mind. How do you stop? How do you stop that whole thought, you know, that whole connection machine that calls that "that" instead of just letting it be what it is?

JS: You just learn how not to trust yourself so much that your mind becomes blank on it, I guess. It's like asking Willie Mays how do you hit a curve ball? You don't really know. It takes years of work to do it, and it's really the trick of being a poet more than anything else, I should say — being able to divorce yourself from what you think the poem is saying. And, in some sense you never can. Just like a batter can never keep himself completely from saying this guy's going to throw a slider now and I'll anticipate a slider, which is just the way to have a .198 batting average.

The same thing is true with a pro in poetry. I think that's really where writing poetry for a long time makes you better. Unless you just decide that you love what you want to say yourself so much that you don't bother with it, you gradually learn how to keep the connections out of your mind and let the connections go the way they want to instead of the way that you want to. Not to say, well now, the path really should branch out over here because that's logical. I can hear water over here, therefore I'll go this way. You get lost in the woods that way — every time.

WT: Now just take the woods. You know perfectly well that there are thousands of forests to study in literature. When you're in your forest do you apply the same process that you're describing now, and keep out the sacred grove and the forest that the Tin Woodsman was in, and all these?[19]

JS: I hope so. I never even thought of the fact that the Tin Woodsman did rust in the forest. I never even thought about that. I wasn't even tempted with that particular connection when the poem was going on. There are connections that come in afterwards, and they're nice to have, but . . .

DL: Well, what about all the Merlin connections? I think that section is what I would say is highly political.

JS: Oh it certainly is. Yes.

DL: Well then, did you know? At what point did you know it was political? Not when you were writing it, you said.

JS: No. Almost as soon as Merlin started talking. Merlin is another one like Gwenivere. I didn't have too much trouble with myself coming in. Merlin had things to say. I don't know if all of you know this, but one of the few things which persisted through English folk poetry—say broadsides, that kind of thing—all the way from the start and you get them as early as the fourteenth century, before there's printing, are Merlin prophecies. They're always political prophecies, and they're always done in kind of a masked language to outwit the Mounties of the time, and to get the political message across. Merlin seemed to have that. Why Merlin got so hung up with the Spanish Civil War and sang their songs, I don't know. I could use that.[20]

Q: How are purity and Long Island Sound equated?

JS: Purity and Long Island Sound? Oh no, to identify yourself with the landscape is as stupid as identifying the Grail with purity, I think.

Q: Galahad, I think.

JS: Galahad, right. "Contemplating America from Long Island Sound"— in other words, from absolutely the farthest out place. I'm not sure that it is geographically in America, but Montauk Point, at least to a westerner, seems just about the farthest way to look at America, as Whitman did. Just getting right at the end of it and looking out over the whole thing and thinking that you could find it. I mean, Whitman did visit New Orleans once, and that's about all he ever did. He didn't ever go West. Using purity to catch the Grail is the same thing. Unfortunately, Galahad did and Whitman did, but it's still foolish.

Q: Even though they did, you still sort of say they shouldn't have done it that way.

JS: I think that Galahad rather thinks that he shouldn't have. He is rather ironic about his role. He's almost as sterilized as a space man and finally disappears, just like the spacemen will, off, you know, to some place, leaving us there. Although I certainly don't think that is in the poem. He disappears in the poem in the holes between things. And myself, I have a prejudice against purity and against Galahad. But at any rate, the paradox of being able to contemplate America as America from the farthest point on Long Island Sound is the same thing as contemplating the Grail—which is something which is more than just not fucking with people—by not fucking with people. And yet both Whitman and Galahad receive the reward and both of them left us going up into the air with really nothing below but the dead forest. At least that's the way I read it.[21]

Q: So Whitman is a Grail searcher too then?

JS: In his own way, yeah.

WT: Jack, what's the difference between the Grail in your serial poem and the moth in Robin's serial poem? Is there a similarity or is there a total dissimilarity? No connections?

JS: Well, Warren, I think if you put it in terms of threes, what is the difference between the Grail, the moth, and the snark in "The Hunting of the Snark"? They are all sorts of collective things to be searched for. Robin's was immediate appearance. Mine in this poem was through poetics: Gawain's big thing about the empty cup and the full cup. You see, the Grail was, in Irish mythology, something that you could always eat from. It was always filled up with food. And in the Christian versions it's the thing that Christ bled into, which is the empty thing. The moth is the occurrence of the Real, I'd say. It's the same moth, obviously, although the moth dies several times, and so forth. But it's the Real intruding on things for Robin. And for Lewis Carroll, the snark is something which turns into a boojum.[22] It's a great poem of Carroll's, but it's not a serial poem on account of the fact that I still think he knew the ending when he started the beginning of it.

WT: Would you add Yeats's Crazy Janes to what you're saying now?

JS: No. I think those are just using the same voice over and over again. I don't think if you put all the Crazy Janes together out of all of the books that you'd have anything. Crazy Jane, if anything, is like "The Structure of Rime" is for Duncan. The Crazy Janes will appear at various places in Yeats's time when he wants to have a certain voice, and that's about it.

DL: What about Edwin Muir's poems? Aren't they all very much tied together?

JS: I hate to confess it but I have not read Edwin Muir. He was sort of a friend of . . .[23]

DL: He translated Kafka. He was Scottish.

JS: Oh no. He isn't even the person I thought he was that I hadn't read.

DL: Well, all through your poem I was thinking of Muir.

JS: Really. Well, I'll have to read him. The only Scottish poet I know who's good is Hugh MacDiarmid, who I think is very good.

DL: Oh, he's quite different from MacDiarmid, but he lives in this world of receiving all the time even though he's putting things into these quite structured poems. But all of his poems seem to me to be a wheel revolving, all saying the same thing from different points of view.

JS: Gee, I'll have to read him. What are his years?

DL: He only died two or three years ago, but he did a lot of work in Germany before the Nazi takeover and he, as I say, translates most of Kafka.

JS: Being a person who dislikes Kafka intensely, that doesn't help me much. But he sounds good otherwise. I'll take a look and see.

Q: How did the Australians get in the poem?

JS: I guess they just marched in like they marched into Greece. [Laughter]
    There are several things that happen in the poem which have to do with other wars: the Tarawa and the Battle of Java Sea and the burning oil and the thing with the Australian soldiers.[24] Our friends the British, who had already decided to get out of Greece when the Germans invaded, had the Australians hold the line above Athens. As a matter of fact, it was the line which was connected with Thermopylae, which was rather nice historically.[25] The Australians were marched in from North Africa. So they went in, thinking everything was wonderful, and they were singing,

"We're off to see the Wizard, the wonderful Wizard of Oz." This was their song. I think about ninety percent of them were killed. The British had only about five percent casualties. But those are ancient wars, like the wars of the Grail.

Well, unless you have more specific questions about the poem . . .

WT: I have one more. Since there are a great many vessel things in the poem — boat, armor . . .

JS: I wouldn't say a "boat" was a vessel in the poem. Armor connects with the shell that Merlin made his own jail from, and the various other things. I think that these images are quite separate. The Grail is something which is open-ended. I mean, a vessel is something which is more open at the top than at the bottom.

WT: Well, what I was getting toward is, since the Grail as a vessel is elusive and a mystery, is part of your process about what the serial poem is not? Is there a "not" process that works there, or am I just completely off base? A not making, a not finding it; you can only find it by not finding it?

JS: Well, Galahad found it and screwed up everything by disappearing with it. When I knew it was a Grail poem, as I did I guess, probably, when that damn witch Gwenivere came in and was denouncing the Grail so much — when I knew it was a Grail poem — I certainly didn't make any effort to find it because I knew I wouldn't find it for myself. I let them thrash around, like eels, as Gawain says in the first thing — the sick king. I just let them thrash around, and they found it. Or at least Galahad found it and went up in spaceship X-59 or something, which didn't help anything. But I certainly didn't expect to find it myself. I just expected to get through the forest somehow or other, and when you're at the end of the forest, you aren't much better than you are before. You're at the same kind of a town, the same kind of a clearing, and all of that. It just doesn't have so many trees. And if I'd found the Grail, maybe I would have disappeared too, and you'd never have seen me.

Q: That's interesting because I thought of the poem as, in a sense, a poetics poem, too.

JS: Oh, Gawain certainly does. I think it goes into more the human condition in relationship to the divine, taking the human just like "Textbook" took the divine in relationship to the human. I think this takes the human in relationship to the divine, and we look pretty silly. Like looking down at a crowd of people from the Empire State Building, and this chasing after the Grail. I mean, Gwenivere is right in a lot of ways. But at the same time Arthur is right too in saying that he was king, and he's *rex quondam et futurus* which was actually supposed to be a gravestone that they report in the fifteenth century in Glastonbury in a cave. And this "once and future king" thing is a pretty old legend, although Glastonbury was a tourist trap then and got all of the credulous people to go there and buy souvenirs, get a sliver from the Round Table, and so forth, so they're perfectly capable of faking it.

   Long before I wrote the poem I read all the Arthurian stuff, and one of the things I was really taken with was in a nineteenth-century guidebook of Glastonbury, that said that in the eighteenth century somebody made a machine there that could write poetry in Latin hexameters. Just arbitrarily, any poem, you know, just like the modern experiments with computers writing poetry. And so it's still a place that has some things happening, even if Arthur isn't under the hill.

Q: You mentioned you just wanted to get through the forest when you answered Warren's question. Is that the same sort of forest as in that section of Robin Blaser's poem, "The Medium," where he talks about the holy forest?[26]

JS: Well, the holy forest to Robin is something different. When I was asked about why Robin had another poem after *The Moth Poem* is over . . . He's had for some time a suspicion that all of these poems—the poems he hasn't written and the poems that he read and some other things which may be included—are part of a large book called *The Holy Forest*. But I think his holy forest is rather different from the Grail forest, where you simply meet odd beasts and odd maidens and knights that get mad at you for some reason, or as Percival says, people either tell me to do something, which I do do or don't do because I get angry. That's the kind of forest that I'm talking about. It's probably the *silva oscura* of Dante more than anything else, which is also known as the human condition.

Q: But he talks about being lost, doesn't he? Where he has two people, one before and one after, I think it is—two friends.

JS: Yeah.

Q: He talks about being lost, too. So that would be the forest in which the path of the dictated poem is in.

JS: Well, forests are places that people are lost in with the spooks or the Martians; whatever you are going to use as an image, it is an image that people have had for centuries. Where you get lost is in a forest. It resembles the human condition in a lot of ways. You don't need to know Jungian archetypes or anything else. There are forests around almost everywhere, except maybe in the Gobi Desert, and I suppose then the poets there would use sand dunes. But pretty much where you get lost is in the forest, as you people, God knows, should know with all the trees here and everything. It's even true in southern California where I grew up.

WT: Jack, Creeley has a lot of forest images in his poems, and the forest is very . . . treed. Does this ring a bell for you?

JS: I think you're right in mentioning trees rather than forests. I sometimes think that Creeley doesn't know the forest for the trees. I mean, the images are almost always tree images rather than forest images. You're thinking essentially in terms of this discussion of the three ladies in a tree, aren't you?[27]

WT: Well, there are lots of them. The trees have eyes.

JS: Yeah. The three ladies in the tree are the essential thing. It sort of has his mystique on that. But it's always the business of one tree which you get to, and you explore that tree very carefully, and so forth. The person who walks through the forest—what is the French Canadian word for that?

Q: The *coureur de bois*.

JS: Right. I mean, he ain't interested in any particular tree unless he wants to put a marker on it. And I think there are tree people and there are forest people. Denise [Levertov] has trees too, and she never has forests.

GB: Maybe it has something to do with how long your lines are.

JS: I suppose it does. You can't afford, if you're writing a short poem, to have a whole forest in it. I think, in a way, I know what the New England hills Creeley came from are like. It's pretty hard to get lost in them. You feel more that they're made of stone than made of trees, even though there are trees growing. There are more abandoned farm houses—blocks of stone from a farmhouse built in 1800 which is now gone—than there are trees. It's a different thing.

Of course, Bakersfield, where Duncan came from, doesn't have too many trees, but you can go twenty miles away from Bakersfield and find all the trees to your heart's content. I do think there's a difference—that western poets tend to have the business of the wilderness that you have to get through, and the eastern poets look at the tree as some kind of miracle which is planted very carefully in some park. Denise is an eastern poet. In fact, she comes from London originally, and her stories about her nature experiences all have to do with parks rather than forests since I don't think there's been a forest near London for a long time. I don't know. Maybe there has.

WT: Just one other thing. Since you mention Whitman and Long Island and it comes from that poem, and since you've mentioned Gatsby a number of times, what about Gatsby's Long Island?

JS: Well, Gatsby's Long Island is mine. The way that I think of Long Island as being out—the farthest way you can go east. It's a kind of exile of the spirit. His forest is the forest of ashes with the eye of Dr.—what is his name?—Eckleburg, or whatever it is.[28] He actually says it's a forest and gives the image of a forest of ashes and so forth, which is different from the forest that he knew when he went up about thirty miles from St. Paul and found real forests up in Minnesota. And to him, this is just as startling and as frightening as the man who fixed the World Series. And very similar. It's a crime against nature in a real sense. I don't mean to imply that Fitzgerald liked baseball. He didn't, but he did have Meyer Wolfsheim.[29]

WT: He liked football too.

JS: Yeah, he liked to get drunk at football games.
      Does this thing about the serial poem make any sense to you people?

DL: Is the order or sequence of each seven fixed? You wouldn't dream of changing it?

JS: Oh, you dream of changing it and wish to hell you could but you know damn well if you do that you're going to go up your own path and not the path that you're on.

DL: In the dream there's another poem.

JS: Well no, I think in the dream there's the business of saying what you want to say, and I always am very unhappy when I say what I want to say. In some sense that's the thing that makes me dissatisfied with parts of "The Book of Lancelot"—the fact that it was saying what I wanted to say. Or where the "I used to work in Chicago in a department store" was one way of me talking using the song [in the "Book of Percival"] and is rather unsatisfactory, then the "Lance me, she said / Lance her, I did / I don't work there anymore" comes up absolutely real and absolutely true [in the "Book of the Death of Arthur"]. As I said last time, it's the poem taking care of the grain of sand which is in the oyster's digestive system and encasing it. So it works where it originally was sort of the thing that I was just allowing myself.

That's what I mean about the fact that you can't trust these things. If you're really on the right path, you can strew all sorts of rubbish on the way and it will be picked up by the animals of the forest and carried by Smokey the Bear, say, to the nearest dispose-all unit. Or do you have Smokey the Bear up here?

Q: Yeah.

JS: Yeah. I think he's as eternal as Mickey Mouse.

ELLIOTT GOSE: What about "Notes toward a Supreme Fiction"?

JS: What about it?

EG: Is it like a serial poem?

JS: No, I wouldn't say so.

EG: I asked because I read some explanations by Stevens of what he was trying to say in that poem, and they sounded sort of like your explanations.

JS: Hm. I really wouldn't think so. I think he knew where he was going before he started out.

EG: Well, he knew the total plan.

JS: Yes, but if you have a nice map and you know you want to get from here to the north tip of Vancouver Island, then it sort of isn't the same thing as if you just sail out and don't know where you want to go, and let the wind carry you.

EG: What about a poem like "The Man with the Blue Guitar"? You spoke of Stevens's early poetry.

JS: Well, the only later book of poems I'd say has something of what *Harmonium* has is an almost serial thing, but an edited serial thing, his *Transport to Summer*, which may be because I like "He is not here, the old sun, / As absent as if we were asleep"—you know, that "No Possum, No Sop, No Taters"—and all of the other poems seem to revolve around that one.[30] The awful thing about Stevens that I've noticed is that everybody in English departments who hates poetry, which is just about everybody, loves Stevens. I liked Stevens a great deal more before I saw that. You get somebody who you know very well just hates poetry, like some people hate baseball or hate French movies like I do. You know, there's just a real weird hatred. Well, they always like Stevens, all of these people. And the more they hate poetry as it is in process, the more they like Stevens. So although Stevens moves me, I've gotten more and more distrustful of him.

EG: Why do you suppose that is?

JS: I haven't the vaguest notion.

Q: I thought they always loved W. H. Auden.

JS: Oh no, no, no. They would be accused of odd sexual adventures if they said they liked W. H. Auden, at least in America. He's been around at the universities in America.

GB: When I think of a serial, I'm thinking of movie serials. I think of writing a serial poem as like going to the movies.

JS: Yeah, well, it's a bad name.

DL: What about serial music though? Isn't it related?

JS: I don't know. It's just a name I dreamed up trying to figure out what it was like that Duncan and Robin and I were like that other people weren't like and this was a name. It's a lousy name. It simply means that you go from one point to another to another to another, not really knowing where you are from point A to point B.

GB: That's why I think it's a good name, because you don't know, since the whole point of serials is that you're not supposed to know what's coming. You don't know where you're going to go to. Like serial comic strips, like stories in magazines. That's just my local.

JS: Well, Dickens wasn't a bad serial writer. *The Pickwick Papers* certainly is in terms of novels what the serial poem is in terms of poems. I never thought of that before you mentioned that, but I'd say that in *The Pickwick Papers* Dickens didn't have the vaguest notion what was going to happen in the Journals of the Pickwick Club from month to month as he submitted the thing. It's the only place where I think Dickens is completely free of that, and also, Mr. Jingle is the first surrealist in all of novels. I mean gee, the stream of consciousness of him.

GB: The only one I've read is *Bleak House* and it took me a couple of years to do that.

JS: Oh. Well, Mr. Jingle will go on about various things, and he was talking about a two-story omnibus: went past a sign, woman eating a ham sandwich, sign cuts off her head, sandwich in her hand, no head to eat it with.[31] *The Pickwick Papers* are great.

GB: That sounds just so contemporary.

JS: Yeah, well, as long as we don't go into Pop Art.

GB: Do you think that *Naked Lunch* relates to serials?

JS: No. I don't like *Naked Lunch*, so I don't.

GB: I was thinking about the stories that are like pieces picked up in motels on four or five continents and shoved together by a committee of people and so on. The stories where Burroughs had forgotten some of the things he did that eventually showed up in the novel somehow.

JS: Well, I think Burroughs is always conscious of himself and doesn't ever forget himself or doesn't make any effort to forget himself. It's just one of those things that I don't like—like I was saying about English professors not liking poetry and liking Stevens. I don't like Burroughs. Although I did like *Junkie*, which he wrote as a potboiler and seemed to me a much better novel than *Naked Lunch*.

What about you people out there in the boondocks?

Q: Do you sort of write reams and reams, and then have the little lights and then pick them out, or does it all come at once? Do you kind of warm up and then it comes or what do you do?

JS: Do you mean for an individual poem, or for a book of poems?

Q: For this poem, for instance. In that nine months, did you have lots of stuff and then cut lots out?

JS: Oh no, no, I didn't cut anything.

Q: That just came?

JS: Well, that's what I think a serial poem needs. Not to say, well no, this thing isn't, this path isn't going anywhere; it looks like it's going to a big chasm and I obviously can't go down a chasm. You simply follow the path regardless.

Q: What if you found that some of it is on the path and some is straying, or something doesn't fit in that you don't find, and the rest does? It seems to click. What do you do? Do you cut?

JS: No, you don't cut. As I was saying, this "Book of Lancelot" had a lot of stuff which was obviously straying off the path, but the path caught up with what it strayed off of. That's why I said, "I used to work in Chicago."[32] You know the song, don't you? It picks up on the thing and later makes it into something which it wasn't when it was first quoted in "Lancelot" and was rather cute.

ET: You can do that now because you have all sorts of things working for you that you don't have to use consciously. But when someone's just starting out, they're starting to write, would you feel they should follow the same process?

JS: I've seen them follow the other process of sweating through and saying, oh this isn't good enough, or oh I had better change this, or oh I'd better do this and that and so forth, and that doesn't work, almost ever. It doesn't work for me. And it didn't work for me when I was that age. So I don't see any reason why they shouldn't start out. They may write a very bad serial poem, but they're goddamn well probably going to write bad poems anyway, whether they revise or don't revise. I think you might just as well take more chances and not worry about it.

DL: Perhaps what she meant was that you have so much more actual experience of the furniture.

JS: Sure. You don't strike out if you've been in the major leagues for five or six years and you're good. And if you come up like Willie Mays did for the first nineteen times at bat, he struck out fifteen times, didn't get a hit. He wasn't used to major-league pitching. But the way to get used to major-league pitching is not to sit on the bench, and it's not to play in the 3-I League. It's to go up to the major leagues, or try to go up to the major leagues anyway, and try to hit a few balls. So you pop out, or you strike out. So what? You're going to pop out or strike out in the 3-I League too and not learn nearly as much.

I'd say that I wasted quite a great deal of time trying to write perfect little poems, and I sort of resent the time I wasted. My advice for somebody like Dennis, who's starting out, would be to try the most complicated things and fall flat on your ass doing it. There's no point in not doing it. If you want to be dignified, there's no reason to be a poet. I mean it's the most undignified thing in the world, other than the person who hands out towels in the Turkish bath. [Laughter]

No, my advice for a young poet would be just to try all of the things. I think that this emphasis on craft which you get in universities in the States, and I've noticed it here, is just a bunch of hogshit. I mean, there is a real kind of craft but it's a kind of craft of being able to manage yourself vis-à-vis what is coming into you on the poem, being able to receive the poem. It's not a craft any more than you can have Ted Williams write a book saying how to bat .400 in the major leagues. There's no use to that at all. You learn it by doing all sorts of wild things, by following the paths that open up to you, and if they don't open up, you wait and see. Make sure that the paths do open up. If they don't, then you aren't a poet.

Won't somebody argue with me? [Laughter]

Q: What did you spend your nine months doing on the poem? Did you just have sort of little times phased out?

JS: Let me put it this way. I usually write late at night and up into the following morning and so forth on these things, sometimes pausing three or four hours between one line and the next because I want to write a line, the next line, which I think is great but the poem doesn't. There's that time.

Q: Again, are you following your own lead?

JS: No, I'm trying not to follow my own lead. When a line comes up and it's beautiful and I really like it and it says exactly what I want, then I stop and wait and wait and wait and wait.

Q: Why? Isn't what you recognize to be of value to the work legitimate?

JS: No. I don't think it is. That's what I want, not what the poem wants.

Q: Do you ever explore more into what you've done?

JS: Do I read my poems over again?

Q: Yeah. Try to figure them out.

JS: Oh yeah, yeah.

Q: And try to go on from there?

JS: No, not go on from there. I try to figure them out because I figure the poem is giving a message to me as well as to other people, and so I naturally read them to myself. I read them out loud and try to get what bothers people about them. Occasionally things come up where I suddenly understand. Like say, I hadn't connected the Tin Woodsman with the woods, oddly enough, and I understand the poem a little bit better now.

Q: Don't you think then that the poem is just a matter of chance?

JS: Chance? Let me just see if I understand what you mean. Would you say that if I turned on the radio now, it would be just a matter of chance that the words were in English rather than in Albanian?

Q: No.

JS: The point is that you're not the thing which is broadcasting. You're the receiver. If you're good enough, you can get so much out of yourself that you're almost as empty as a radio tube or a transistor or whatever you're using, and the message comes through. The message may not be important. A lot of the stuff that comes through isn't important, or at least doesn't seem important to me. But if it's really coming through, I read it again and again and see whether it is. The fact that you don't have anything to do with it, that you aren't doing anything more than relaying something, doesn't seem to me anything to be particularly perturbed about. At least I'm not.

Q: What about the "yellow eye" poem, that one that was in *The New American Poetry*?

JS: "The Imaginary Elegies," yeah. What about it?

Q: Were they more planned than this one?

JS: They were the first thing I got into really which became serial. They were written over a period of years. I wrote the first three, I think, in regular sittings, but I did revise them later. The fourth came afterwards, about five years afterwards. Yes, it says five years in the poem. And the revision of the whole thing came after that. It's sort of a mixed-up kind of thing. I'd say it's half-dictated and half-made, and I wouldn't say it was serial in any real sense although I have written a fifth and a sixth elegy after that. So it may be very much like Duncan's "The Structure of Rime," something which will stay. But although I like the poems, I mean I like the "Elegies"— they're fine, they're very brilliant poems and technically they're lovely— they don't tell me very much more than what I knew when I was writing them, and that's the sign of, to me, a poem which is good but unsuccessful.

Q: If you have this poem, and you found you were discovering more through it, what if you kept on going from there and kept developing it with what you discovered through it, until you finally came to the end and you had something that didn't give you much more because you'd gotten everything out of it and written it all down? Doesn't that make it a more complete and true poem?

JS: Well, you've got me, it's like saying what would happen if you were able to bat, say, .997 or something like that. The point is that this threat never comes up, of being able to get everything down which is being transmitted.

Q: But you'd get lots more down if you kept working through the original.

JS: I don't think so. It may be true with some people. Yeats certainly was able to improve his poems and actually get more dictation by revising them, and I've seen other people who could do it. But I find that I start imposing my personality on the poem. I start saying, well this *should* be the message, goddamn it, even if it isn't. Then, by the time that four or five revisions have happened, the poem that wanted to be heard is sort of lost and something which is more brilliant and more easily understood by the public, and by me because I created it, is left. This is all very well, but it isn't, I think, what a poet is supposed to do.

Q: I think you've gained there rather than lost because you've made something comprehensible to yourself.

JS: Well, I got very few surprises from the "Elegies," and I get very few surprises. I mean it was the "Elegies" where I did get some dictated revisions. In the second elegy, the business of the castle made of glass and skin and the "da dada da" was a dictated thing which came long afterwards. But that's the only place where I actually wrote some revision where I still don't quite understand (or at least don't like) what the poem is saying. It came to me like an original poem would. And it's quite possible that some poets can do that often. But that's about the only time when I fooled around with a poem that I didn't hurt it rather than help it.

EG: You seem to equate passivity with unconscious skill.

JS: No, I don't. Passivity is not the same thing as clearing your mind.

EG: You know, even if you make analogies with baseball, you can also make an analogy with music. Beyond a certain point a musician doesn't think about his technique because he did think about it at one time, and he formed a particular technique. The same thing is true with poets writing in traditional meters. Take Stevens. Excuse me for taking him again but . . .

JS: Oh, let's take Wallace Stevens.

EG: I've already been put down for taking him once, but take his use of blank verse. He writes blank verse very easily, and probably pretty unconsciously because he wrote it for years. So it seems to me that there's a kind of unconscious skill which comes as a result of having mastered a particular skill and done it very consciously. The best analogy I can think of is the analogy of an instrumentalist. Yet you seem to be trying to draw away from something, from anything like that. In other words, the technique you seem to be recommending isn't a verbal technique but a kind of meditative technique.

JS: Well, fundamentally that is what I recommend, whether you learn to be able to write in blank verse or anything else.[33]

There's no magical reason this should be true, but I'd say on the whole distrust revisions.

Q: Yeah, but it could be the medium thinking that you didn't get the right furniture, therefore I'll communicate again.

JS: Sure, sure. It could be. It's just that I've seen so many poets that get hung up on revising poems, like Tate's "Ode to the Confederate Dead," which he revised, I think, a hundred and five times and published in about fifty versions, and it got weaker and weaker as time went on.[34] You know, you can spend a whole life revising one poem, and I suppose that would be very interesting. I think Stevens could actually do it—getting back to your Stevens thing.

EG: Well, I don't think he did, later.

JS: He didn't. But what I mean is, I think he's probably the only poet who might have been capable of writing something like the "Ode to the Confederate Dead" and each revision would be something which was adding up to something else.

EG: Well, the question I had really was that maybe we do have different conceptions of poetry. My notion has always been that the poet masters language the way a person masters an instrument, and that finally it reaches a point where it is unconscious, in much the way you're speaking. But I wondered if the preparation wasn't a little bit more conscious than you want it to be.

JS: Well, this is the thing that I grew up with and I think everybody grew up with. In painting, first you have to learn how to paint a representational painting before you can paint a nonobjective painting, and all of that sort of crap, which is untrue, as a matter of fact.

EG: I think that a poet finally should be exactly what you describe him as. But I wonder if the preparation isn't or shouldn't be . . .

JS: Well, you used music. Now, to begin with, music has a problem and an advantage in transcribing that poetry doesn't. If you can't transcribe the music that you hear, then you're not going to be able to write the damn thing down. In transcription you have to know something about key signatures and all of that. Just like a poet has to at least be able to know how the language goes. He can't write something in a language he doesn't know anything in. But past that, I don't know.

EG: Take an analogy with jazz then.

HARRY ADASKIN:[35] Let's go back to baseball then.

JS: No, let's take something aesthetic, because I think he believes that there is a difference between the aesthetic world and the non-aesthetic world of game.

EG: No I don't, I think the analogy with any game is a good analogy.

JS: Oh.

EG: I think the analogy with baseball is a fine one. In fact, it's a perfect one for the point I'm trying to make.

JS: Okay. Good.

EG: But take the analogy with jazz, which is often made. A jazz musician plays "These Foolish Things." Fine. But after he's played it every night for a couple of years, the reason he can be passive, the reason he can allow his unconscious to operate, is that he has patterns in his fingers and these patterns are so firmly in his fingers that he can allow them to take their own head and do what they want to.

JS: I would agree with that. But at the same time, you get the kind of thing which you've had in jazz since Parker died, with the exception of Monk, where at least I am not moved any more, where you are just showing what you can do with the things which are in your fingers or in your mouth or wherever the thing is.

HA: It's utterly boring.

JS: Yeah. Cool jazz becomes cold jazz.

EG: But your preparation has been a little more conscious maybe than you want to admit. I mean, you've stocked your mind.

JS: That's furniture, though. That's furniture which the spooks can move around any way they want to.

DL: Yes, but a young person wouldn't have nearly as much furniture.

JS: That's right. But the only way to find out what furniture you need is to lack it. You go to a place, and the green Martian spook doesn't find anything in the room he can possibly sit in. This tells the poet, for chrissakes get another chair for the room. And I certainly think that a poet ought to supply as much furniture as possible but then ought to be very careful about not saying, "oh *please*, sit down in this new armchair I've just gotten."

As far as the business of reading—education—I think that unfortunately the universities hinder it rather than help it usually because they make reading and education a chore rather than something that you enjoy doing. But certainly I think that any poet who is going to write decent poetry in this modern age where we don't have the ballad tradition anymore, where you could get by with practically no furniture, and let's squat on the floor, ma'am, and that sort of thing—I do think that just the average young poet ought to read as many books as he can and they ought to not be in paperback. They ought to be books that nobody's read and that aren't fashionable, and things which are about animal husbandry or what saline solutions are like with octopuses or something like that. It doesn't really matter too much. But he certainly ought to have more stock in his mind than he has.

As far as practicing the forms, I think this is something which people did believe, but I really don't believe it now, except for being able to write the forms down.

Let me just give you an example and see if this makes some sense to you. There's a very good poet in San Francisco, or an on-and-off very good poet, named Jim Alexander. Nothing of his I think has been published in anything you'd have seen. His best poem is "A Jackrabbit Poem" published in *J.*[36] Now, Jim has a big thing in his poems, in his poetic, about breaking words, you know, which is perfectly reasonable. Joyce did, too—making words into portmanteau things, and all of that. So spelling is extremely important. Unfortunately, the kid can't spell. And so it is impossible to know often whether the thing is an error in the fact that he thinks that "there" meaning t-h-e-r-e is spelled t-h-e-i-r. In other words, whether it's intentional or not.

This obviously is something which does hurt his poetry because there's no rational way of really telling. But you can often feel where the things are. Now this obviously is something useful. On the other hand, knowing the language in the sense of knowing what a *terza rima* is or some goddamn thing like that seems to me something that should come later. I've seen a couple of poets go in for sonnets after they'd been writing all sorts of wild stuff which was about as far away from a sonnet as possible. Ebbe Borregaard is an example of that. Then he comes up against Shakespeare's sonnets and some other Elizabethan sonnets and writes sonnets, but he writes sonnets in a way that they originally worked for the Elizabethans—songs rather than anything else, and not necessarily fourteen lines. He has the freedom that he's gotten by being free, and then he takes the form and sees what he can do with it. And it turned out very successfully.[37]

It seems to me, just like I think most artists would say, that the best thing to do with a kid is not to encourage him—not to discourage him—but not to encourage him to be representational. Then again, with nonobjective painters, the Black Mountain School—Tom Field, for example.[38] He went from the absolutely nonobjective to the representational, and he goes back and forth. But he was able to get the focus on the thing from the fact that he had the forms and the colors first and then the objects came afterwards, and if he'd learned how to get proper perspective and to draw fingers and toes and so forth, I doubt it would have come out as successfully as it did.

EG: The trouble with talking about learning forms or practicing the forms is that we all pretty much agree that those are conventions that aren't too useful. So if you practice writing sonnets to begin with, you're likely to be writing something that is almost immediately dated. And this would appear almost to be true with blank verse, too. But take a poem like Hart Crane's "Voyages II," which is a great poem. I suppose you agree.

JS: Yes, I know.

EG: Yet that poem shows an immense control of blank verse. And I doubt that Crane could have written it if he hadn't had something of the openness that you talk about. I'm sure that no good poem is written without that kind of openness.

JS: Well what Crane did was to make all of his openness not metric but in terms of vocabulary.

EG: Yeah, but still metrically.

JS: I know, but he would use the metric as something that he took as fairly stable and the vocabulary exploded all out over the world. In "Voyages V,"—"Meticulous, past midnight in clear rime"—that "sleep the long way home" poem is one of the finest poems in English.[39]

EG: Yeah.

JS: These words which I wouldn't dare to use, and most modern poets wouldn't dare to use at all, he does. He does it because he's allowing himself this Elizabethan aureate language, because instead of using the line as the thing where he stretches his legs, he's using the vocabulary as the thing he stretches his legs in. I don't think it makes any difference. I think a person can write very nicely using the vocabulary as the thing that's allowed expansion rather than the line. I don't think it matters much. Although Crane is rather an oddball in terms of things like that. He's about the only example I can think of that.

EG: But isn't one of the pleasures in poetry seeing a person take language and do what he wants with it, and control it, because he's practiced and practiced doing things—not necessarily because they turn out as poems, but simply practiced them for the sake of getting control of language, to go back to my original analogy with learning how to play an instrument.

JS: I don't think so. I think that's one of the things I object to in cold jazz.

EG: Well, in hot jazz it would work as well.

JS: Not really. Well, jazz is not my subject, so there's no point in getting into it. But in terms of poetry, in the first place, I don't think poetry should be a pleasure for the audience any more than it should be a pleasure for the poet. I don't think it's meant as a pleasure. The pleasures are sort of incidental, if they do exist, and haven't really anything to do with the poem.

And it seems to me that the poets who are showing their great control are very much like the bad things about Willie Mays—since we did say that we could talk about baseball. He'll make circus catches when he doesn't have to, and that will please people in the audience who say, oh gee, he caught this terrible thing, and you know, had to throw his cap back and go back and do a ballet dance like he studied Catherine Dunham and all of that, but it's a routine fly ball, you know. It's a nice way to pass a boring, windy afternoon in Candlestick Park, but it ain't baseball.

EG: Well, what you're saying is that technique for its own sake is bad, which I would agree with.

JS: Yeah we just disagree on what a younger poet should first concentrate on and I don't think it should be technique.

DL: Surely it should be then simply the rhythm of the language that is impelling him.

JS: Well, I think he ought to do just exactly what somebody would do in one of those mystical Asian sects that Ginsberg likes so well—trying to get his personality out of himself and letting something else come in, whatever the hell it is. I think that the first thing of becoming a poet is a kind of a spiritual exercise, and it's emptying yourself as a vessel. Then the language is one of the pieces of furniture, or maybe just the way the walls are built. That's more than pieces of furniture, I guess, in the analogy.

The language is there, and it has to be learned, and you have to really know the shadows of the words and all of that, eventually. But the first thing, if you're going to build a house and furnish it and set a table and all of that—the first thing to do is make sure that you have a guest. I mean, it's like the recipe for rabbit stew. First catch the rabbit.[40]

EG: I hate to sort of throw your attack at me back at you, but it seems to me that maybe you're more interested in truth than in poetry. It would seem to me that the person who's interested in poetry is interested in language first of all. And he may be interested in truth, or finding something secondly. Whereas I really think that you're interested in finding truth first, and that poetry is secondary.

JS: I'm interested in being a conveyor of messages, whether they're the truth or not. There's no reason to suppose that a message necessarily because it's conveyed from an outside source to a poet is true. As far as not being interested in language, it's probably because I'm a professional linguist.

EG: Yes, I had thought of that as I was saying it.

Q: You said that poetry wasn't for pleasure.

JS: Yes, I really believe that. I think it's very nice to get kicks out of poetry, but I don't think it's for pleasure any more than I think baseball is for pleasure or chess is for pleasure.

HA: Or music.

JS: Or music. Yes. Exactly.

Q: I thought it was.

JS: I don't think so. There's something Duncan quotes in, I think, "Domestic Scenes" from Aristotle's *Poetics*: "One cannot expect every kind of pleasure from tragedy."[41] The pleasures are there—the pleasure of almost anything happening that happens and hits, just the pleasure of being able to hear somebody when you haven't heard somebody. You know, you're in a room for two or three hours and you hear somebody say something idiotic, there's a kind of a pleasure in it. But I don't think that's it.

I also don't think that I'm looking for truth as it helps human beings. I'm not sure what poetry is for. All I am sure of is that it's not for pleasure, although it does give pleasure.

EG: Certainly not exclusively for pleasure but, after all, you read it for pleasure, I think.

JS: I don't.

EG: Or at least if you don't get pleasure while you're reading it—and I think this is true of music too, actually.

HA: It's not true. I don't play for pleasure, and I don't listen to music for pleasure. I get something very serious out of it, but pleasure would be the last noun I should think of.

EG: I don't want to reduce it to pleasure.

HA: It would be a purely incidental thing. Let's put it that way.

EG: Well, pleasure's a word that can be used pretty seriously too. By picking on that word it makes it seem that we're reducing it to nothing but pleasure. Or I would say that we're reducing poetry to nothing but baseball, because I thought that people watch baseball for pleasure too, actually.

Q: Maybe what he means is something like poetry is for itself. It's not for anything.

HA: Baseball isn't pleasure to the people who play it, surely. I mean, it's a very serious business.

EG: It must be pleasure to the people who watch it.

JS: Well, it's not really. Lord, I don't know. In Vancouver, I suppose, the Mounties you almost have to watch for pleasure. When the Giants are playing the Dodgers, even if the Giants win, I'm a nervous wreck after the game.

EG: Well, it's a pleasure.

JS: It may be a pleasure, but I feel like I've run cross-country and am a shaking wreck.

HA: Pleasure is always, I have always thought, where music is concerned, a sign of a dilettante. I can't even conceive of Heifetz getting pleasure out of his violin playing, or Toscanini out of conducting.

EG: It's unfortunate that pleasure should be the term we're playing with here because it implies superficiality, and it implies something trivial. I was just saying that it seems to me that it always has to be there. And furthermore that there's pleasure in pain. There's pleasure in drinking.

Q: Does this mean, as an audience, that you're pleased after you've heard something, or while you hear something?

Q: In other words, it can't leave you blah. It's got to do something. You can't define the something.

JS: I can't imagine anything less pleasurable than the later Beethoven quartets. But at the same time, they're compelling. I mean, if someone wanted to play the fifteenth to me when I wanted just to relax and have a good time, I would just . . .

EG: It seems you're attaching trivial meanings to the word.

JS: Well, no. I mean, I could be forced to have that pleasure but it would be almost a kind of rape.

EG: I was about to go that far.

ET: I don't want to change the subject if someone wants to pursue it, but I'm still concerned about one thing, about the poems that you throw away, namely the ones that you want to write.

JS: Since I write serial poems, I throw the whole thing away—including the poems I didn't want to write which are poems—if I come up to poems that I want to write and I can't get away from them.

Q: You just intrude.

JS: Yeah. I mean, there are plenty of poems. One of the nicest things is when you learn that you can throw poems away—that you don't have to save good lines and things like that.

EG: There weren't really serial poems written before the twentieth century though.

JS: In the sense I limited them to, there weren't any. Of course, there were. "The Hunting of the Snark" is near to that. *The Countess of Pembroke's Arcadia* by Sidney is certainly sort of like a serial poem.[42] And the way that Spenser's *Faerie Queene* was constructed, I'm goddamn sure he didn't know where things were going from one path to another. There have always been things like that. Skelton's "Speak, Parrot" and things like that were certainly serial poems, in a broad sense.[43] Lear's "Jumblies," which is a lovely poem.[44]

WT: Jack, does your ruling yourself out have any connection at all with Eliot's idea of impersonality and getting rid of personality?[45]

JS: Yeah. I think that Dante is the first one. No, Horace as a matter of fact mentions it. It's probably what poets have always known. I don't think it's anything that Mr. Eliot suddenly discovered.

EG: What about Eliot saying that he knew nothing more about his craft than a carpenter knows about his? Or what about Pound's preoccupation with craft? You would appear to be sort of antipathetic to this.

JS: To begin with, craft is a very funny kind of thing. If a carpenter had to restrain himself from sawing in a non-straight line because his personality wanted to saw not a straight line but a curved line, then, in a sense, his craft would be learning to go a straight line and having the straight line take over him. I don't know. I think that both Pound and Eliot certainly had, in their youth, this crap about craft and never really changed in their essays what they said. But it must have struck Pound as odd that he was able to write the most moving, the most immediate cantos when he was in the monkey cage, without any books. And this must have kind of made him think, well, maybe all of this isn't quite the way that it seemed to me.

EG: But it seems to me that sounds perfectly consistent with the point I was trying to make. The reason they were the most moving—I suppose you're thinking about . . .

JS: The "Pisan Cantos."

EG: "Pull down thy vanity" is because he had written all the rest of them.

JS: Yeah.

Q: But why do you keep wanting to make Jack's poems be not what they are?

EG: I wasn't talking about his poems.

Q: Even calling them meditative, because it puts a whole trap on them.

EG: It seems to me that they are.

JS: Meditative?

EG: Yeah.

JS: Did you say that tonight?

EG: Yeah.

Q: But that's a way of talking about them so that you don't see what they are.

EG: Well, any way of talking about them is going to be superimposing terms. I mean, finally perhaps we can't talk about them.

JS: No, I'm interested in meditative though. This seems so out in left field that it probably has something to do with the poems. What do you mean?

EG: Well, the reason I used the word was that you used terms which might come out of Saint Ignatius or something.

JS: I see, you mean meditative in that way. I'm sorry. Yes, in other words, like spiritual exercises. I didn't get the Catholic use of the word "meditative."

EG: I was thinking that you've talked about spiritual discipline. I keep thinking of Saint Ignatius.

JS: Yes, except that there's a difference. Saint John of the Cross maybe. Saint Ignatius, no. Although Saint Ignatius had the right methods.[46] But Saint Ignatius would prepare all of this, as Jesuits do, for something to come in. But they make the cell so bare, so barren of furniture, that nothing can possibly come in. They're afraid of having any furniture because they're afraid of being taken over by the furniture, or having the Christ child sit on a chair which isn't exactly nice for the Christ child to sit on.

EG: My only point in using that term was it seemed to me you're more interested in meditation than in poetry, in that you talk largely about techniques of meditation or meditation in this Ignatian sense.

JS: I think that's the first thing for the poet, yes. I think that for a poet starting out, say like Dennis [Wheeler] and Sherry are, that probably the best thing that people can give them is the business of telling them to empty themselves out of themselves first and start receiving, and then go on from there.[47]

EG: I don't disagree with that at all. Not for a moment. All I was thinking is that possibly that's one thing, and it might provide subject matter for poetry, but then the poetic technique might be something further.

JS: I certainly agree. I mean, it's a question of what is the basic first thing. Do you teach a person to throw a slider or do you teach a person to throw a fast ball? What I'm saying is the basic technique is to do the simplest thing first which is to empty out yourself from the room and start adding furniture as things start coming in, and you will use these crazy pitches later on, and your screw balls you use when you're forty or so and going over the hill.

EG: The conversation has taken a turn which has made it look as though I'm totally antagonistic to what you're saying. I'm not at all.

JS: I don't think you are. Meditative in that sense—you understand what I'm saying quite well, and it's exactly that. Except that I think that I have been talking as if everybody in the room was starting out in poetry, because I think it's about the only way that one can honestly give one's opinions, starting from scratch. Obviously, this advice to Duncan or to Brother Antoninus or to Ginsberg would be absolutely useless. They've gone their way. I'm just saying that I think if you're going to start out writing or start a real change in your writing, that this is the right way to do it.

Notes

1. In this instance, the term "book" is complicated, because the entire book, *The Holy Grail*, is made up of seven chapters or sagas, each of which bears an individual title: "The Book of Gawain" or the ("The Book of Percival," and so on. For an in-depth analysis of the intricate weaving of form and figures, and the interlocking narrative structures in *The Holy Grail*, see Riley. For a discussion of seriality, see also Conte.

2. Elliott Gose (b. 1926) is the author of several critical books, including: *Imagination Indulged: The Irrational in the 19th-Century Novel* (1972), *The Transformation Process in Joyce's "Ulysses"* (1980), *The World of the Irish Wonder Tale* (1983) and *Mere Creatures: A Study of Modern Fantasy Tales for Children* (1988). In 1959–1960, he was a founding editor of UBC's *Prism* magazine, now known as *Prism International*. He came to UBC the same year as Tallman.

3. The New Design Gallery reading in May 1965 was organized to demonstrate the serial poem. The readers were Spicer, Robin Blaser, and Stan Persky. The order was as follows: Blaser—"The Moth Poem," "Cups." Spicer—"Billy The Kid." Blaser—"The Park." Persky—"The Lives of the French Symbolist Poets." Blaser—"The Moth Poem" again.

4. See Lecture 1, note 39.

5. In a letter to Ariel Parkinson, Spicer writes that "that Gawain poem your show inspired has become part of a long Holy Grail poem which I am about half through."

6. *Medieval Scenes* was begun in February 1947 in the context of Spicer's and Duncan's discussions of poetry and magic while they were living at 2029 Hearst Street. According to the biographer of Duncan's early life, Ekbert Faas, Duncan "decided that for ten consecutive evenings, he would sit down at the round table, pencil in hand, and not get up again until he had finished writing a complete single poem," the sum of which would form the series *Medieval Scenes*. Faas reads the poem in terms of Duncan's attraction to both Spicer and Hugh O'Neill. Inspired by Eliot's notes to *The Waste Land*, Duncan also wrote six pages of "Notes to *Medieval Scenes*" (Faas, 226–29).

7. In previous years, Creeley and Duncan had also given talks in the same series at the Tallmans'. In response to my questionnaire to audience members, Jamie Reid wrote of the difference between the three poets' lectures: "Creeley always gave the sense at first of speaking haltingly, embarrassed and reluctant, but gradually warming to the event as he found his feet. . . . Duncan, by contrast, was always and immediately voluble. Duncan just kept talking, generating jokes, lore, aperçus, impromptu theories, etc., until everybody was worn out and finally went home. . . . Spicer seemed more interested than the other two in finding out what the audience thought, and sometimes placed questions directly to individuals as a means of finding out."

8. Duncan, Blaser, and Creeley all create a matrix of superserial composition in works like "The Structure of Rime" and, later, "Passages" (Duncan), the "Image-Nation" series (Blaser), and the "Echo" poems (Creeley).

9. See also his letter to Robin Blaser in *Admonitions*: "Poems should echo and re-echo against each other. They should create resonances. They cannot live alone any more than we can" (A, 61).

10. Lewis Carroll's "The Hunting of the Snark" is composed in eight "fits," plus a preface. As Spicer suggests, the snark is not discovered to be a "boojum" until the last few lines of the poem, but "boojum" is a neologism of Carroll's (which, if it were in a dictionary would go between "boo-hoo" and "book"), so the narrative's discovery of the murderer, as Spicer would have it, is replaced by a trick of language. "The Snark" is the narrative of the search for an object that, like the Grail, is not there except as a construction of language.

11. Robert Duncan uses the phrase "Cheat at this game" in the first poem of the "Structure of Rime" (*The Opening of the Field*, 13).

12. Spicer is probably referring to Weston's most influential book, *From Ritual to Romance* (1920), but see also her earlier treatise, *The Quest of the Holy Grail* (1913). Weston ascribes the legend to pagan ritual rather than to Christian or Celtic origins.

13. Tony Sherrod and Tony Aste were two young men who were on the North Beach scene (Ellingham and Killian, 221 ff.).

14. In the first letter of *Admonitions*, to Joe Dunn, Spicer writes similarly: "In these poems the obscene (in word and concept) is not used, as is common, for the sake of intensity, but rather as a kind of rhythm as the tip-tap of the branches throughout the dream of *Finnegans Wake* or, to make the analogy even more mysterious to you, a cheering section at a particularly exciting football game. It is precisely because the obscenity is unnecessary that I use it, as I could have used any disturbance, as I could have used anything (remember the beat in jazz) which is regular and beside the point" (A, 55).

15. The capital of a British colony in the central Pacific, Tarawa was occupied by the Japanese from December 1941 until November 1943, when it fell in a particularly bloody battle with U.S. Marines. (See HG, 195.)

16. Frankie Frisch, "the Fordham Flash," first played for the New York Giants (1919–1926), including four World Series. He became a record-breaking second baseman and then manager for the St. Louis Cardinals.

17. Ellen (King) Tallman (b. 1927) was married to Warren Tallman. She attended UC Berkeley and was a close friend of Blaser, Duncan, and Spicer. She is preparing a memoir of her friendship with these three figures.

18. *The Fool Killer* (directed by Servando Gonzalez, 1965) starred Anthony Perkins and Edward Albert. Based on the novel by Helen Eustis, the film is set in the post-Civil War South, where a twelve-year-old orphan runs away from his foster parents and learns a horrifying legend about an axe murderer who kills people who persist in doing foolish things.

19. In L. Frank Baum's *Wizard of Oz*, the Tin Woodsman (who seeks a heart), first appears as a disembodied groan Dorothy hears in the forest. Once he's been oiled up, he tells the story of being in love with a "Munchkin girl," but her mother conspires with the Wicked Witch of the East to prevent their marriage. The witch enchants the young woodsman's axe so that it cuts off first one of his legs, then another, then his head, all of which a tinsmith is able to replace. When the witch makes the axe chop through the woodsman's body, the tinsmith gives him a tin body but is unable to replace his heart; hence, his love for the Munchkin girl is lost. Symbolically, his quest is perhaps the most Grail-like (Baum, 33–34).

20. For a discussion of the Merlin prophecies, see the Merlin chapter in Butler's *The Myth of the Magus*, in which Virgil and Merlin are discussed together in relation to incarnation and divination. Of further interest, see also Ashbery's poem "Sortes Vergilianae" and Creeley's poem "Heroes," both of which make use of Butler.

21. In Spicer's "Some Notes on Whitman for Allen Joyce," he writes:

> He was reaching for a world I can still remember. Sweet and painful. It is a world without magic and without god. His ocean is different from my ocean, his moon is different from my moon, his love (oh, God, the loss) is different from my love.
>
> In his world roads go somewhere and you walk with someone whose hand you can hold. I remember. In my world roads only go up and down and you are lucky if you can hold onto the road or even know that it is there. . . . Forgive me, Walt Whitman, you whose fine mouth has sucked the cock of the heart of the country for fifty years. You did not even understand cruelty. It was that that severed your world from me, fouled your moon and your ocean, threw me out of your bearded paradise. . . . Calamus cannot exist in the presence of cruelty. Not merely human cruelty, but the cruelty of shadows, the cruelty of spirits. . . . So when I dreamed of Calamus, as I often did when I touched you, or put my hand upon your hand, it was not as of a possible world, but as a lost paradise. A land my father Adam drove me out of with the whip of shadow. In the last sense of the word—a fairy story. (ONS, 81–82)

See also "Landscape & Seriality" in the Afterword.

22. See note 10 on "boojum."

23. Edwin Muir was a working-class Scottish poet and, with Willa Muir, a prolific translator, most notably of Kafka. His *Collected Poems* was published in 1960 by Faber and Faber.

24. The Battle of the Java Sea in February 1942 was a disastrous defeat for the Allied forces, after which Java was left open to invasion by the Japanese. It took place shortly after the Japanese takeover of Tarawa (see note 15). "The burning oil" is a possible description of the Battle of Java Sea, in which Allied ships were sunk near the coast of Java and sailors were left floating in burning seas. This apocalyptic image appears again in the third poem for the Vancouver Festival in *Book of Magazine Verse*.

Churchill recalled the Australian soldiers singing "We're off to see the Wizard" during the "buoyant days" of the North African campaign in 1941 (Churchill, 615–16). Henry M. Littlefield cites the passage in his article "The Wizard of Oz: Parable on Populism" (Baum, 221–33).

25. Thermopylae is a narrow pass between the cliffs of Mount Oata and the Malic Gulf. Here in 480 B.C. the Spartans lost to the Persians under Xerxes.

26. In *The Moth Poem*: "the story is of a man / who lost his way in the holy wood / / because the way had never been taken without / at least two friends, one on each side" (*Holy Forest*, 45). As it appears in *The Holy Forest*, *The Moth Poem* contains one poem more than the original edition.

27. The poem is "The Three Ladies" (Creeley, *Collected Poems*, 61).

28. In *The Great Gatsby*, the neighborhood of Wilson's Garage, where ashes flourish like wheat, is overseen by the godlike eyes of Dr. Eckleburg's billboard for eye care.

29. In the novel, Meyer Wolfsheim is the crime boss who fixed the 1919 World Series. In his poem "October 1, 1962," Spicer conflates the Black Sox scandal with the lack of team spirit and fair play among the contemporary San Francisco poets and the sense that poetry too had been "fixed" by its bosses (ONS, 87). This sentiment is echoed in his discussion of bosses in Lecture 4.

30. Spicer chooses a particularly dark and enigmatic poem that works by negation. One can't help hearing the oblique reference to Eliot in the title (Stevens, 293).

31. Jingle's Joycean commentary is: "Heads, heads—take care of your heads! . . . other day—five children—mother—tall lady, eating sandwiches—forgot the arch—crash—knock—children look round—mother's head off—sandwich in her hand—no mouth to put it in—head of a family off—shocking, shocking!" (Dickens, 11). Aside from its use of serial form, *The Pickwick Papers* would probably appeal to Spicer in a number of ways: first, as the account of a somewhat secret society with rules of order and loyal members; second, as an urban society situated in and around pub life; and third, as a text whose fictional author is both corporate and posthumous. Dickens's full title is *The Posthumous Papers of the Pickwick Club*, and Spicer's practice of dictation entails a nonunified voice in a text that exists only in the poet's posthumous future.

32. The "I used to work in Chicago" song tells the story of someone who is fired from his job because of a pun or misunderstanding that changes an innocent request into a sexual encounter. Among sports clubs the bawdy song is still in play with infinite ad-libbed and updated verses available on the World Wide Web. The text is sung to a tune resembling "The Bear Went Over the Mountain." A sample verse goes: "I used to work in Chicago in a department store. I used to work in Chicago, but I don't work there anymore. A lady [or man] came in for some paper, some paper from the store. Paper she wanted, a ream she got. I don't work there anymore." Other verses include: "a balloon he wanted, blown he got" and "a translator she wanted, a cunning linguist she got."

33. At this point, there is a break in the recording.

34. In fact, Allen Tate published "Ode to the Confederate Dead" in 1930 with the subtitle: "being the revised and final version of a poem previously published on several occasions to which are added Message from Abroad and The Cross," but he revised the poem several more times before the 1937 version that was published as a final draft in his *Collected Poems* in 1977.

35. Harry Adaskin (1901–1994) was a concert violinist. He taught music at UBC and was a music commentator for Canadian radio. He was appointed an Officer of the Order of Canada in 1974.

36. James Alexander's (b. 1940) "A Jack Rabbit Poem" was later collected into his chapbook *The Jack Rabbit Poem*, designed and printed by Graham Mackintosh for White Rabbit Press in 1966. The poem first appeared in Spicer's magazine *J*.

37. See, for instance, Borregaard's *Sketches for 13 Sonnets* (1969), published under the pseudonym Gerard Boar. Borregaard (b. 1933) was a poet active in the San Francisco scene of the time and a participant in Spicer's legendary workshop "Poetry as Magic," held at the San Francisco Public Library in 1957. Other participants in the workshop included Helen Adam, Robert Duncan, Joe Dunn, Jack Gilbert, and George Stanley.

38. Tom Field (1930–1995) was a student at Black Mountain College who moved to San Francisco in 1956, where he remained and painted for the rest of his life. In fall

of 1996 there was a retrospective show of his painting at 871 Fine Arts Gallery in San Francisco. Robin Blaser, in his note to the show, describes him as an "undergrounder" and "outsider."

39. The refrain in one of Spicer's most emblematic poems, "A Diamond"—"there is nothing in the universe like diamond, nothing in the whole mind"—is strikingly similar to the sentiment and syntax in Crane's poem, "Voyages V" (AL, 22; Crane, 39).

40. The last three sentences of this paragraph were made into a broadside by the Arif Press.

41. The 1947 manuscript copy of "Domestic Scenes" is entitled "Upon Jack's Return: Domestic Scenes." First published in the *Quarterly Review of Literature* in 1952, it is reprinted in Duncan's *The First Decade: Selected Poems 1940–1950*, retaining a dedication to Spicer. The Aristotle quote appears in the "Electric Iron" section of the poem (48).

42. Sir Philip Sidney's *Arcadia* takes two forms: the earlier *Countess of Pembroke's Arcadia* (also known as the "old" *Arcadia*, probably written in 1577–1580) and the "new" *Arcadia* (unfinished at Sidney's death in 1586). Sidney embeds over seventy poems and a running commentary on English verse culture within the old *Arcadia*'s overall structure of romantic comedy. The weaving through of serial composition and critical commentary within a thickly impacted narrative of romantic liaisons complete with classical backdrop provides an interesting correspondence to the poetry of the "Berkeley Renaissance." In the mid-1940s, Spicer writes "An Arcadia for Dick Brown." It was published posthumously with Robert Duncan's "Ode for Dick Brown" in *An Ode and Arcadia* (1974).

43. Originally published in 1519–1522 as "The Boke Compiled by Maister Skelton, Poet Laureat, Called Speake Parrot" or "Speke, Parott," the poem is a thinly veiled attack on Cardinal Wolsey, who tried to get the laws of the sanctuary changed and who appeared to be trying to negotiate his way into the papacy. The poem reads as a verse drama and includes a section on the "Grammarians' War" of 1519–1521 (in essence, an argument between two different camps on the methods of teaching Latin). In terms of serial composition, the poem was probably written over two years' time and published in various incomplete versions since the first sections seem to date from November 1519 and the end of the poem cites events of December 1521.

44. A poem in six parts about going "to sea in a sieve," "The Jumblies" was first published in *Nonsense Books* in 1843. Edward Lear was reigning monarch of Victorian nonsense and ranked first in John Ruskin's "List of the Best Hundred Authors."

45.
> The progress of an artist is a continual self-sacrifice, a continual extinction of personality. . . . I have tried to point out the importance of the relation of the poem to other poems by other authors, and suggested the conception of poetry as a living whole of all the poetry that has ever been written. The other aspect of this Impersonal theory of poetry is the relation of the poem to its author. And I hinted, by an analogy, that the mind of the mature poet differs from that of the immature one not precisely in any valuation of "personality," not being necessarily more interesting, or having "more to say," but rather by being a more finely perfected medium in which special, or very varied, feelings are at liberty to enter into new combinations. . . . The emotion of art is impersonal. And the poet cannot reach this impersonality without surrendering himself wholly to the work to be done. And he is not likely to know what is to be done unless he lives in what is not merely the present, but the present moment of the past, unless he is conscious, not of what is dead, but of what is already living. (Eliot, 7–11)

46. See Saint Ignatius Loyola's *Spiritual Exercises* as well as the poetry of Saint John of the Cross.

47. Dennis Wheeler (1946–1977) was a young filmmaker who died of cancer. His film work includes *Potlatch: A Strict Law Bids Us Dance*, and *Shadowcatcher*. He edited and contributed to the volume *Form & Structure in Recent Film* (1972), and published an important interview with the late Robert Smithson. Sherry Sandwell Killam is married and lives in Vancouver.

VANCOUVER LECTURE 3

Poetry in Process and Book of Magazine Verse

JUNE 17, 1965

🔊 The third Vancouver lecture is in many ways the most contrary and least accessible of Spicer's lectures, but it may also be the one that most repays the study it requires. On the surface, the lecture strays and rambles, but interspersed in the repartee of questions and answers are some of Spicer's most interesting and enigmatic statements on his art.

At this point in the lecture series, Spicer and the audience have become intimate enough to lose patience with each other, challenge each other's basic tenets, talk loudly at the same time, and burst into laughter at the slightest inside joke. As Spicer may have intended, the audience itself has begun to appear divided on the basis of just how seriously they take his propositions. Spicer, in turn, while declaring that he wishes he could stay in Vancouver, proceeds, directly and indirectly, to insult the local magazines *Prism* and *Tish*.[1]

Again, it is important to realize that Spicer repeatedly creates and sustains around him a vortex of dissent, but he is no less utopian in his thinking because of it. In many ways, dissent *is* Spicer's utopia. Since a community of heterogeneous members could never live in agreement without becoming a tyranny, it seems the only hope would be to value instead its disagreements, to see argument as progressive, and to create a context for heterodoxy.

For Spicer this means creating a community or "city" that is open at its center, and through the course of the lecture this open center becomes represented by the baseball diamond that he places at the heart of the city—a kind of absurdist's town square, which is publicly shared and therefore always potentially "in play" and in which no individual player is allowed to dominate the "game" but everyone, in turn, is required to participate. It's a community of informed and engaged constituents who are committed to the regionalism and teamwork of their shared game.

It turns out, in fact, that baseball works for Spicer as a model of individual *and* social composition; in the lecture he uses it to describe his practice of dictation and in his last book, *Book of Magazine Verse*, the diamond becomes an incarnation or synthesis of heavenly and earthly cities. If magazines are societies, as Spicer reiterates in Lecture 4, then this, Spicer's last book of poems, constitutes a community of peers with belief systems that are ordinarily not on speaking terms but are here brought into play, echoing and contradicting each other: *The Nation* (Politics), *Poetry* (Verse Culture), *The Sporting News* (Game), *Ramparts* (Theology), *Downbeat* (Jazz), etc.

For Spicer, as for Blake, this contrariness is generative. Gesturally, the confluence of Spicer's last book (*Book of Magazine Verse*, which he refers to as the building of a city), his last line of poetry ("People are starving"), and the last words in his lifetime ("My vocabulary did this to me") constitute either his deepest moment of correspondence or a true magician's great and final trick: to disappear while remaining everywhere manifest, appearing and disappearing in the margins of things, as in the startling poem he dedicates to himself in *Admonitions*.

> Tell everyone to have guts
> Do it yourself
> Have guts until the guts
> Come through the margins
> Clear and pure
> Like love is . . .
>   (A, 63)

On these grounds Spicer's use of Christianity makes sense; it is both more heretical and more ecstatic than it first appears. In his poems for the Catholic magazine *Ramparts*, he is at once mocking and faithful; his Christ is the magician whose greatest trick was his own incarnation.

Spicer loves to use low terms to discuss high aesthetic practice, especially when it jeopardizes the authority of critics over the work of the poet. His practice is very Keatonesque in this sense; he is most in control when he appears to be most offhand. Though Spicer claims in Lecture 1 that his choice of the term "Martian" is not to be taken too literally, its choice is purposeful. Likewise, Spicer uses baseball humorously as a metaphor for poetry, but thereby grounds poetry in a profoundly appropriate vocabulary of fair play, teamwork, democracy, and popular culture, particularly the culture of radio. For Spicer, baseball offers an ideal correlative to poetic composition with its model of mutuality, reciprocity, fraternal competition, gaming, and even "stealing" for the greater good. Neither player nor poet can exist alone. Both are absolutely dependent on the rules of their trade, their ability to cheat, the existence of tradition, and the regionalist team spirit of their peers. In addition to undermining the militaristic seriousness of the avant-garde, Spicer's baseball vocabulary offers a joust at Olson's theory of composition by field, especially considering it as the very heart or projective center of the ideal city, Olson's "polis."

At the outset of the lecture, Spicer wants to convey that he's taking a risk, sacrificing himself to the experiment of reading one of his own poems still in progress, for the sake of better understanding the process of poem-making in spite of his overstated fear that this may interfere with the process of the rest of the poem. In any case, he is violating the rules of serial composition which he elucidates in the first two lectures, by looking back. In Spicer's cosmology, the "not looking back" is, as for Orpheus, a kind of ideal, a rule, but one that is inhuman, a rule one can't help but "cheat" at. For Spicer, rules and cheating are, conceptually, of equal importance for the poet. As much as Spicer argues for not looking back at a serial poem and not revising one's work, he drops a number of clues that this is not necessarily something practicable.

Discussing a poem in progress and performing its process are in fact historically crucial to Spicer's practice. The community ritualizing of the writing process has been one aspect of Spicer's work since the Berkeley days, through the Magic Workshop, the Sunday poetry meetings, *Open Space* magazine, and his long-term friendships with Blaser and Duncan, which included extensive, playful, and sometimes scathing critiques. His tactic of group intervention is reminiscent of the Magic Workshop when Spicer assigned his students to write a poem that would make him write a poem.[2]

As a charlatan and dissembler Spicer also seems to delight in creating the drama of an Event, like a magician who shows the audience the daggers that are about to pierce the box with the body in it. The daggers are real but the scene is accomplished with one of Spicer's most impacted metaphors for composition: the composite mirror that reflects the poem back at him through its readers.

JACK SPICER: Tonight I'm going to try something which may foul up a poem for me. It's a poem which is in process, and I'm going to try talking about a poem in process and then reading it right in the middle of whatever process it's in, if it hasn't gone to a dead end.

I think what I would like you people to do, if you would, is to ask me questions about how I would treat a poem in process. I'll tell you just a little bit about the background of it, from my own standpoint, of dictation and of the business of the serialness of poems—the dictation of form as well as dictation of content. I'd like to get some questions . . . Imagine that I was just starting to write a poem, which I am, I guess, about one-quarter to one-half way through, but you don't know that yet. Ask me questions about how I would operate in terms of what I have said. And then see from there how the poem actually goes. I'll then give you a synopsis of the chronological thing of how the poem has gone and where it is either becalmed or not becalmed. In other words, I'd like to get a response from you from the two previous meetings on just exactly how I would treat a poem I was starting now, and you'd go back to the fact that I started it in late January. Is that too much of a challenge?

Q: I don't understand your question.

JS: The challenge is this. I've been trying to tell people how I think poetry ought to be written, what methods and all of that. Now I'm in the middle of a poem, and there are plenty of places undoubtedly where you were skeptical. Once you've finished a poem—once you've caught the rabbit and cooked it—it's very goddamn simple. You can say, oh yeah, you can catch the rabbit, and you cook it. No problem at all. You may get tularemia or something, but no problem at all really.

But this rabbit ain't caught yet, and what I'm asking you to ask are the things which would make me nervous in reading the incomplete poem, in presenting it to an audience. In other words, what are the things that I'm worried about in writing the poem?

ELLEN TALLMAN: We have to wait to hear the poem.

JS: Well, no. I would rather have you ask it first.

Q: No.

JS: No?

Q: You want us to write your poem for you.

JS: No, I certainly don't. That's the least of these things, although one of the worries that comes from reading an incomplete poem is the fact that you're afraid that the poem will be written by the people who hear it, and I'll probably stay a week away from the poem on account of that. Which is the first good question. Now another one.

HARRY ADASKIN: What are you worried about? You were saying that you're worried.

JS: Well, when I came to Vancouver I wrote two of the three poems pretty fast and pretty accurately, both of them with dictation, and the third one too. The third one presents a kind of mountain cliff that is very difficult to climb. This is a section of a long poem called a *Book of Magazine Verse*, and tonight I figured out what the section is called for this part, which I hadn't known before. But what I would like to do is to have you think back on the previous meetings and challenge me on the kinds of dictation and the kinds of talking about the serial poem. It's so easy for a poet to talk about the serial poem, to talk about dictation and all of that when the thing is finished. What I'm asking now is for you to challenge me while it isn't finished.[3]

Q: I have a question. You were talking on Sunday about dictation. Is this poem to be a series of maybe twenty-five or thirty parts where you sit down and you write each part at a blow and then two days later you write a second part and then two days later a third part? Or are you sort of look-ing at it and rearranging parts as you go along?

JS: Well, I've lost you on the word "blow."

Q: Okay. At one single sitting you write maybe twenty lines and you call that "One," and then "Two" and then "Three," and then you wait until you're ready again.

JS: Yeah, you see where things section out if they do section out, and you know pretty well when that happens.

Q: Does this mean if you write a part, then you look at it and decide whereabouts in the poem this part is going to fit in?

JS: Oh, no, no. Not at all. I'm glad you asked that because there are things I'm sure I didn't make clear. I was listening to part of the tape and it sounded like I was talking all the time and not making myself clear. No, things go one, two, three, four, five. They can go in opposite numbers from what they seem to go, but they have to go in terms of the sequence of the writing. The only exception would be if something is repeated. Now, a poem is repeated in this in two different magazines.

The structure of a *Book of Magazine Verse*, incidentally, came long after it started being written. I didn't know what the hell the name of it was or the structure of it was. But the first thing that happened was the idea of writing poems for magazines which would not print them. So far, I have a hundred percent average. [Laughter]

But I must say I've sort of stacked the cards.

DOROTHY LIVESAY: You could try *Prism*. I'm the poetry editor. You could try me. [Laughter]

JS: Yeah, well.

Q: One-hundred-and-one percent.

JS: No, it would be a defeat if any of the people did print them. [Laughter]

DL: You don't want to be in *Prism*! [Laughter]

JS: Uh, no, no, no. Go to jail. Go directly to jail.

GLADYS HINDMARCH: Jack, at this point do you see several directions at once?

JS: I try not to see any directions, but this is actually a test of just exactly what happens. I mean, I have a feeling that this book, although I think it's good, is not so good that I can't take a chance with it. It may go all down the drain, reading it tonight. It's possible. It's one of the kinds of experiments that I think that poets ought to do. You know, you tell kids, well, just, you know, experiment; don't care about what happens. Yet you don't do it yourself. You play it safe. I'm not playing it safe tonight. And this is scaring me—quite a great deal.

GH: The question I was trying to ask is exactly how empty your mind is. Remember how you said it should be like an empty vessel?

JS: Well, that's why I won't write for another week. Because now it's fairly full. I can see where connections are, and so forth, but I'm right in the middle of the poems for the Vancouver Festival and I don't know how many poems there are. And it's "*Blank* Poems for the Vancouver Festival."

HA: At last the Festival will pay for itself, won't it?

JS: I hope not, because that would jinx the book. You know, it's very complicated. You are sort of riding on a one-wheeled bicycle and going through all of these things, and you know if you make any mistake you just fall on your ass. At the same time you have to take chances because if you don't you get like Ginsberg or, in my considered opinion, Duncan, where you cease taking chances and you don't end up on your ass but you end up in Kansas City or some place like that, that you don't particularly want to go to, doing the same thing that you were doing before.

GEORGE BOWERING: Hey, Jack. There was a question I wanted to ask the other night, but I got involved in something else. About dictation and about chronological series—isn't it possible that the voice could tell you the third part first?
   [Background noise of a cat fight]

JS: God, the voice is telling us.

Q: Sounds like a cat fight.

ET: It was.

Q: I think it's another poem coming in.

JS: I think so, yes. As far as adjustments and all of that, I'm very conservative about them. As a matter of fact, looking over one of the Vancouver Festival poems, I saw that the refrain which was going through it should come at the end, too. And this seems like a reasonable thing. I haven't ever really changed chronological order, but I don't see why a person couldn't. It depends on whether you are tempted to, which I often am. I'd like to re-make history. You know, to make things in a logical order and everything else. And whatever you want to do is a very bad idea to do in a poem.

In other words, if the one, two, three, four, five doesn't help your audience understand what you were trying to do, that's fine, because it probably does what the poem is trying to do. It's a kind of discipline, just like this business with the sonnet is a kind of discipline. You take certain rules and you follow them. But any poet, I think, can take different rules as long as he takes rules, which keeps his damn personality from intruding in the thing, and the rules are rather arbitrary.

The "cheat at this game" thing that I talked about Tuesday night is perfectly right if you have rules that you can't cheat from. And you ought to change the rules every once in a while.

I remember when I was a kid, there was a rich kid in the neighborhood and we invented a game called Bleevers which we would change the rules to all the time, and the rich kid didn't know it. We'd bet on things, and he'd get four aces, and you'd say, "well, no, in Bleevers that is just the same thing as three of a kind" — that sort of thing. It can be done, but you have to have a structured poker in order to play Bleevers.

ET: Well, are you cheating at this game?

JS: That I don't know, but I'll find out.

ET: No, no. I didn't finish . . . at this game, if you use the dream?

JS: I don't think so, if the dream is insistent enough. Ellen's talking about the fact that the first poem in the Vancouver Festival is taken from a kind of editing of dreams that I had when I came here the second time, this last part of May. I think a dream is just about the same thing as any other piece of furniture in the room. I don't think the dream is dictated. It never has been to me. It's part of the furniture that can be shifted around for these folks to sit on. I don't think it matters terribly much. I don't see a dream as a dictation thing.

Now, in the Middle Ages they did, and they had the whole idea of the poem being a dream poem. Except the dreams in, say, the "Book of the Duchess" of Chaucer were obviously unlike any dreams any human being has had. They weren't really dreams. I doubt if dreams are any more significant than your excrement or anything else. I would doubt it very seriously. They certainly do tell the future as well as the past, but I don't think that's terribly significant either. I think that human beings probably are perfectly capable of telling the future for a brief time without terribly much good result from it happening. I imagine within a hundred years they'll probably figure out how to do it electronically. But I think it's furniture. I don't think it's the same thing as the world that the poems come from. Is that the answer?

DL: How do you feel that? How do you know that?

JS: I don't know that. It's just a question of thinking. I mean, if I suddenly got a dream that changed my mind, it would change my mind. But I don't really think that the dream world is any more real than the real world is, which isn't terribly goddamn real. It seems to me that there's a world in between them that goes into both of them. But the dream world is so very incoherent. I mean, when you explain a dream in the morning, you're almost creating a poem, because it wasn't the dream you had. The dream is pretty damned incoherent and doesn't have all of these sharp edges and all of the things that your explanation of the dream does. And, I don't know, I imagine that most of you have told dreams to people, and I imagine that just about all of you have felt like you were liars when you told the dreams because the dreams weren't that sharp and you were editing all the time. You were doing like Don Allen did with Kerouac—just slicing away whole things and putting everything together in a nice unit that you can use in public relations. I don't know. Dreams are to be trusted as much as the real world, but no more, and both of the things are furniture.

WARREN TALLMAN: Jack, do you think that dictated thoughts come to you just during the day while you're walking around or talking to people, and that you do or do not recognize them at times?

JS: I find very few dictated things ever come to me when I'm talking to people.

Q: Are you in a specific place usually when this happens, a place that's familiar to you?

JS: I usually am. It's usually late in the evening in San Francisco and I'm in a specific place, yes. However, again, in this Vancouver thing, I was able to write one of the poems during the daytime, rather than the nighttime. And I think it's perfectly possible to change your location. I'm just sort of lazy and don't like to.

Q: But would the location that you changed to, would it be quite familiar or quite like the situation or place that you normally use?

JS: Well, no. The situation is not familiar. But I certainly try to make it as familiar as possible—just like a cat when he goes to a new house—try to get things which are like the old house and get associations and all of that.

Q: But she means a place you feel easy in.

JS: I think she means more than that, a place where you actually can get something coming.

Q: I mean, is it almost like a physical situation—I'm finding it very hard to express.

JS: I know what you're talking about, and I just am not sure what the answer is because I think that a lot of *my* thing is laziness. I certainly prefer the same situation for writing poems of the same book and all of that, but I think that's probably just real laziness, acedia, the kind of thing I really shouldn't do. I should probably climb a mountain writing one poem and go into Death Valley in another, but I'm too lazy to do that. I don't really think it makes that much difference because your laziness simply opens your mind. But I really don't think that this has anything to do with any advice to any other poets.

GH: Still, laziness is a habit?

JS: Well, what the hell is laziness but habit?

Q: Is there sort of a ritual involved in the preparation for the dictation? Or can it happen when you're just sitting in your chair that you usually write poems in?

JS: Well, again, I can just talk about me as an individual. I can say for my-self that, yeah, there is some kind of ritual, but you have to realize that about half the time no poem will come, and that the time when you want to read the mystery story that you got in paperback, and you're halfway through and you really would like to finish it and go to bed—this is the time that usually a poem will crop out and the ritual gets all disturbed to hell because you wanted to read the mystery story and this poem is intrud-ing on you and you say, go away, go away. Like somebody knocking on your door at three in the morning, you know. And you try to pretend that you aren't breathing. That's what you do with the poem. If the poem's strong enough, it comes through anyway. And if it isn't, then it can just roll out the door and go someplace else.

Q: Is your dictation usually in words or in images or a combination?

JS: It certainly isn't in images.

DL: In rhythms?

JS: Rhythms sometimes.

DL: Hopkins said he kept hearing this insistent music and his mind kept pushing it away and finally he suddenly had to write "The Wreck of the Deutschland."[4]

JS: Yeah. Which is a goddamn good poem.

DL: It was the music, the rhythm, that was in his head.

JS: Well, you remember the Arthur poem—"a noise in the head of the prince" [HG, 213], and so forth. There is that kind of noise and it does sometimes dictate itself in rhythm, which is always a rhythm that you don't want. I've never seen a rhythm that I wanted in a poem. At least a good poem. But, I don't know, this gets down to the just barely personal. All of these things are just habits of an individual rather than the poet. I think that you can get poems almost any way if you can empty yourself and know how to empty yourself, and for everyone there's a different way of doing it. Even the dumb Zen Buddhists know that different people have different ways of being able to get a complete emptiness, and you have to learn your own way, and your own way is not your master's way at all. It's your separate way.

But the point is that you have to be able to get this kind of receptiveness and know when it's coming. When you're reading a mystery story and want to keep on reading the mystery story, you ought to resist it as long as you possibly can and then throw down the mystery story and write the poem. And both of them should be simple acts. Often it isn't simple, but it should be.

Q: Denise Levertov talks about the craft and intelligence of the poet. Where does this enter in, like when, in a week's time, you write the next poem?

JS: Well, intelligence is part of the furniture, and craft is part of the stuff that you're wanting to get out of the house so that enough ghosts can sit in the house—so that they're all comfortable. I mean, like the television set is out of this room right now. You have to take your craft out and just use the most elemental parts of the craft that you've learned and, Lord, writing for five years you learn plenty of craft. It's no problem at all. It's just like with a pitcher. You learn plenty of things that you can do and can't do. But if you don't actually go for whatever kind of pitch is your best pitch—these things which are craft—they should be used on a 3 and 0 pitch, a 3 and 1 pitch. They shouldn't be used regularly.

Well, let's go to the poems now and see what happens.

[Reads *Book of Magazine Verse*, "Two Poems for The Nation," and "Six Poems for Poetry Chicago" 1 and 2 (BMV, 247–48)]

DL: Why is that there when it was earlier? [The second poem from "Six Poems for Poetry Chicago" is the same as the first poem of "Two Poems for The Nation."]

JS: That is one of the things I was talking about—the fact that it is repeated. When I first read these, I thought that they were two separate poems, all of them. I'd sort of clued you people in that they weren't, but they are two separate poems, too, in context.[5]

[Reads "Six Poems for Poetry Chicago" 3 through 6 and "Three Poems for Tish" (BMV, 249–52)]

"Four Poems for Ramparts." *Ramparts* is a Catholic magazine in San Francisco. It's a pretty good magazine. They haven't not accepted them, but they will not accept them, on account of Pope John, as you'll see later.

[Reads "Four Poems for Ramparts" and "Four Poems for the St. Louis Sporting News" (BMV, 253–58)]

And the last thing are the "Poems for the Vancouver Festival," which aren't finished.

[Reads "Poems for the Vancouver Festival" 1 through 3 (BMV, 259–60)]

That's the last poem.

Q: How long have you been working on this one?

JS: The first poem was written two days before I went to Vancouver in February, or January I guess, last January.

Q: Where were the Vancouver poems started? Here?

JS: The Vancouver poems are written here, but I think that some of the other poems had to do with Vancouver when I was last here.

You can see what kind of a mess the thing is in now. It doesn't know what it wants to be, and I certainly don't know, and I have to figure out how not to try to dictate what is going on. Warren, when I showed him the last poem of the Vancouver Festival thing, which wasn't called the Vancouver Festival thing then, said that he thought it was an ending poem, but it can't be, in terms of anything I can see.[6]

GB: How do the Vancouver Festival poems fit into a magazine series?

JS: I figure it's about as much of a magazine as the *St. Louis Sporting News*. I mean, you have to be expansive. You look at it and write it for the CBC, and they'd probably accept it.

GB: If you could call it the Vancouver Festival Program or something.

JS: Or Overture, like Brahms.

Well, what are your general reactions to the thing? Did the voices come through, and what voices do come through and what don't?

WT: This one seems to me to have many more what seem like disparities, where it jumped a long way to a different area.

JS: Well, in terms of the groups of poems or in terms of the individual poems?

WT: Not in any one individual one.

JS: The groups certainly jump from one thing to another, but I'd be interested if you saw any individual ones jumping in the group, which I don't see. I'd sort of be happy if they did.

WT: It's only an impression I have, that it's a jagged, ragged, more jagged, more disparity, more ragged between poem and poem than I had a sense of in other ones that you've read.

JS: That was sort of what I wanted, and I guess the poem wanted it too. It may be just being a Jesuit and that sort of thing, as we said the other night, but one of the things that convinces me of things is when they don't fit to any real extent; they seem to be actually going better and more *really*. Where did you find the disparities? Do you remember any of them?

WT: I've got a different word for it now and that's more disheveled. Does that do anything? I keep casting around for what it is. It might have been your reading that was doing it, too. I can't tell.

GB: I got a lot more concrete things in this than in the other two poems you read. I'm not sure about the Arthur thing because I don't know it very well. But there were things in here that I can move around in more than the other ones—the baseball things and the Vancouver images and a whole pile of images. It's more images, I think. More visual images.

JS: Yes. I think that the poem, if I guess right, is going to move toward building the city instead of the celebration of the city as the "Textbook of Poetry" did. It feels like it to me except for the fact that the last poem is a real stopper for me right now.

GB: The Vancouver ones seem to me to be a little bit aside from the other ones, but this might just be because, like, we know this place more than we know the other places.

JS: How aside?

GB: It seems to me that the style or the line of the rest of the poem up until the Vancouver poems is quite steady, and they just seem to have a different line.

JS: Yes, certainly that. You can't see the dead catcher being in Vancouver?

GB: Yeah, I think the images aren't apart from each other, but I think it's more the sound of the poem, how it goes.

JS: I know what you mean. The whole rhythm of Vancouver is different from the rhythm of San Francisco and I do think that there is something to that. I hate the word "measure"—I've always despised it—but there is some kind of natural measure to a city that does change things.

GB: You don't just mean "measure" in terms of . . .

JS: No, I meant "measure" in terms of Williams and Wieners's magazine and all that sort of thing.

GB: Yeah, I suspected that was why . . .

JS: Yeah. Well, somehow or other it all has to get fitted together which is rather difficult, to say the very least. Jamie, what did you think?

JAMIE REID:[7] I thought that the Vancouver poems were connected intimately with the rest of them—the baseball image of the city building up from the diamond, and the idea of the diamond as the big cliché that everybody lays on Vancouver, as the diamond or the pearl of the sea or whatever.

JS: I never heard of that.

GB: I never did either.

JR: Yeah, well, occasionally the young writers of Vancouver, when they start writing, start talking about it in terms of a jewel or whatever—and then to extend it into a baseball diamond.

GH: I remember a story called "Diamonds Red and Yellow." I don't know if they remember that.

JR: Yeah, it's often referred to in travel magazines as the "jewel of the Pacific coast."

JS: Well, actually the city wasn't about to be built in Vancouver. It was about fifty miles north of Squamish.

Q: That inland sea thing . . . I remember you mentioned Vancouver.

JS: Yeah, as far as the Grail, same thing as Glastonbury. Well, that connection never hit me until we talked about it. It was just the business of the islands being in the way and the waves coming up and sweeping them away and the diamond staying there. I think I wrote the thing after I went the first time to that awful place where all the ferry boats are. Where is it?

ET: Horseshoe Bay. It's not so awful.

JS: Well, it looked very picnicky. But I could imagine what was in the mountains beyond them and I still could when I went to Squamish. Is it Squamish?

ET: Yeah.

JS: Ridiculous name. I suppose San Jose is too.

Q: I don't understand. You said "measure" and George said he understood it. I don't understand what you mean by Vancouver as being measured, or more measured than . . .

JS: No, it's not that. Like, say, you are walking with your grandmother who is seventy-five years old. You walk different. You have to get a different pace to your legs, and that's what Williams and everybody has meant by "measure," if they meant anything. It's the kind of pace of walking. There's a pacer and a trotter and a racer in race horses, and so forth. It's the way you use your legs. And in a way, it has nothing whatsoever, so far as I can see as a linguist, to do with the metrics of poetry. It's a kind of thing that does happen differently in different cities, and the difference in the city undoubtedly has made a difference in the metric. I don't know how much of it is simply the alienation or finding a new country. I suspect it's finding a new country from the way the poems go, but I'll wait till I get back to San Francisco to see. But, you walk different in Vancouver.

DL: Well, but surely the gait is a part of the whole body's rhythm which comes from breath, and the way you breathe.

JS: Yeah, but the gait also comes from where you're walking. If you're walking on a catwalk, twenty stories high, you walk different than you do when you're walking down a street, you know, or through the Broadway tunnel, which you'll hear about tomorrow night if you people come to hear *Language*, the walking through the Broadway tunnel with the signals and all of that. You just walk with a different gait. And you also walk with a different gait with a different person that you're walking with. This is about a mile of tunnel. It's a two-way thing, each way one way, and a kind of catwalk above it and echoing car sounds.

GB: And trucks!

JS: Trucks don't usually go through it.

GB: Something big went through one time. Scared the hell out of me.

JS: Well, they could, but they usually take Bay Street which is much more sensible. But drunks throwing firecrackers or beer bottles and all of that, and you walk fast through that.

What I'm trying to say is that I think that the difference that a town makes in poetry is this kind of way of walking, and this probably doesn't have anything to do with dictation at all. It's just that if the green Martian tells you to walk somewhere, you walk different if you have seven ribs broken than if you don't. You know. It's that kind of thing, and I think it's rather accidental. That's why I'm not terribly happy about celebrating measure as something that is really important.

Like I said the other night, the difference between Crane using fairly conventional blank verse in "Voyages" and us using fairly unconventional lines and conventional images and words—I mean, Crane can use the words to do the thing. It doesn't really matter. What matters is getting from place A to place B, and you do that whatever gait you use. It certainly is a different gait.

DL: Well, the metric, like the use of vocabulary, or what have you then, is in a sense part of the furniture. But beyond that, surely there is a basic rhythm that comes from the way you actually speak, and is "you," which isn't the furniture. It's your only possible voice.

JS: I don't think so, really. I've had other people read my poetry who have just the most absolutely opposite voices imaginable, and although I always want to strangle them after they've read them out loud, there still is the thing coming through regardless.

DL: That's because you have placed it in a certain way in relation to the way you speak and read.

JS: What I mean is that you don't write for the voice like, say, you write for an oboe if you're an oboist. You have to pay no attention to your own voice in that sense. Who the hell was that violinist who wrote all of those things for himself?

HA: Kreisler?[8]

JS: Kreisler, yeah, that sort of crap.

HA: He made a lot of money.

JS: Yeah, he made a lot of money, but if you wrote something for piano, then it would be because you couldn't play that on the violin on account of the piano isn't strung in a way that you could possibly even transcribe.

HA: Conceived in the idiom of the instrument.

JS: In other words, you take an instrument which is not yours and you have to use it that way. If you take your instrument, you're cheating, I think.

DL: Oh, no, I don't. Explain that.

JS: Okay, let's just go on with the music thing. Stravinsky, as a matter of fact, did do a transcription of the *Firebird Suite* for piano and violin, which was a real odd thing, much different than the *Firebird Suite* originally sounded. Now, the point is that he was demonstrating, it seems to me, the way that you can take almost anything and make it into anything else, as long as it has some internal relations to itself. But it doesn't really matter. Even if the two things are in dissonances, as the piano and violin actually were in this transcription, it doesn't make any difference. You can get away with that because the essential thing is there.

DL: Which is a relationship and a recurrence.

JS: A recurrence which can be retranscribed for almost any [instrument].

DL: Well, then it's a basic rhythm which comes from . . .

JS: I'm not sure what the answer is, but it isn't in rhythm or measure. It's in something else. It's that you really can flub the dub all over the place and still have the kind of thing that works. If it can be transcribed to various voices, various metrics, these things are furniture, and the basic thing is coming through. And when it doesn't come through, it doesn't come through.

WT: Jack, haven't a number of the questions that have been asked you all three meetings been directed to a quote suspicion, which is not being suspicious of what you're saying, but just doubt that Jack Spicer, Jack Spicer's personality, Jack Spicer's skills, Jack Spicer's accomplishment with language are truly ruled out when the Outside is dictating the thing. That is, aren't there a number of people who are saying aren't you there, or doesn't acquired skill that's peculiar to Jack Spicer control here?

JS: I don't think that there's anyone here who believes me when I say these things, if that's what you mean. I realize that, but I think that they might get to believe me more if they tried it.

WT: But you would go back to the point that at no point at which this is discussible is the dictation attributable to you.

JS: No, I'm afraid I can't say that. I'd say that I was a great poet if I could make that statement. I'd say that at a minimum number of points I've eliminated myself—depending on my skill in getting the static out—that's about as far as I could go. I think that's probably what Cézanne would have said in his last period—who is, I think, my favorite painter.[9]

WT: And you see this as a meditative process rather than as some technique of poetry. Or is that a fair statement?

JS: Well, gee, I don't know. I'm sure that Cézanne as a painter never meditated a bit in his life, and his wife wouldn't let him. He probably was just worried about the grocery bills and all of that. But he managed somehow or other to get his last ten years of painting fairly pure of anything he intended. Which someone like Kandinsky, who's a nice painter, never did because he was always worried about the plot he was in. We've gone to music and painting. I don't expect anyone to trust me on this thing, but I would like to see people experiment and see what they can do in terms of their own lives.

JR: Oh, you want us to give away our secrets. That's what you're doing.

JS: How many secrets do you have, Jamie?

JR: I was going to ask you, do you have any idea right at this moment where your poem's going to go? I mean, do you have any ideas in your own mind, or any feelings?

JS: I try not to.

JR: Your mind is a blank?

JS: No it isn't, unfortunately. It's trying to be a blank. And trying to be a blank is utterly different from being a blank. Again, this guy who was talking about Jesuit exercises was absolutely dead right, on course, on the thing. The point is that you can't really make your mind a blank. You can't really get to receiving God, which Saint Ignatius wanted, or receiving poems, or doing anything. You can't. It's impossible. There's this utter animal spirit which is coming out and saying, well, gee, can I lay this person if I write this line, and all sorts of things like that. It's just impossible to make your mind a blank. You just do as well as you can, just like you're playing a horn or playing a violin or playing a piano. You try your best to make your mind a blank, but you don't. I'm sure of that. Well, when you're playing, what happens? Can you completely get yourself out of it?

HA: You have described it perfectly. I don't see how I could add anything to that. It's exactly true. It's the best and most accurate description of the production of art that I have ever heard.

JS: I do think that everybody has his own kind of balance for this and you can't make your mind a blank in other people's terms. You have to use your own. But at the same time I think that everybody ought to, if they're going to try to write poetry, or maybe anything else. I don't know, since I'm not a musician or a painter or any of the other things, but as far as poetry's concerned, I think it's a fruitful way of going about things and that it wouldn't hurt anybody. That's about all I can say.

HA: Copland once said, in listening to various performances of music, that the best performances always are those just this side of disaster. And that's so much like what you said the other day, about taking a chance and risking it, which is exactly what he meant. And those are the most memorable and the truest performances, where you dare to the extent of facing failure very nearly.

JS: Yes. And sometimes failing.

HA: Sure.

JS: I remember one time Ernest Bloch was at Cal when I first came to Cal and he was very pleased by the fact that Toscanini said that he wouldn't play anything by Bloch because it was too bloody, too filled with blood. It wasn't the English expression. It was just too bloody. And this was the failure and the success of Bloch. He recognized what Toscanini was saying. He also recognized he was too bloody. And the two things—he didn't dance between them.[10]

I suppose with this dance thing that everyone likes, you have to dance between being too bloody and being too accurate, like Marlowe was too bloody and Shakespeare was too accurate—both as poets, not as playwrights. But you have to dance between the things and it's really difficult, particularly since you're dancing with somebody controlling you and you're dancing one step and the Martian's dancing another, and it's awful.

Q: What bothers me is, say you're sitting in this room that's familiar to you and it's late in the evening and something comes through. How do you judge it to be a true message and how do you judge it to be what you want to say? This is the craft, I guess.

JS: It's just a matter of, again, the analogy of the pitcher. Actually a poet is a catcher more than a pitcher, but the poet likes to think of himself as a pitcher more than a catcher. This, as a matter of fact, is why I believe in the *St. Louis Sporting News* poem, because I wanted to be a pitcher and I was a catcher and I was denouncing pitchers. The thing is that when you get something that you really want, some ball that you really want as a pitcher—now I'm talking from the standpoint of a catcher—the guy is likely to hit it out of the park the next time. I've seen it happen over and over again. Who the hell was that pitcher, Warren, in the last game that we saw?

WT: Lindblad.[11]

JS: Lindblad. He pitched two balls, one just absolutely beautiful, an inside slider, and so he pitched it again, and the guy hit it out of the park. He still won the game, but a pitcher gets pleased by something he does and then the guy hits it out of the park. [Laughter] After a while, you kind of get used to that. You're both catcher and pitcher, I guess, as a poet. And you get quite used to things.

Q: You don't get to catch the ball if it gets knocked out of the park.

JS: That's true. You can sit back and just gloat and smile at the pitcher and say, see, I told you to throw an outside curve. [Laughter]

Q: The thing you said in the poem about the inside, I think it was an inside curve?

JS: Yeah.

Q: And he threw an outside curve. Now that's you being a poet as the catcher and the pitcher being the Martian.

JS: That's right. Only I think it's more split up than that. I think the pitcher that the baseball poem was written to is partly me and partly younger poets, and less likely the Martian. I think that "No kid, don't enter here" is sort of a reminiscence of Dante. And the part of your personality which is extended in younger poets is the thing that you're lecturing to, and you're old, like Yogi Berra or something like that, and you tell them what not to do, but you can't tell them what to do.[12]

Q: Why wouldn't the *Louisville Sporting News* print the one about the . . .

JS: St. Louis.

Q: Or the *St. Louis Sporting News* print the one about the pitcher and the catcher saying I knew what Warren Spahn was doing all the time?

JS: Well, they would have to print the whole series. They've been sent it.

Q: You just made the terms too narrow.

JS: Well, what I want to say is "rejected by the blank blank blank blank blank blank blank blank." No, I mean, it would be just a great sell if one of them accepted it. That's why I haven't given the *Tish* poems to *Tish*.

Q: He's hoping we won't print another issue.

JS: I think it's a fairly reasonable hope. [Laughter] Unless Alvin Dark comes to Vancouver and becomes manager of the Mounties. Which is possible, God knows.[13]

WT: Jack, when you started talking about this magazine verse poem, I don't know whether you said "I'm" or "if," and I don't know whether it's "becalmed" or "not becalmed." It was just an inadvertent phrase you used.

JS: No, it's not. It wasn't inadvertent. It was in the imagery of *The Holy Grail*, and becalmed simply means that you don't get no wind, and you can't sail and you have to scuttle the ship.

WT: But I'm wondering if that last poem which has the oil slick on the water . . . if there's a connection between . . .

JS: Yeah. I don't know.

Q: Are you a ghost?

JS: *Holy.* I didn't think you could tell. [Laughter]

Q: Is that the Logos or the Lowghost?

JS: Well, that's a problem for the future.

Q: Did he say locus?

JS: No, a Lowghost or a Logos. Yeah, a locus or a solus.
     Well, what did you people think about the lemon? [BMV, 248–49]

GB: I understood the working with the lemons, but I didn't understand
the statement about the shape of the lemon.

JS: Well, take an orange and a lemon. They are different to handle.

Q: It's not really oval, though, is it?

JS: Oh, I see what you mean.

Q: I think that's the wrong word because, you know, what gets me about a
lemon is the relationship of the taste to the shape. Like an oval has this
serenity, but a lemon goes phhtt—what's it called? There's some sort of
mathematical term for that.

JS: What is it? A spheroid?

Q: There must be some sort of real word for it.

Q: Do lemons grow around Chicago?

JS: I've never been to Chicago.
     Well, lemons are certainly different than oranges in their shape, what-
ever it is. But oval is the wrong word.
     Can you imagine "ellipsoidal" in a poem? That's what Hart Crane
could get away with.

Q: Well, maybe that's what's so annoying about a lemon.

JS: Yeah. Well, we'll call it oval. I think everyone knows what oval means
in terms of the thing—that actually it is something in terms of poetry. I
mean, if you set up the terms right enough, I don't think there's anyone in
the room that didn't see the lemon and the orange being different, one
easier to peel, easier to eat, and everything else. And whether the word is
"oval" or some word in Martian like *tycheame* . . .

Q: Mathematically.

JS: But you don't need that. The point is that you just need a word that distinguishes one thing from another and that says, you know, "the fruit of the poor lemon is impossible to eat." By the way, did they sing that [lemon tree] song in Canada at all?

Q: Oh yeah.

Q: I was going to ask you, did you sing it intentionally that way, or is that your peculiar way of singing? [Laughter]

JS: My way of singing is always peculiar.

Q: But you did sing that differently, with more of a sort of put on something or other, than when you sang the other night.

JS: Yes, because this was a popular song, and the things the other night were folk songs. This had to be an entertainment type thing. It also had to have the same thing where it was "limon" with an *ih* in the first thing, and the limon flower is sweet, the fruit of the poor "lemon," with an *eh*, is impossible to eat, which is the way it goes in the song, and the way it goes in the printing of this thing. This particular vowel before nasals doesn't get distinguished in very many places but California, but it does there.
    Well, what about it? What about the poem? I'm asking you people now.

Q: It looks like a romantic poem to me, as compared to your other stuff. At least I read *Heads of the Town Up to the Aether* and some of the other things, which gives me your bitterness, and these poems have a kind of a sweet . . .

DL: Vancouver softens everybody up.

JS: I guess it does.

Q: Beware, beware.

JS: Well, I'm trying to become an orange. [Laughter] What about that last poem in the baseball thing? Did you see the connection with the oranges?

Q: I didn't see the connection with the oranges, no.

GB: I saw the connection with the poet all the time.

DL: He's not supposed to be there.

Q: A baseball diamond, really, for Vancouver, I thought it was a joke. Anyway I'm still looking to see if it's there.

JS: Well, it's not there. It's about a hundred miles up in the hills after the road stops at Squamish. That's where the baseball diamond is set up. If you take a square going in each direction, a square ray from each baseline, you start a city. [Overlapping cross talk]

DL: But it's an American game. Here they play soccer and cricket.

JS: I would agree with you. I've seen the Mounties play three times, and I agree with you. You're better off playing cricket.

GB: Yeah, but nobody plays soccer and cricket in Canada.

DL: Vancouver does.

GB: Vancouver and Toronto are the only places they play soccer in Canada.

DL: What I mean is baseball is purely American.

GB: No, it's not. I would say the ratio of baseball to cricket in Canada would be about one thousand to a half percent.

Q: But baseball isn't a Canadian sport.

DL: No, it certainly isn't. It's an American import.

JS: Do you know what the original inventor of baseball's history was—Abner Doubleday?[14] Abner Doubleday was the first president of the American Theosophical Society under Madam Blavatsky, and he was also a rather good general in the Civil War, on the Northern side.

GB: You know the league that Vancouver used to be in—the Class A league? It was one of the three oldest baseball leagues in North America. I think it was the third oldest.

JS: Yeah. It had Twin Falls in it, didn't it? But I think it had Twin Falls in it, which Robin Blaser's father is a third owner in.

ET: But baseball as an analogy or an image or anything . . .

JS: Baseball is the most perfect sport in the world.

DL: But it's not Vancouver. It doesn't belong here.

Q: No, it's definitely not.

GB: It does! It was here before . . .

Q: A lot of people play baseball when they're kids, but baseball isn't a fundamental part of your life, let's face it.

GB: It is mine.

Q: It is with a lot of people.

Q: In the small towns, baseball is a very important game. In the springtime they have announcements in all the papers . . .

GB: It's the only game ever played in our town.

Q: I hate baseball.

JS: Just what do you know about baseball? You're being quoted now, on the tape recorder.

Q: How did the diamond get up to Squamish?

JS: It's past Squamish, long way past Squamish.

Q: Have you ever tried pitching oranges?

JS: Oh, lemons are much better. You can get a very good spitball with a lemon. But damn it, peeling it at second base is pretty terrible. It dissolves in your hand.

Q: Well, that's the way to peel it.

JS: It's a fingernail ball.

ET: More than being Canadian or American, I think that moving from a Los Angeles street to Vancouver or to a hundred miles up from Squamish gives a sense of coast, which is what Vancouver and British Columbia really are—a part of the West Coast more than anything else.

Q: But the ocean really is down here. You're right about that. It's inland water all right.

JS: I'm also right about the Fraser River being a kind of a spook, on account of Fraser couldn't even find salt water. He was all the way to Westminster and just gave up on the goddamn thing and said there weren't no ocean, it was about a hundred miles to the south. Unfortunately I spelled Fraser when I wrote the poem F-r-a-z-i-e-r, which is the name of a park, one of the big wilderness areas in southern California, beautiful area, as a matter of fact. And unfortunately, he spelled his name with an *s* and an *a*. Very bad.

Q: If you pitched an orange to your own catcher, do you think he would catch it? In terms of that poem, I'm still puzzling.

JS: I'm sorry. I don't get the point. Do it again.

Q: If you pitched an orange to your own catcher—you yourself, writing . . .

JS: You mean the catcher's catching this batter up?

Q: Does he catch the orange, or only the lemons?

JS: Well, is there a batter in between the catcher and the pitcher or not?

Q: I don't know.

JS: I guess the confusion is where I said that in this particular poem the poet was both the catcher and the pitcher. The batter is the green Martian, the ghost, the spook, whatever, and it depends entirely on the batter and also on the pitcher, whether he pitches a screw ball or something like that which a catcher can't ordinarily catch, or has to have big gloves to catch, and so forth. But essentially, there's the third party in the thing, who is the batter, and the batter is the intermediary between the pitcher and the catcher.

Q: I was thinking of that poem, actually.

JS: I know. So take the orange thing. Obviously the lemon would be easier to slide by the batter than the orange would.

GB: Did you have any sense of pun with lemon and pitcher, or was that completely out of . . .

JS: No. Completely out of even my dialect.

Q: What about the sugar that they fed the lambs?

JS: That I don't know about. That's obviously the future. Do they ever feed lambs sugar?

Q: Gee, I wish I knew.

JS: They feed hogs sugar, I know, but lambs? That was one of those things that just flipped me when I wrote it. I had no idea why, and I still don't.

Q: Just when you were talking to Sam [Perry][15] about this lemon and orange deal, you know, "the fruit of the poor lemon is impossible to eat," I got the idea of orange as something that you want, like you getting between yourself and the source; whereas a lemon, even though it's not easy to eat, is more true than the orange.

JS: Put it this way. Suppose you're a poet, and you are both catcher and pitcher, and something is coming to you. Now, as a poet you would really like the batter actually to hit the goddamned ball, and an orange is more easy to hit than a lemon, and the kid in the poem, the kid pitcher, can pitch all sorts of junk balls, these halfway sliders, various other things, which are going to ruin his arm by the age of twenty-five. You'd rather have him pitch fastball oranges which the batter, namely the green Martian, will either hit or not hit, than you would this nice clever lemon, which is rather like a spitball.

Q: In the remark you made about Ginsberg and Duncan—do they fit in that way?

JS: I'd better not.

WT: Jack, in a lot of his poems, Yeats simply out-and-out explicates and tries to demonstrate that we live in a non-tragic universe. Do you have a sense that the news coming to you is of a non-tragic nature or of a tragic nature, or does that figure at all in your work?

JS: "No kid, don't enter here." That's the answer. I don't know if it's tragic or not, but I just know that you better make certain that you don't get in on the things unless you really want to pay the price for them.

WT: Are you speaking there of the poet or what will come to the poet?

JS: Well, both. I think that anyone's a fool to become a junkie or a poet.

Q: Why both?

JS: Well, it's the same kind of hook really, and it has the same withdrawal symptoms if you ever try it.

Q: How about the fool?

JS: Well, the fool is the same thing as the pitcher. There's no question about that. Percival is obviously the same thing as the pitcher that the catcher is getting mad at, but the catcher always strikes out still, although he hit these home runs off of Spahn, which is very easy, incidentally, in case people don't know it. Spahn—you hit home runs off of him or you strike out, even before he played for the Mets, where I hit singles off of him on account of the Mets.

Q: What about the guy who's instructing what should be thrown. You talk about that a lot.

JS: You signal. You look to the third base side and see what they tell you to do, and then you signal what kind of pitch, and somebody, especially in Wrigley Field, is out in the scoreboard looking to see the signal, and they're signaling back at the batter.

Q: There's a sort of manager and he has to listen to somebody else?

JS: No, the catcher usually tells the pitcher what to pitch and the pitcher will throw off the sign then. I didn't read that "who stole the signs" thing in *The Heads of the Town*, but essentially the business is that the catcher signals to the pitcher, like, "I would like you to throw an outside fast ball there." You have him o and 2 and an outside fast ball he sometimes swings on. So he does something like this with his hands and the pitcher then will go like this, to shake off the sign, and then you give the second thing that you'd like him to do if he doesn't pitch an outside fast ball. And finally, you find, after he's shaken off three or four signs, that he just wants a fast ball to the plate, and so you give him the sign for that, and the guy hits a home run.

There are some batters like Mays, the catcher doesn't ever say anything about. You just let the pitcher figure out what the hell he should do for Mays because nobody can figure out Mays. But you have a rookie, or even somebody two, three years—say, Jim Ray Hart, a very good example of the Giants—the catcher knows how to pitch for him much better than the pitcher knows and he'll give the sucker pitches for him. For someone like Mays or Ernie Banks, there's no sucker pitch. Either they're in a slump or they aren't, and it doesn't really matter what the hell you do. You might just as well let the pitcher figure the thing out.

Q: The time in the poem, where the batter and the pitcher both knew what the ball was going to do . . .

JS: Spahn and the catcher, yeah.

Q: You work towards that?

JS: No. It's the kind of thing which happens with age. I think Spahn and the catcher, who is probably Jim Hegan of Cleveland, according at least to Warren . . . wasn't it Jim Hegan?

WT: Hegan, it was.

JS: Yeah, who must be dead, because he wouldn't appear in the poem otherwise.

Well, the thing is that after a certain amount of time, you know and life knows what the hell is going to happen pretty much. You can't tell individually the exact second, but Spahn knows when he throws the pitch at you, and you know whether you can hit it or not, and Spahn fools around, you fool around, and you hit three home runs off of him. And you probably don't win any games by doing it, on account of the fact that Spahn pitches you those fast balls at a time when it wouldn't make any difference whether you hit a home run or not. This is getting old.

Q: That's politics.

JS: Yeah, it is.

Q: You don't think the poets ever throw away their masks and their bats and go do something else?

JS: Well, Rimbaud did. And then came back.

Q: Are you afraid of doing this?

JS: Oh, shit, I'm so old that Rimbaud already died before I was my age. In Marseilles, with a vision.

No, I don't see any point in throwing the bats away particularly. You can sure get pissed off at ways of you striking out, or hitting home runs against a bad opposition, stuff like that.

Q: But you're a poet because you do funny things with bats.

JS: I think our baseball thing has gotten all confused.

DL: Basically, we don't know anything about baseball.

Q: How long do you think it will take to finish that poem, Jack?

JS: As I say, I think it's about half over, so this is just a real prediction which will probably foul up the prediction coming true, but I'd say off-hand from my previous experience, November. But I don't know. I've got stuck on this oil slick right now, and I don't know where to go. And furthermore, I don't want to leave Vancouver. There's that to it—the business of really not wanting to go back to Berkeley and San Francisco, wanting to stay here and not being able to. There's that thing, which gets in the way of any poems which are aimed toward me. It's going to be a rough few months, and I have no idea what will happen to the poems in this time.[16]

Q: Are you actually going through a transition in your writing?

JS: I'm going through a transition. In fact, I don't have no job, and I . . .

Q: No, I mean in your actual writing.

JS: Well, if the radio set has three batteries which are gone and one that's still left, that isn't a transition in the radio broadcast. It's a transition in the radio set, namely that you don't have very much power. And these things that happen to you in life are like that. If you're only going on one transistor and you're a four-transistor radio, you're not going to be able to get in the outlying stations very easy. KFI doesn't come in.

Q: How long ago did you write the poem that you read on Sunday night?

JS: Was that *The Grail?*

ET: No, *Heads of the Town.*

JS: Oh, *Heads of the Town.* I would say that the "Textbook" was written in '62, maybe early '63, something like that.[17]

Q: That was more assumptions and ideas, and the poetry that you read today seemed to be on concrete hooks. For instance, the image of the oil slick.

JS: Or the image of the hook, if you remember the line.

Q: Well, I didn't intend to make that reference. See, that's the problem— every time you mention something, you've got it in a poem somewhere.

JS: Nice thing about poems, I guess. It scares the shit out of me, too.

DL: It seems to me a different kind of poem from the others. I couldn't get with this the way I was with the others. That may be because a lot of the references are quite alien.

Q: I didn't mean to make it a point of weakness. I'm just wondering whether you're actually in your own mind when you're going through a change of personality or a change of outlook or whatever.

JS: As I say, I think that the changes are due to environment and not anything else. I don't feel any real need for a change in attitude for poetry, although I wish I did. It's always exciting when one does. I don't. But just the fact that I leave from San Francisco to Vancouver—this is a change. It's a change in all sorts of things. My bowel movements change. My eating habits change. Everything's changed because I've moved from one place to another. And naturally, the part of me that's receiving poetry changes, too. I have no idea what that means, but I am certainly in a transition period in terms of my life, and that would probably mean in terms of my poetry, too, I would think. It would be logical, although I've sometimes been able to write in the most ghastly times in the world without any static coming through. In general, what happens to you in your life has some reflections in your poetry.

JR: I remember when we talked down in San Francisco, and you said that you can write without any static coming through, and while we were talking, I had the feeling—it was funny—that it seemed that your physical body had shut off functioning, and yet your mind was still coming through. Your lips weren't moving, and your eyes weren't moving, but there was still a voice coming through from someplace. It was rather an interesting experience. I remember that.

JS: How long ago was that?

JR: This was around March the 20th. We were down at Gino's.

JS: Yeah. That was in the middle of the lemon poems, the poems for *Poetry*. Jim, I must say that it was quite true.

WT: I suppose you've answered this fifteen different times in other ways, but does the thing that's speaking or dictating work through what the poet happens to know?

JS: Furniture, yeah.

WT: Say baseball was not an interest of yours. Say hockey was.

JS: Or *schkertl*, which is a Martian sport played on Mars.

WT: Then, what's the connection between that and the that which is speaking or that which is dictating?

JS: As I said, if a Martian comes into a room and sees a baby's alphabet blocks, he'll obviously use them to communicate. He won't understand what they're for or anything else. He'll simply rearrange them into an order which makes very good sense Martian-wise, and doesn't too much Earthman-wise, and he'll just use them. No, obviously, baseball is not going to last as long as these poems. If they're good poems they're going to last. But I don't see any of it makes too much difference.

ET: I know what I feel in the last section of the Festival poetry. It's that the cautions and warnings that I so often feel in other poetry—I don't know whether it's there or not, but that's how I feel—aren't there in the last three poems.

JS: Yeah. It scares me too.

Q: Why does it scare you? I'm a little bit confused when you say it scares you.

ET: Because it's so open.

Q: What do you mean, open? Open? Open to what?

ET: Vulnerable.

Q: I'm still confused here. Why would you be vulnerable writing this positive kind of poetry? [Laughter and more cross conversation]

JS: As somebody said in Stalin's purge trials, when they asked if he murdered his grandmother and raped two nieces and delivered all the plans for the dam to the Nazis and the question went on for a long time, the answer was "You have found the very word."

ET: Sure.

Q: Then let me ask you who are you vulnerable to?

JS: Ghosts.

Q: This change of geography—is it important to most poets, and to yourself specifically? Does it bring about this change that Allen has noticed and other people have noticed, the measure and all that?

JS: I'd say so. "Gait" is maybe a better word than "measure."

Q: Is it important that the poet get that different gait?

JS: No, I don't think it's important to the poem. It certainly makes a difference to the poet, whether he knows it or not.

Q: That's what I meant. Is it important to the poet that he do this, or can the poet remain in the same gait?

JS: It's pretty hard to if you're on a different kind of street. I mean, shit, if you're walking down a sandy beach, you obviously aren't going to walk the same way you walk through the Broadway tunnel. There's a different resistance and everything else. That lovely American astronaut that we had playing around in space—he obviously didn't walk the same way he walked down Main Street of his hometown, but at the same time, he was the same person and the same loss of gravity and everything else were possessing him. He had to learn how to walk out in space. But there are different kinds of levels of gravity and Vancouver has a different level than San Francisco does, and it's one I prefer.

DL: It doesn't really matter which.

JS: It doesn't matter in the long run. To people who write your biographies it certainly doesn't matter. To these awful English students fifty years from now at UBC or somewhere like that, it won't matter a good goddamn what happened there, but it does matter to the person because the person's a person and not just a poet.

Q: There's one more thing that I wanted to ask you about. Valéry in *The Art of Poetry* talks about going to a lecture. You brought up the university. He talks about going to a lecture at a university about his own poems, and he said, "I felt very strange because it wasn't me or my poems that they were talking about because I had the memory of all the trials I had gone through to get this down properly, and I felt as if they were talking about a ghost of myself."[18]

JS: Yes. As a matter of fact, his poems talk about the ghost of himself ahead of time.
     I think Valéry was sort of playing footsie with the whole thing of being a ghost of himself when he took off for twenty-five years or however many years he took off for, playing hookie. He was really making this an important thing. I don't know. I don't trust him, although he's good.

WT: Jack, a while ago, while I was asking you about that tragic/non-tragic, I was really trying to get to something else, and that is what I sense as a comic dimension in your poems. Do the Martians play tricks on you, or do you play tricks on them? Am I making any sense at all?

JS: Yeah. But my answer to playing tricks on the Martians is a poem by Ogden Nash. It's a lovely two-line poem: "When called by a panther / Don't anther."[19]

Q: Well, I was a little confused. Are you concerned right now that the ghosts aren't operating you? Or do you want to be totally operated by the ghosts?

JS: I just want to lead a simple life. [Laughter] I mean, the question is sort of ridiculous. I don't know what I want myself, and if I did know what I want, it would be the wrong thing to want.

Q: Now this is what I don't understand. If you know what you want, why is it wrong?

JS: Well, on account of the fact that I ain't myself only. I'm a member of the team. And like Ted Williams always knew what he wanted and the Red Sox never did win the pennant. I'm sorry, but let's face it.

GB: Lay off Ted Williams, that's all.

JS: He gave that marvelous finger. I was there in Boston when he was giving it. It was a marvelous finger. But he didn't get any hits in front of him or behind him. He still stayed at the plate and took it very easy, and you know, he'd take a base on balls if he wanted a base on balls because he felt he couldn't get a hit, and it wouldn't matter that the Red Sox had a one-run deficit and it was the ninth inning or anything else. He still would take the base on balls and that kind of thing. He was a goddamn lousy team player, which is nice, but I don't really think that it works if you want to win pennants, and I think that I do and my poetry does.

Q: You always talk about yourself and then that very other thing, the ghosts, and I keep wanting to say there must be a position where you don't notice the distinction so much, where that's not what gets you about the two things — that they are one thing.

JS: What you mean is what Warren said, that nobody believes me when I say that there is a distinction. I still believe there is. But I don't think it's a psychological distinction or anything else. I don't think it's something the electroencephalogram would get. I don't think it has anything to do with what's in my skull. I think there's something Outside. I really believe that, and I haven't noticed anyone really, in all of these people who come here, who did seem to believe that I believed it, but I do.

   And I don't care if you don't. It doesn't matter a good goddamn to me. But I just want to say for the record that I do believe it, that there is something *Jenseits* that has nothing to do with me whatsoever, and this I believe.[20]

WT: Jack, in part I think it's not disbelief. It's that, as you very well know, poetry in Vancouver has been very much centered on the handling of the language as prior and then what comes in as following on that handling. Whereas yours seems to reverse that. I think that's where the static and the confusion is.

Q: It's the coming through, the idea of a message always to be received, but it can be thought of as just an event occurring, which is also a trans-mission between two things.

JS: Yes, but then that comes down to "happenings"—that kind of thing that art galleries call. And you beat apart a piano like in Six Gallery, and you say that's a happening.[21] Well, shit, that's just beating on a piano.

Q: But when you write a poem and you say, ah, there's something coming through in that poem, I'd read that poem and I'd just say there's some-thing really happening. I feel very different when I read this poem than when I read other poems. And I don't see it as a message transmitted via that poem.

JS: The messages don't come through that way. Certainly, for these poems I read tonight I've only gotten two or three things from them as messages to me. "No kid, don't enter here" is about the only thing which is absolutely clear and has told me something about what I should and shouldn't do in my life and so forth. And the lemon poem still is very, very difficult for me.

In the poem on Eliot's death, which is really about the death of Churchill—it was written because of that, and Eliot came in on Suspi-cion afterwards with a capital *s* in the poem. That was just before I left for Canada. Churchill had just about died then, or had died. And it was the first time—not the first time he died—the first time I came to Canada.

But the things don't come through very fast, and it's quite true that you don't get messages like, "arrive tomorrow at 7:30, plane so-and-so" and so forth and so on. It doesn't come like that, obviously. But they do come as messages nonetheless. And not just for having pleasure, which was the thing that the guy probably misunderstood the other night—that pleasure was the thing about poetry. It isn't. It has to do with messages. But they come through awfully unclear and you don't really know when you're even delivering them whether the person you send the telegram to is going to sock you in the eye or give you a quarter tip.

ET: At what point did you allow these messages to take over or start hap-pening in your poetry?

JS: It happened about halfway through when I was writing *After Lorca*, when the letters to Lorca started coming and being dictated and the poems, instead of being translations, were dictated. Then I sort of knew what was happening. And when the final thing happened, in the poem, the business of the last letter, I really knew that there was something moving it. Before, I never did. I just had the big thing of you writing poems and isn't that great, and they were sometimes great, sometimes good at least. But after that I never really had any ambitions to do anything else.

DL: The first Sunday when you spoke, you were asked whether this message was important to your life. My impression was that you said no. And you were asked was it important to other people hearing it, and again you said no.

JS: What I'm trying to say is that when I say "not important," it is the kind of thing that—you want a job, you want a million dollars, you want someone to sleep with—no. That doesn't help a bit. It is important to your life in the sense that you live your life not just as a human being but as something more than a human being, and I don't know how much it is. In terms of biography, I doubt if poems that you write or poems that you read by others really change the course of, or the flow of events, of things. But at the same time they do in a fundamental way.

It's again like music. It doesn't really mean a goddamn thing, and yet it does. It's this kind of halfway into reality and halfway out of it that does seem to me important—at least important enough to be hooked with as one is hooked with poetry.

Q: Here's another question, Jack. Are you writing with any special purpose or purposes when you're doing that? I'll give an analogy. Yeats tried to define his metaphysical system in his own mind, and let's say Eliot tried to clarify religion.

JS: No. Yeats did not try to define his metaphysical system in his own mind. The spooks told him, "We have given you metaphors to write your poetry with" and he was . . .

Q: He tried to understand them, didn't he?

JS: Sure he did. Yeats was completely uninterested in the long run in what the metaphors really meant because there was no point in his trying to understand it. And Yeats occasionally would face things. Well, "Nineteen

Hundred and Nineteen" is, to my idea, just about the best poem he ever wrote, and he faced these things with bitterness and all of that, but things came through that were just completely wild to the political poem he was trying to write. And he just left it alone, and he didn't revise "Nineteen Hundred and Nineteen" at all.

I don't know. Take "Among School Children," where he talks about it himself—his business of being the "smiling public man" versus the business of the "Ledaean body, bent" and so forth. He faced the thing and it ends up in a chestnut tree, which is about the only place you can end up in. I mean, it is a kind of a growth, and a growth between two things, ground and a tree, or whatever the hell it is. You have to get your roots firmly in the ground first. Put your feet on the ground first. Money doesn't grow on trees. You know, I don't like the dance image, but there is a kind of dance.

Q: I beg your pardon.

JS: I say I don't like the dance image which always occurs when you try to figure out where the poet is doing things, and it's like a dance, maybe, of the Indian fakir on hot coals, but it ain't very much like a dance that I'd like to dance of choice. It is a kind of a thing where you go between one thing and another, I guess as trees grow roots, and the smiling public man is the same thing as the chestnut tree, the "great-rooted blossomer."

Q: Let's put it this way. Fifty years from now, what would you expect an English student to get out of your poetry?

JS: Term papers. [Laughter]

HA: Fast mark.

WT: Jack? The that from Outside which is dictating—you mentioned ghosts. Does this have anything to do with former poets? Can former poets be part of that Outside? Or is this something that simply dictates to anyone who is in poetry?

JS: I think in some sense it can. Has anyone in this room read Dunbar's "Lament for the Makaris"? Dunbar, a Scottish poet, fifteenth century. Well, *"timor mortis conturbat me"*?[22]

I think it's more a tradition of the past. I've never gotten any poet but Lorca, which was just a direct connection like on the telephone. Which wasn't the poets of the past but was Mr. Lorca talkin' directly. But my most unsuccessful book for myself is *Lament for the Makers,* which was going after the Dunbar thing and didn't really make it at all, although it did in some places.[23] I think when you pay attention to a tradition like Eliot does, you get into all sorts of the most soupy static that you can possibly have, so that you don't know what is your reading of English literature and what is ghosts. The fact that I didn't know Spanish really well enough to translate Lorca was the reason I could get in contact with Lorca.

WT: Is that which is outside you the same thing that is outside, let's say, Blaser or Duncan? Are the messages the same? That is, is each poet to give a different reading, but of the same messages?

JS: I wouldn't say so. I think if you had to identify the ghosts of Robin's poems, they'd be ghosts of the Northwest, going from Mormon country up through Idaho, and they're pretty specific geographical ghosts. Duncan's poems, where the ghosts did come, I'm not sure what they were. It's hard to remember since Duncan's gotten all his Egyptian gods coming in and fucking up things. But I think essentially they were probably purer ghosts, probably nearer to the central image, than either Robin or I have achieved. But again, it's hard to tell, because he's gone off now into some Blavatsky-Guggenheim spirit world.[24]

ET: Oh, Jack!

JS: I'm sorry. You can cut that out of the tape. [Laughter] No, that's actually the way I feel about where Duncan has gone in his poetry.

WT: Then Vancouver poetry of this kind would be cognizant of, or dictated from things that are in this locale. Does that make sense?

JS: It certainly does make sense. These poems haven't been completed yet, so I don't know, but it makes sense that they are. And I do have a sense that, well, the baseball diamond poem certainly told me something about the country which I hadn't really felt, except I had dreamed about it. I don't know how much this is just the personal thing of liking Vancouver and wanting *it*, and how much it is a thing that is going more toward, well,

Blake's "London." You know—is it London or is it the spiritual world or what? It's pretty damned hard to tell, for Blake or for anybody, and I don't know myself on this.

WT: In the summer of '63 there was a morning discussion about Lorca's *duende*.[25]

JS: Which started at a very bad time.

DL: Yes, but isn't the *duende* supposed to come from the Latin *dominus*, the spirit of the house?

JS: That's one theory about it.

WT: Do Lorca's distinctions figure in your own thinking about it?

JS: No, not a bit.

Q: It does tie in with a little bit earlier statement, where Lorca says that *duende* is not the trick but the ability to actually be on the horns. I mean, there are plenty of bullfighters, he says, that can be on the horns, so you get scared and this is some kind of art.

JS: Yeah.

Q: And that *duende* is to actually be on the horns, but it's not recognizable you're on the horns.

JS: The way I understand *duende*, and the way I think Lorca means it, is more like singing a song than being on the horns of the bull, although that's what it means.

DL: But in the Spanish folk music and folk song, the *duende* is some sort of spirit or demon that takes over.

JS: It's being able to carry the tune in the sense that I can never carry a tune, but I can carry a tune every once in a while. When I was with Warren singing "Lloyd George Knew My Father" with Stan, we were carrying a tune. It was a great tune.[26] And it's sort of that thing, that the bull's horn is the tune. I don't want to use the word measure, and I'm not going to, but it's something . . .

ET: It's a mode.

JS: Mode is very good.

Q: Like Billie Holiday when she sings, you know. She was on television the other night, and you realize that the rules of her singing are that there are just certain points which she's got to hold to, but all the rest between is risk.

JS: Did you ever hear Billie Holiday sing when she was good? Yeah. She could do that.

GB: You mean soul?

JS: No, it's not "soul." It isn't. It's playing on the bull's horns. When she sings "Strange Fruit" or "I Cover the Waterfront." The late records don't show that.

When I was a kid, I went to Fairfax High School, and there was a bar called The True Bill which was nearby which would let in anyone who was over fourteen and could pay for marijuana, which they sold. She was singing there with Snuffy Smith as the accompanist. And there wouldn't be one note which wasn't off, but she'd just exactly know where to go off and where never to go on, but it would always be the same thing. "Gloomy Sunday." Again you have just the records of her later life there, but on her earlier stuff, she could just go right between the bull's horns and hold them, and everything else, and still remain unscathed, and get this kind of a balance. It's a marvelous thing to be able to do, and of course she died like Marilyn Monroe did.

GB: What I was going to say is that soul is a thing that you can't get from a master. You can't pick it up in a grocery store or something.

JS: I'm not sure about that, George. I really am not. Though a lot of people say that and it may be true.

Q: Like *duende* in the cabbages.

GB: As a matter of fact, there's a toilet paper in Mexico called Duende, but I wasn't thinking of that. This is just what a friend told me.

JS: Poor lost *turista*.

GB: Yeah. It means "soft" in one sense.

Q: It seems to me there are parts of Miles Davis's technique that get that quality. There's not enough in it. Well, it's too orchestrated, but you get a sense of that.

JS: Well, more in Monk than in Davis. Davis—I think the same thing that I was saying in that nasty statement about Duncan.

Q: Yeah, but there's a phrasing, right?

JS: Well, there are a hell of a number of phrases which are great. But the thing is the cop-out thing, which Monk has never done, and Billie never did, although she sang lousy the last half of her life. She never copped out on us.

Q: When she came to Vancouver, they used to put her down for singing off key.

JS: She certainly did that. I think that any poet who doesn't sing off key ought to be very careful because singing on key is . . . Well, all poets sort of know that, nowadays. One of the few things we have learned is that you have to learn how to sing off key in some way or another. Again, you have your infinite resources in the furniture. You can make the vocabulary the off-key thing, like Crane did, or you can make the metrics the off-key thing, or you can make the whole structure, or anything else, and then the ghosts come and decide differently. I don't know. Fundamentally I think that the thing that I've seen about Canadian poets, which is mainly in *Tish*, is the lack really of trying to experiment with their own stuff.

Q: *Tish* won't allow it.

JS: Oh, I know everyone says that, but I don't think it's true. I think that *Tish* is about as much of a creation of all the people not wanting to take chances as it is any particular editor not wanting to take chances.

Q: Have you ever dealt with Frank Davey?[27]

JS: I have, and I would imagine very strongly that if I were nineteen and writing a poem, that he would probably accept it if it were the kind of poem I would have written at nineteen. I don't really think it's that. I think it's the people being scared of trying out things on them. Have you tried out anything on *Tish* that's been rejected, Jamie, that's good to you still?

JR: No. Finally, I would push through the things that I thought were good.

JS: That odd poem you have in *Tish* this time, the wet dream poem, that's as about a far-out a poem as you could publish anywhere. I don't mean as far as content, but I mean as far as going away from what *Tish* is or what your poetry has been.

JR: Yeah. *El Corneo* took it for a while but didn't print it finally.[28]

JS: What is *El Corneo*?

Q: *El Corneo* is from Mexico . . .

JS: Oh, God. Sounds like a breakfast food.
    Any further questions to ask me before we go?

WT: I've got one more. In the summer of '63, Olson said that he has a visit from his angel in March of that year. Does this make sense to you, in terms of what you've been talking about?

JS: Do you know what angel means in Hebrew? It means messenger.

WT: Messenger?

JS: And Jacob wrestling with the angel. Actually, one of the things I've found up here is that nobody has ever read [Hans Jonas's] books, which do deal with just exactly that kind of thing. I imagine Olson hasn't either. But the [Jonas] series gives you a pretty clear picture of what an angel is. It's a pretty historical thing, really.[29]

WT: I think Olson made the statement in connection with the Lorca essay on the *duende*. They were talking about what Lorca meant by "angel."

DL: Is this the same as Rilke's angel?

JS: No, it's not. Rilke's angels, I guess, come from thingness rather than from the opposite way of the wrestlers. Although, I suppose you can wrestle with things as well as you can with Outsideness, but there are two different things. It's what I said in the first meeting—the Williams thing of the nimbus around things, around objects, and everything else. The sort of thing that a thing has besides being a thing—the fact that they can name it "the chair," that kind of thing. That's Rilke's angels, I think. When he cries, who hears him? It is essentially things, I think.

And with Lorca, it's not. It's essentially a conflict between the world outside of things, which has its own things maybe, its own kind of "the chair" which probably has its own nimbus and everything else, but it's different. I don't know. The *Duino Elegies* are lovely, but I prefer the *Songs for Orpheus*.[30]

We can't end on that. Someone ask me a last question which we can end the tape on.

WT: Who's going to win the pennant?

JS: Well, I predicted Milwaukee at the start of the year, and so far it seems more accurate than my last-year predictions in the book *Language*, which predicted Philadelphia would win the pennant. Although they still should've, and I suspect Milwaukee will end up one game behind the Dodgers.[31]

Notes

1. *Prism*, later called *Prism International*, was a literary magazine connected with the Creative Writing Program at the University of British Columbia. *Tish*, edited by Frank Davey, George Bowering, David Dawson, Jamie Reid, and Fred Wah, was founded in 1961 partly as a reaction against *Prism* and partly in response to Robert Duncan's then recent series of lectures. Warren Tallman wrote of the *Tish* scene: "the *Tish* poets were very much like the fools who rush in where more cautious men fear to tread. And did rush in, managing to create a wonderfully garbled, goofy, and in many ways ludicrous Vancouver version of the poetics Duncan had turned loose. But great energy and liveliness were exerted, interesting poems were written, and talent had a favorable milieu in which to gain footing and grow" (25).

2. For a description of the Magic Workshop, see Ellingham and Killian (89).

3. At the time of the lecture, Spicer is in the middle of composing *Book of Magazine Verse*, his last book. By inviting the audience in to witness or participate he is coming full circle with the performative aspect of Duncan's originary serial poem *Medieval Scenes*.

4. In a letter to R. W. Dixon, Gerard Manley Hopkins wrote about the composition

of the poem: "I had long had haunting my ear the echo of a new rhythm which now I realized on paper. To speak shortly, it consists in scanning by accents or stresses alone, without any account of the number of syllables. . . . I do not say the idea is altogether new; there are hints of it in music, in nursery rhymes and popular jingles, in the poets themselves, and, since then, I have seen it talked about as a thing possible in critics" (Hopkins, 14–15).

5. It's interesting to note that the one poem unintentionally repeated happens to be about a funeral procession for someone who "died in agony," which obliquely returns us to Creeley's poem "After Lorca," a funerary poem about an impoverished burial ritual. The only other repeated poem in Spicer's opus is in "Homage to Creeley" (HC, 129, 138). Spicer dies shortly after this book's completion and his ashes are buried in a public grave.

6. Warren Tallman's comment about Poem 3 for the Vancouver Festival is certainly justified given its apocalyptic image of the sunset over dark oily waters.

7. Jamie Reid (b. 1941) was a founding coeditor of *Tish* and a frequent contributor to its pages. His early poems show the influence of Spicer as evidenced in *The Man Whose Path Was on Fire* (1969). His most recent books are *Prez: Homage to Lester Young* (1993) and *Mad Boys* (1997).

8. Fritz Kreisler (1875–1962) was an Austrian-American violinist who wrote operettas and works for violin. In 1935 he revealed that a number of pieces he had performed as obscure works by great composers were in fact his own compositions.

9. Meyer Schapiro writes of the paintings of the late Cézanne: "Each area approaches an ultimate of movement and depth, within the limits of simplicity and grandeur of form. . . . In this impulse-charged rendering of great masses, the smallest inflections count, without appearing contrived. Its simplicity belongs to the greatest masters." His paintings become "passionately free, to the point of ecstatic release. . . . The contrasts are not simply of the stable and unstable, as in his other works, but of different kinds of movement and intense color" (122–24). I offer these quotations as a parallel reading of Spicer's *Book of Magazine Verse*, a deeply abstract composition that voices some of Spicer's most lyrically turbulent passages.

10. Composer Ernest Bloch (1880–1959) was director of the San Francisco Conservatory from 1925 to 1930 and Professor of Music at UC Berkeley from 1940 to 1951.

11. The baseball players to whom Spicer refers in the lecture are as follows:

Paul Lindblad was a pitcher for Kansas City starting in 1965.

Yogi Berra (born Lawrence Peter Berra) was a legendary catcher and excellent hitter for the New York Yankees from 1946 to 1965. He managed the team in 1964 and again in the 1970s.

Willie Mays (nicknamed "Say Hey") played for the Giants his whole career (1951–1957 in New York and 1958–1972 for San Francisco). As Spicer suggests in Lecture 2, he was known for his crowd-pleasing antics, such as taking off his cap and facing the crowd every time he got to first base (Dark, 76).

Jim Ray Hart was a third baseman for the Giants from 1964 to 1972. Spicer called him "Dr. Strangeglove." As a rookie, he hit his first home run off Warren Spahn in April 1964. Also in that season Willie Mays replaced him at third base after Hart was hit in the head by a ball and hospitalized, bounced out of the box. Hart seems to be the rookie in the second poem for the *St. Louis Sporting News*: "Somebody so young being so cagy, I / Got three home-runs off Warren Spahn but both of us understood where the ball was (or wasn't) going to go. You / Are a deceit and when you get to the age of thirty (and I live to see it) you're / Going to get knocked out of the box, / Baby" (BMV, 257).

Warren Spahn pitched most of his career for Boston (1942–1952) and Milwaukee (1953–1964). He played for both New York and San Francisco in 1965, the year he retired.

Jim Hegan was a catcher for Cleveland. He played for San Francisco in 1959 and retired in 1960.

Ted Williams (nicknamed the "Splendid Splinter," "Thumper," and "The Kid") was a legendary batter and outfielder for Boston, 1939–1960.

12. A good definition of Spicer's role in all this.

13. Alvin Dark (b. 1922) played shortstop for the Boston Braves (named Rookie of the Year in 1948) and the New York Giants, and he played in the World Series for both teams. In 1961–1964 he managed the San Francisco Giants, who won the Series in 1962. He was notorious for losing his temper with team owners and provoking animosity in the press; he was fired in 1964 for alleged racism, though he claimed the press had misconstrued his remarks and that to be a good manager, his treatment of the team was necessarily colorblind. (Dark claimed he was fired because of an extramarital affair.) He wasn't hired to manage Kansas City until after the 1965 season, so at the time of the lectures he was unemployed. His autobiography, published in 1980, is strikingly Spicerian in its seriousness about the game, its warning tone, its sense of the ignorance of the owner-bosses and the inordinate importance of social behavior over talent, and its retrospective awareness of the importance of managing oneself well. Like Spicer, Dark had great ambition within his field and a deep hatred of indifference. In the early sixties in San Francisco, Dark had a radio program that was broadcast during the morning traffic hour (Dark, 77).

14. Popular legend has it that Abner Doubleday (1819–1893) invented the game of baseball in 1839 in Cooperstown, New York, but records show that Doubleday was at West Point at the time. The legend appealed to baseball advocates like FDR who liked the connection between baseball and the heroism in Doubleday's Civil War career. (Roosevelt even went so far as to allocate New Deal money to restore the "original" field at Cooperstown and establish the Baseball Hall of Fame.) The legend would appeal to Spicer in its combination of otherwise divergent discourses: theosophy, war, and games. Blavatsky did, in fact, place Doubleday in charge of the Theosophical Society in New York.

15. Sam Perry (1939–1966) was a young filmmaker influenced by Stan Brakhage. He made three films. His essay *Personal Locus: Maximus of Gloucester from Dogtown, Charles Olson* was published by Tish Books in 1965.

16. The sentiments expressed here are evidence of Spicer's inner turmoil. He dies exactly two months later—long before November.

17. *Heads of the Town* was written in 1960–1961 and published in 1962.

18. Paul Valéry writes that reading "what has been written about you is as nothing to the peculiar sensation of hearing yourself commented on at the University in front of the blackboard, just like a dead author . . . I felt as though I were my own shadow" (Valéry, 141–42).

19. In Nash's collected poems, *Verses from 1929 On*, "The Panther" has six lines (Nash, 97).

20. *Jenseits* or *Jenerseits* is German for the "other world."

21. Spicer was one of the "six" of the Six Gallery. It was the site of the public inauguration of the Beat generation with Allen Ginsberg's reading of "Howl" in 1955. Of the event Spicer refers to, Rebecca Solnit writes: "The Six Gallery died with a bang in November of 1957. Pianist and sculptor Ed Taylor organized what might have been called a Happening if it had happened back East, though he called it 'Collective Expressionism.' A participant cut off Taylor's tie to launch the event, then six poets read

their work simultaneously while someone shouted 'the horses are off and running.' Everyone then demolished the gallery's decrepit piano with axes, blow torches, and sledgehammers" (72).

22. William Dunbar wrote "Lament for the Makaris" around 1508. The refrain of Dunbar's poem, *"timor mortis conturbat me"* (the fear of death troubles me), comes from the *Responsorium* to the seventh lesson in the Office of the Dead. Levertov also uses it in her poem "Who Is at My Window" in *O Taste and See* (1964).

23. Spicer's book *Lament for the Makers* (San Francisco: White Rabbit, 1961) features the acknowledgment page from Duncan's *The Opening of the Field* (New York: Grove, 1960). The original version of the main poem of the series quotes Matthew Arnold's "Dover Beach" and sends up Pound's doggerel salute to Browning's "Sordello." But instead of publishing the poem with the original: "Hang it all Robert Duncan / there can only be the one bordello" (LM, 110), Spicer replaces Robert Duncan with Robert Browning. Perhaps this book is a failure for Spicer because he wrote it out of personal injury rather than as a strictly dictated poem. Or maybe the poem never elicited the proper response from Duncan.

24. Spicer's assertion that Duncan's ghosts were "purer" is an extremely high compliment in the context of their fraught relationship, which often included scathingly honest critiques. He balances it, of course, with the critique of Duncan's current ethos (particularly his recent allegiances with the East Coast) which, he seems to be saying, has compromised poetic "purity" in the interest of upward career mobility.

25. Lorca's essay on *duende* deals primarily with song and with the physical quality of creative acts, placing the event outside intellect. Spicer's first public talk similarly asserts that there is more poetry in Sophie Tucker than there is in John Crowe Ransom.

26. "Lloyd George Knew My Father" is collected in Winn.

27. Canadian poet, editor, and scholar Frank Davey (b. 1940) was the primary editor of *Tish* (1961–1963) and went on to edit *Open Letter*. His books of poems include: *D-Day and After* (1962), *City of the Gulls & Sea* (1965), *Weeds* (1970), *Arcana* (1972), and many others.

28. *El Corneo Emplumado* was edited by Margaret Randall and Sergio Mondragón in Mexico City.

29. The name on the tape is unclear but the person Spicer might be referring to is Hans Jonas, author of *The Gnostic Religion: The Message of the Alien God and the Beginnings of Christianity* (1958). John Granger makes good use of Jonas in his essay on Spicer, "The Idea of the Alien in the Four Dictated Books."

30. Spicer of course means the *Sonnets to Orpheus* which in many ways do behave like songs. One reason he might prefer the *Sonnets to Orpheus* is it is one of the major examples in this century of a dictated text (Rilke's term). The poems came, Rilke wrote, from the occasion of reflecting on the news of the death of a friend's daughter and were written down, he claimed, without censorship, in the course of about one month. Rilke was finishing his *Elegies*, a project of over a decade in the making, when the sonnets "came" as a purely dictated text. Rilke writes:

> The angel of the Elegies is that creature in which the transformation of the visible into invisibility, which we are accomplishing, appears already fulfilled. For the angel of the Elegies, all past towers and palaces are extant because long since invisible, and the still standing towers and bridges of our existence, already invisible, although (for us) they still physically continue. The angel of the Elegies is . . . therefore "terrible" to us because we, its lovers and transformers, are still clinging to the visible. —All the worlds of the universe fling themselves into the invisible as into their next deeper reality. (*Sonnets to Orpheus*, 135)

Note: The angels of the elegies are comparable to the figure of Vera Knoop which creates the orphic circuitry for the *Sonnets to Orpheus*. In their own way these figures of Rilke's correspond to Spicer's "Lowghost." Vera Knoop also corresponds roughly to Maxim, the young man whom Stefan George loved and who was "brought back" through the efforts of the *Georgekreis*. (Spicer may prefer the connection with the *Georgekreis* because it is a gay culture and its "bringing back" of the lover is more overtly erotic.) See Edward Halsey Foster's *Jack Spicer* for a discussion of Spicer's own "magic circle" in relation to the *Georgekreis*.

31. As it turned out, the Los Angeles Dodgers won. Milwaukee finished in fifth place.

CALIFORNIA LECTURE

Poetry and Politics

JULY 14, 1965

≈ᾇ The backdrop of Lecture 4, "Poetry and Politics," is the controversial and frightening reality of war and the escalation of American troops in Vietnam — two hundred thousand by the end of 1965. Spicer is addressing a student body at UC Berkeley, where one of the largest student anti-war activities in America was about to take place. In this lecture he speaks to current student issues like the Free Speech Movement as one who has experienced the inhospitable repercussions of administrative decisions. Spicer himself was a veteran of Berkeley's controversial loyalty oath of 1950, one of a handful of people who didn't sign, at a time when there wasn't a unified student movement; he was basically alone in his resistance. Spicer is wary of movements, and he speaks to the students as someone who has experienced the loneliness of political conviction.

The Berkeley Poetry Conference (July 12 through 24, 1965) was a major gathering of poets from Donald Allen's seminal anthology, *The New American Poetry*. Spicer was one of seven featured poets to give a lecture. The others were Robert Duncan, Gary Snyder, Charles Olson, Ed Dorn, Allen Ginsberg, and Robert Creeley. Spicer's lecture was given to a large audience on the Berkeley campus on Wednesday, July 14, at 10:30 A.M.

Because Spicer is addressing young poets, he tries to train his perspective on their point of view. Imagine Diogenes giving a freshman orientation. The lecture is filled with purpose, cynicism, and mother wit. In contrast to the more informal Vancouver Lectures he gave a month earlier, he is slow, precise, and methodical in his answers. He is speaking on his own turf, there is an element of caution to his talk, and, as with the Vancouver Lectures, it is evident from his tone that he feels his message is particularly important for the young.

In classic Spicerian form he takes an unpopular stance, given the political climate on campus and the students' zeal for self-expression. Spicer's argument that poetry does not in itself effect political change is, understandably, met with some resistance. His message is not against political activism but against having any illusions that poems in themselves have political effect. It is important to remember that while Spicer argues the futility of political poetry it is not because his poems are devoid of political content. While he suggests that overtly political poems seem to be more self-gratifying than effective, his poems and plays acknowledge war as the backdrop of all writing. As Zeus puts it in the prologue to Spicer's unpublished play *Troilus* (1955):

> The Trojan War has been going on for the last 3,000 years and it hasn't stopped yet. All the stories you've heard about the destruction of Troy are just daydreams Ulysses invented to keep himself sane. You've probably dreamed like that yourselves, waiting for a war to come to an end. One thing, though—the people in the play don't seem to know how long the war has lasted. They have the idea that it's only been going on for nine years or so. I don't know why. Human beings don't have a very good time sense. (2)

Spicer asserts that writing poetry does not absolve one of political responsibility, but if one expects to use poetry as a vehicle for political activism, it is likely to be bad poetry. He is not against political action; on the contrary, he suggests that instead of writing a bad political poem one should write a letter to one's congressman. This suggestion is not dismissive. Spicer himself wrote a number of such letters in his life, one of them to the *San Francisco Chronicle* protesting its racist coverage of the Vietnam War, which recounted overwhelming losses among the Viet Cong less sympathetically than much smaller losses among American troops (I, n. 24).

Political content finds its way into Spicer's poems in a number of ways. His work often contains references to specific wars and war stories: World War II, the Trojan War, the Spanish Civil War, and the American Civil War are all embedded within his poems. As a given of human experience, war is one of the many grand narratives that inform and structure human meaning. Beyond the outrageous humor of having Lorca posthumously write the preface to his first book (*After Lorca*, 1957), Spicer's invocation of Lorca is also an honorific summoning of someone who died for a cause; when Spicer, on his deathbed less than a decade later, says to Robin Blaser, "My vocabulary did this to me," he proclaims himself a casualty of poetry, placing himself in a correspondence with Lorca and even with Whitman as a politically subversive gay poet living in a time of civil war. But maintaining an absurdist's sense of the Real, Spicer also crosses politics with dada; in his book *The Holy Grail*, the horse Lancelot rides is

"Dada" and the Australian soldiers march into battle singing "We're off to see the Wizard," to name just two examples. As implied in his "Unvert Manifesto" (CB, 341), nonsense for Spicer is the overarching condition of the universe and war is its most evil and absurd manifestation in reality.

But the most important function of this lecture is to offer practical advice for young poets about how to "manage" themselves as artists within such uncertain times. Since war is perpetual, Spicer suggests that the dangers for the artist are not just the Vietnam War. He's more interested in illuminating the politics within the poetic community which form a dark correspondence with political power structures, as he provocatively compares the visibility and power of Olson to that of LBJ and argues that Ginsberg's popularity mars his later poetry. He wants to draw attention to the political aspects of all self-governing bodies and to point out that the poetic community is no exception; it has its own tyrannies of style and personality which are equally debilitating to the rank and file. His message is quite literally to "stay loose." He reiterates that the enemy is whatever keeps the poet from making poems. But this lecture isn't only admonishing. In the end, Spicer presents a positive model of poetic community through his assertion that "a magazine is a society," as exemplified in the discussion of the project *Open Space*.

In this lecture Spicer reminds us that poetry has always been threatened by the overpopularity of movements, individual star machines, the misappropriation of the academy, and general misguidedness; that to be a poet is an enormously difficult and vulnerable position to occupy; and that, finally, there is no better (or worse) time than the present to be a poet, when it couldn't be more inappropriate.

THOMAS PARKINSON:[1] I think we can start the lecture now. This seems to be old home week. We have Jack Spicer with us, as we have off and on now for about twenty years, and it's always a pleasure. Jack first came here in 1946 as a student and stayed on here for some time doing research work and has traveled widely.

JACK SPICER: Really? I got as far as Vancouver. [Laughter]

TP: Well, there are people who are under the illusion that Jack Spicer was in Boston . . .

JS: Oh, well, yeah. [Laughter]

TP: . . . and Minnesota, and even once went as far as Palo Alto.

JS: Yeah. That was the worst.

TP: That was going pretty far.

JS: Yeah. That was absolutely the worst. The aborigines there were just terrible.

TP: His only foreign country. Now, Jack seems to be eager to talk . . .

JS: No, not particularly.

TP: . . . and I'm not going to stop him. I think I've created enough silence so that we can get on with the business of the day. You all know Jack's bibliography. His latest book is *Language*. Some of you already know Jack, and the rest of you will soon have some idea of Jack. Isn't that right?

JS: I guess so. I hope so anyway.
   Well, when you talk about poetry and politics, it gets pretty desperate.
   You've all read your morning paper, and you know what's happening as far as our escalator or whatever it's called in Vietnam. This is not what I'm

trying to talk about. What I'm trying to talk about is for you people who are poets and want some idea about how the strategy is for you to become poets who both write good poetry and also don't sell out to the bosses. There are bosses in poetry as well as in the industrial empire and everything else, and what I want to talk to you about today is simply that—how to manage yourself in your own individual way, I guess, since no poet who's worthy of the term doesn't. But also, where to avoid mistakes that one has, say, the mistake of saying "Gee, I'm a great poet and somebody wants to print me." And you have say, five, six poems. They're good, but they aren't that good, and so forth. What do you do?

The point is that, essentially, the enemy—as I think I quoted in one poem from Rosa Luxemburg—is in your own country.[2] I mean, you're not going to be able to do a good goddamn thing about Vietnam—that's absolutely out—because President Johnson is not terribly interested in whether intellectuals don't like Vietnam or not. As a matter of fact, I imagine he thinks whenever an intellectual says something about Vietnam, that it's a very good thing for him. [Laughter]

No, I mean seriously just that. Seriously, there is no possible way of getting at anything about the American system that I've been able to figure out in forty years. Maybe you people can. It would be marvelous if you could, but I don't think so.

The point is then, if you're poets—not too many flashbulbs, huh?— you ought to figure out what the power system is within your own community. Your enemy is simply something which is going to try to stop you from writing poetry.

So what do you do then? It's a good question, and being battered around for forty years, I'm not sure of the answer. But one of the things I do know is that you try to figure out the terrain. This is, I'm sure, subversive jungle fighting—Mao Tse, who was a damn good poet, and probably still is, and also Ho Chi Minh. You have to blend with the scenery, but at the same time not open yourself up to the kinds of attacks which these very lovely people, reasonable people, nice people, people who believe in poetry, want to give you.

It's a terribly hard thing to be a young poet—I'm a young poet, I have two poems, four poems, whatever the hell it is—and say no to various publishers. But I think you ought to. It's hard to say, because I've been talking about poets being united for years and they aren't united. They have some silly-assed thing with the IWW now that might unite them, and if so, I'm all for it.[3]

But the point is that most people will exploit poets. They'll exploit the older ones for the knowledge they have, and they'll exploit the younger ones for the promise they have, which somehow or other gives the people some kind of thing that maybe they have promise too, which they don't.

Essentially, what I mean is, stay loose. Stay absolutely loose, and don't accept any offers whatsoever.

But you're not just a poet. You're also a human being who wants to be recognized and everything else. One of the best things that I heard on that was last night on KCBS where some guy—his name was Anderson—was talking about peach farmers, and he said the peach farmers didn't know a good goddamn thing about the number of peaches that were needed in the market. In other words, they would send in peaches, and peaches would go down to one cent a peach, or whatever it was, and that this had a great deal to do with farm labor.

What I'm saying is that you're going to sell out eventually. You have to, just for economic reasons. But when you sell out, know exactly what your peaches cost. Know exactly how many peaches there are on the market. Know exactly what is the price you can sell out for.

This is something that most young poets don't do, and this doesn't sound like it has anything to do with the writing of poetry, but it does. The writing of poetry, essentially, is something which you really can't say any-thing about except that if you violate something deep inside you—maybe even something that you didn't know was deep inside you—you're lost. You don't write, or you write bad poetry. Or you write for the market, which is another nice thing. You manufacture artificial peaches to go to the market at the high price. And all of these things are just not really things to do. But I think of all of the young poets here, just about every one of them will make at least two or three mistakes in this line before they realize it. But what I'm trying to do is to say don't make any more than two or three mistakes.

It's the business of being a person, too. Now, as Tom told you, I went to Cal and I was one of the people who didn't sign the oath in 1950.[4] So, a great deal. I didn't suffer by it. I think that, on the whole, I gained by it, in an economic sense. But I was not really conscious of myself as a poet when I was not signing the oath, and I'm not at all sure that I wouldn't have signed the oath had I been conscious of myself being a poet.

Now there is the lovely Free Speech Movement. Great, I guess. You can say the word "fuck" without any trouble whatsoever, as I did. But I don't quite see that it was the same thing as the oath. The oath was something which actually would have made your professors really scared. There've been five oaths passed by state legislatures before ours, but there weren't any other state legislatures after that that passed any kind of oath. The oath was meaningless. Of the people in the English Department who didn't sign the oath, none of them had voted for Wallace in '48. Two of them had voted for Dewey—God knows why—and the rest voted for Truman. I mean, you can't get the individual politics, the politics you have as a poet, out of the national politics.

When I get upset by reading about Vietnam and what we're going to do there, and so forth and so on, it hurts me as a poet. And—I'm trying to think of the right words for this—there's a poet who's writing poetry, who's a conveyor of poetry, that doesn't have anything to do with his poems if he's a good poet. There's the individual and then there's this society he moves in. Now, Mao Tse said once, you swim in it, like a fish. You swim in whatever circumstance you are in. He's talking about guerrilla war at the time. You swim in it like a fish, but it's pretty difficult to do. These people—these Johnsons or these Olsons or these Kennedys or these any-things—they're better than you are at it. What you have to do is to some-how or other figure out some way to swim in the thing like a fish but not sell out. And I don't know how you do that. I really don't.

I'm getting a hundred dollars to give this lecture, which is extremely generous. But I don't know if I wouldn't have stopped giving this lecture if it had been no money at all, because I just don't know how this society can be swum in, like a fish, to use that kind of phrase.

Now, I'd like, if it's all right with you people, some questions, and then I can go back on to what I was talking about.

Q: It has been said that poets are the unacknowledged legislators of the universe. Would you agree with this?

JS: I think Plato was much better on saying the thing, where he said that a poet shouldn't be allowed in society. What I mean is, sure, Shelley had this great stuff of saying that, but where did Shelley land?

Q: Where we all do, I guess.

JS: No, not where we all do exactly. I mean, Shelley did land in Italy, and did have his heart saved by some guy who then made a lot of money out of saving his heart. But I don't really think that we have anything to do with it. I would certainly like to, but I haven't been elected by any body of anything to legislate, and the people who legislate are generally about as unpoetical as anyone could possibly be.

Willy Yeats did serve in the senate in Ireland, but Willy Yeats also didn't do anything while he was there. He made about three speeches, which haven't even been reprinted yet on account of the fact that they were so dull. And Willy Yeats I think is a great poet. I don't think Shelley is, but I think that Willy Yeats is, and here's a new nation, coming into being and all that sort of thing. All the place for the great poet to come in to be the great senator, and what happened? Nothing.

Q: But don't they pull the strings behind, you know? They're unacknowledged.

JS: Well, what poet do you think has pulled the strings? [Laughter] No, no, this is a serious question. No, of all the poets in all the world, what poet has pulled the strings?

Q: Of the universe? [Laughter]

JS: Of the universe, yeah, but we're talking about politics, which directly takes out the universe from the discussion. We're talking about the poet, the individual who is a poet, and society. Now, who pulled the strings, of any poet that you've ever heard of, in any society you've ever heard of, even indirectly?

Q: Mao, maybe.

JS: Mao gave up being a poet when he was about twenty-five, and he didn't pull any strings until then. He came, actually, from a fairly rich place in China, if there is such a thing as a rich place in China, which is doubtful. He was upper middle class. He wrote poetry like anyone else did. He wrote some damn good poetry. He wrote poetry after he'd left that, but the poetry was not really anything which, at least to me, had any political meaning. Sure, you celebrate five thousand miles or ten thousand miles or whatever the hell the march was.[5] But there was no meaning to it in the sense that a poet has. Of course, I can't read Chinese. I may be absolutely wrong on all of this.

That was a lovely question because it did bring up an essential thing. Would someone else have a question?

Q: I can see a difficulty in selling out your political ideas, but, as far as your poetry goes, I don't quite understand the difficulty in selling your poetry. If somebody wants to pay you to print your poems somewhere, what's the difficulty, except perhaps personal pride?

JS: It's a good question. And that's the thing I was trying to get at, but I obviously didn't yet.

Well, take it just the most simple way possible. A poet is offered to go into an anthology and the anthology is done by a good person, or at least you think he's a good person. Something like that. The kind of association of your poetry with the other people's poetry makes an entire difference. You feel, when you've been coupled with the other people, kind of like, well, you're a pimp.

Now, magazines, the same way. Sure *Poetry* magazine will pay you—what, a hundred dollars, something like that now, for a poem? So what? I mean, it's not "so what" when you don't have a hundred dollars, just like I'm lecturing here because I don't. But a magazine is a society. I think *Open Space* proved that.[6] You have to behave within the rules of the society, and if you don't, then there's nothing else. In other words, if you publish in *Poetry* magazine, it's great. You get paid money. You get people reading it all through the country. But, in the long run, if you're participating in one of these things, then you have to say "yeah, I read *Poetry* myself"—*Poetry* magazine, that is—which I don't, and wouldn't, because I don't believe in the society that it creates.[7]

That's a rather vague answer to your question. Why don't you ask me another question now, just to make it less vague.

Q: Well, it just seems to me that if you want to make a personal honor thing out of it . . .

JS: Not a personal thing, no. Let's get that straight. I divided three classes of things. One was the poet, one was the individual who was writing the poems, and the third was society. It's a business of the poet's honor, not the individual one. As far as my individual honor, I couldn't care less.

Q: And you think that the poem then is somehow tarnished by appearing in some commercial venue?

JS: No. I think the poet writing poetry, receiving poetry, is not exactly tarnished, but is less able to write poetry than he was before, from this.

RONNIE PRIMACK:[8] What happens to a poet when he gets in cahoots with a non-poet or an anthologizer? When he gets sort of intimate . . . [Laughter]

JS: You can see the answer. [Laughter] No, Ronnie, did you have something more to ask than that?

RP: I really struggled with that.

Q: Did you also mean that if a poet should become vitriolic or very much against a political objective, that he would also damage his other poetry? In other words, does he have any obligation to perhaps speak up against political acts that he doesn't agree with? If no more than anything else, to get it off his chest?

JS: Yeah. Except it doesn't work that way. Of all of the poems I've seen in the last ten years coming from this area, I haven't seen one good political poem. And I think that that's sort of an answer to you.

Q: Would you recommend that he write it and throw it away?

JS: Yeah, or write a letter to his congressman or something like that. It's just as meaningless. I mean, I would bet that at least ninety-nine percent of you were against the Vietnam thing. Okay. So, what do you do? You write a letter to your congressman. You write it down in poetry. But it doesn't come out right then. Again, I don't know of any political poems which have worked.

Q: Do you include among your wholesale condemnation of political poetry Allen Ginsberg's work?

JS: Well, this is something again I have to think about. I hate people who are sitting up on a stage and giving, you know, nice simple answers, which you can do.

Well, now what did Ginsberg change by the *Howl* trial, except for the fact that Mark Schorer had to be disturbed by the district attorney by being asked, "Well, what do you think Mr. Ginsberg means by 'fucked by saintly motorcyclists'?"[9]

Now, it seems to me a totally unimportant point. Ginsberg's later poetry I don't like. And I can't really see the point of it. Certainly, he is not political. If he were here now, he'd say that he's working for love, which is an entirely different kind of thing.

Q: Love is not a political stance?

JS: Well, if you can make it that way. [Laughter]
     Could I have another question?

DAVID BROMIGE:[10] Do you really think the Free Speech Movement was fought solely or mainly so students could say "fuck" on campus?[11]

JS: No.

DB: That's the inference that could be drawn from your remark.

JS: It certainly shouldn't be. But I think that in 1950, when the oath thing was on, and there was the business of whether professors would not only be completely saddled with—well, the word McCarthy is a nice word to use, but it wasn't just McCarthy. It was the whole thing—the Korean War and everything else. But in 1950 there was no student movement whatso-ever. In other words, I'm not sure that having a few things saying this and that and the other and sign this petition, sign that, at Sather Gate is so im-portant. Not nearly as important as the other thing was. I mean, it's nice to have it at Sather Gate. It's a traffic hazard sometimes, but it's nice. But I don't really see that the Free Speech Movement meant anything. Per-haps you could tell me what it meant and I could see more clearly.

DB: Well, for instance, there was the picketing of the *Oakland Tribune* to protest discrimination in hiring practices.[12]

JS: Uh huh. Now, you picket the *Oakland Tribune* and what happens?

DB: Wait and see.

JS: Well, not really wait and see, because the thing is not that simple. You know damn well the *Oakland Tribune* is going to have its same sub-scribers as it had before. You know damn well that the hiring practices, if they're changed, will be changed by hiring one or two Negroes and that's it. You don't know anything else about it. If you wanted to bomb the

Oakland Tribune Building, like they bombed the L.A. Times Building in 19—what, 12, something like that—then that would make some sense.

Q: Perhaps the significance of the FSM was to return the university to the students and teachers, rather than keeping it in the hands of the administrators.

JS: Well, again, I'm talking now as a person in society, not as a poet, and we've been getting off poetry and onto society, which I suppose is reasonable. But look, what's going to happen with the university, which is expanding too fast, which is going to have to have administrators who have to be experts and all of that? It's like trying to go against computers or something. The university wasn't returned to the teachers or the students, which it never did belong to. It was simply made quiescent with a nice tranquilizing thing and you got rid of a man who was going to be fired anyway—Strong—and what else happened?[13]

Q: Well, you're right. We're getting a little off the track here, and the problem I think is that we are all a part of the same imaginative force, meaning the poets, the university, the politics involved. How do you separate any part of it?

JS: It's damn difficult. [Laughter]
    No, I mean that seriously. It is damn difficult, and trying to separate it, I'm simply trying to tell you, number one, don't sell out as a poet. Number two, just remain cool about the rest of the things because you're not going to be able to do anything about it anyway.

Q: And yet you say that no political poetry you know of has ever been successful and it seems Auden says the same thing about Yeats: "the businessmen roaring in the Bourse" and "poetry makes nothing happen." But is that inevitably so, and what can you say about it?[14]

JS: Well, number one, I think that if we all were able—which I'm not, and no one I've seen has been—to remain firm and dedicated, and at the same time know where we're going, not trying to buck the University of California, which is just not buckable, but know where we're going, it's possible, yes. It hasn't happened, and I still would like anyone in the audience to tell me about one poem which changed anything in history.

Q: But didn't you say that "Nineteen Hundred and Nineteen" was a good political poem?

JS: Oh, it's a lovely poem, but it's not a political poem. It's a poem of despair. I mean, my God, "the weasel's tooth"? No, what Yeats is talking about in the poem, much better than I'm talking about, is exactly the same thing. There's no real way that I can see to do it. If there were, I'd do it, in a moment.[15]
    Ebbe?[16]

EBBE BORREGAARD: Jack, earlier you made a correlation between Olson and Johnson. [Laughter] Can you elaborate on that, taking into account things like the Orion poems, projective verse, or *Maximus*?

JS: Olson is probably the best poet that we have in the country.

Q: You meant that he sold out?

JS: No, I didn't mean he sold out. I meant that he was in the same position in poetry as Johnson is in politics. And that's not selling out or anything like that. But you get to be a power figure. Olson was, as a matter of fact, a New Deal functionary in the thirties and has a sense of politics, which I don't. And perhaps all of this lecture is just the business of my despair at the fact I don't have any sense of politics.

Q: I'd like, if you would, to discuss a little bit about the poet and his audience. I think your question, your challenge to us, to name one poem which has made a mark in politics, is not a fair one because no one poem can make a mark which will make any imprint. But many poets and many poems might possibly make a tiny imprint over a long period of time.

JS: Yeah, but . . .

Q: The fact that I'm sitting here listening to you I believe is proof that you all, as a group, are making a big mark on our culture, because if you weren't, I wouldn't be here at all and maybe a few others like myself.

JS: Well . . .

Q: What about the poet and his audience?

JS: Well, this raises about three questions, not one. To begin with, I don't think that you could name a group of poets in any particular historical time who have changed anything whatsoever in the political culture.

As far as the poet and his audience, I just don't believe that there is an audience for poems. There's an audience obviously for poets. They come and they pay a dollar and a half, and that sort of crap. But for poems, it seems to me that you're very lucky if you get two or three people within a five-year period who understand any of your poems. So it seems to me that the only reason for writing poetry is because poetry is sort of forced through the poet and is just there, like Mallory's great thing on Everest. Nothing else. In other words, what impact did the climbers make on Everest? Successful ones—not Mallory and Irvine, who died.[17]

What I'm trying to say is that I don't really think that a poet can have any effect whatsoever on society.

Q: Sounds to me like you're ruling out Bertolt Brecht entirely. That you're leaving out Mayakovsky.

JS: Uh, let's see, what happened to Mayakovsky?

Q: A suicide finally.

JS: Do you think he had any effect on the Bolshevik Revolution whatsoever?

Q: I think he's had a strong effect on the poets who are writing now, in this era.

JS: Well yeah, he's a damn good poet.

Q: . . . and on the young people in Russia, as well as the United States.

JS: I hope so. It just seems to me like the effect of Shelley or something like that on us. You know, revolutionary, but not terribly revolutionary. You can't really have too much of an effect on the younger generation if you kill yourself at what, twenty-six?[18]

Q: You gave me more of an answer right then than you have so far by saying "I hope so." The fact that you say you hope so proves that you have not given up hope that the poets do have a great influence.

js: Not a great influence. My only hope would be that perhaps something like the figure of Mayakovsky might possibly make things a little bit easier in Russia for poets. But other than that, I can't see any real hope. The people who do these things are people like Lyndon Johnson. And, my poetry, no one's poetry as far as I can see, is going to influence Lyndon Johnson.

MARY NORBERT KÖRTE:[19] Perhaps you don't consider this poetry, but what about the labor songs of the thirties and the songs of the civil rights movement? Those certainly have aroused everybody in every facet of society, either to hate or to some kind of an affinity.

js: You've made a very good point, and I can't really argue with it. Certainly the IWW songs—Joe Hill—did have some effect. But my father was a Wobbly, and my father also gave the whole thing up, like everyone else did, when the Wobblies were not getting anywhere, when they were separated from the Communists but not knowing what they were.[20]

Sure, you've got a lot of people to strike, and to do things, and you're right in a way. The popular songs do, but I'm not sure. Take "We Shall Overcome." Is there anything in that that's like [Sings]:

> Long-haired preachers come out ev'ry night,
> Try to tell us what's wrong and what's right;
> But when answered in voices so sweet:
> They will say you will eat, by and by
> In that glorious land up in the sky,
> Work and pray, live on hay,
> You'll get pie in the sky when you die.

[Applause]
Now I don't happen to believe that either.
But you're right. There is something to that. If I could write popular songs, I'd do it. And it's a damn good question.[21]

Q: Is humanity evolving to a point where poetry will be futile?

js: I'm sorry? [Laughter] No, I didn't get the question.

Q: Is humanity evolving to a point where poetry will be futile?

JS: Well, I think poetry's been futile to humanity all the time. I mean, it's not been futile to poets because they get messages from the poems, but as far as humanity—how many hundred billions are there now on the earth? How many people do you think even think about poetry?

Q: Mostly all of them through religion.

JS: What?

Q: Mostly all of them through religion. Through their ancient texts and their myths. It's only in America where we're separated from that, that we don't have poetry in our midst, in the proletariat and the peasantry.

JS: Well, I just don't think that's true. It may be true in terms of popular songs.

Q: The *Rig Vedas* and *Upanishads*.

JS: The *Rig Vedas* and the *Upanishads* were both written in a Sanskrit which the people of the time wouldn't even have understood. In Sanskrit culture I think that you have bigger isolation from popular culture than you do any other place. It's a completely artificial language, like the language of the Latin poets was to a lesser extent. You talk about vulgar Latin and classical Latin, and yet they were speaking it at the time of Martial. The poet has always been isolated by himself or by something else. But in Sanskrit poetry, it's particularly isolated.

Q: I have two questions. The first concerning the Agrarians which I feel had some political influence in that they used both the method of New Criticism and poetry to, say, gloss over the politics of the South for a while and to, say, unite the country in poetry in a way that they hoped would maybe further a union in politics. Now, that may or may not be so. I do think then that the Agrarians have been able, through editing anthologies and just through being leading critics and all, to influence greatly the thought of our country for, say, a good thirty or forty years.

JS: You mean Tate and Ransom?

Q: I mean Tate and Ransom, and maybe Robert Penn Warren.

And secondly, Kenneth Rexroth in the June edition of *Harper's* magazine said that there are no good poems about race, and that is including, he said, LeRoi Jones's poems in which black could be erased and white substituted with no loss. I'm wondering what you feel about this.[22]

JS: Gee, LeRoi Jones and Allen Tate seem to me almost the same thing. [Laughter]
    No. I should get back to what I was trying to say to the young poets here to begin with, and that is that you can get tempted with all kinds of power and I think that both Tate and LeRoi got tempted with it. I don't know, I prefer LeRoi Jones to Allen Tate, but that's only as a poet.

Q: What about the influence of the Agrarians?

JS: Well, the New Criticism is big in universities. I haven't seen it have any effect at all on poets for the last ten years. Anybody knows that a poem is not something which was written at no particular time, which is what New Criticism is about, and that it is written at some particular time. You have to know that. You're a fool if you don't.
    But, yeah, in the factory over here [UC Berkeley], I'm sure that the influence is still there. The Agrarian part of them was the best part, as far as I can see. I don't think they were doing it to subdue the Negro, because he was subdued then. I think that they were simply doing it with the idea of trying to get back from American capitalism, and this was obviously unsuccessful.[23]
    But I'm sure they were all racists in the way that almost any Southerner would be. I can't blame them for that. I can blame them for New Criticism much more than for that. I certainly could blame them for that now, once the Negro has come out as a real issue. But then you stand on something. You either say no or yes. But at that time, you didn't say either no or yes because they were saying "yes, boss" and "no, boss." What would anyone do? It was a crime, but Lord knows we've committed so many crimes in this country. Being one-eighth Blackfoot Indian, I know what happened to our tribe.
    Okay, a couple more questions.

Q: What would you say is the nature of a society like the *Open Space* society?

JS: That's a very good question because that brings it back to what I was trying to talk about.

To begin with, a lot of you probably won't know what *Open Space* was. It was barely circulated in Berkeley by Cody's [Bookstore] sometimes, and it was a magazine which went on for one year and purposely just for one year, which simply had all the poets put poems in it, not at final stage but poems as they were writing them. In other words, to encourage other poets to plow the field sort of, and it succeeded fairly well. I think probably a hell of a lot of good poems came out of it. I know I couldn't have written *Language* without it.

The whole thing that the average younger poet thinks of is I want something in a magazine which is going to last. The idea of making things last is something which just has to be conquered. The idea of *Open Space* was that these things would not last. They wouldn't be given past the East Bay. They were never sent to New York. Well, as a matter of fact, they were, subterraneously, but the official policy was that they wouldn't be. It was a kind of community of poets using one person who was able to take the enormous job of doing it. And it had to come out once a month. And you couldn't postpone your poem saying, "oh well, gee, I'd like to have three more days." There was no question of that. It was a question simply of poetry being exposed as it happened, naked. And that was good. What did Lew sell the copies of *Open Space* for?[24]

STAN PERSKY:[25] A hundred bucks to Cal.

JS: Yeah, a hundred bucks to Cal. They were given away free. That was just last year. It stopped in late December, I believe.

TP: They say it took an act of Congress to get that hundred bucks. I just don't want people to get the idea that we've got hundred buckses floating through the air to buy things.

JS: Oh, yeah, yeah, yeah, yeah, yeah. I know that myself, from my own books.

But the point was that the poets were not thinking of themselves as anything but poets and the society didn't matter. Obviously, if you're smart in society, you get your thing sent to New York. That's the reasonable thing. And you get in anthologies and all of that sort of crap. But this was restricted and restricted properly, with a few unfortunate exceptions.

Q: What was the total printing of *Open Space*?

JS: Stan, could you tell me?

SP: A hundred and fifty a month.

JS: All issues?

SP: No. When I thought people were starting to save sets a couple months I just gave out issues to poets that I knew so that other people wouldn't get sets.

JS: And that's why Lew Ellingham got a hundred dollars.

Q: But you suggested it's a community and not a society.

JS: Well, if you mean what Goodman means by the word "community," yeah.[26] But it's a very difficult thing. The community has been absolutely—I wouldn't say completely torn apart but almost—torn apart since *Open Space* stopped. It seems like you need an artificial thing like that to do it. So that isn't really a community, a place where you live.

But I'd say yes, more or less. Certainly we belong to a community rather than a society, we poets. But I think every poet has to create actively his own community.

Q: Don't you think then that the value of the poet right now in this futile society we're living in would be better if he read than tried to publish. I mean, read first—this very thing you're doing now. The lady across the way over there said this is quite valuable to some of us that are not poets.

JS: Well, again, I just can't say I know the answer to that. I mean, I could give, again, a slick answer to it. But actually I don't know what a non-poet can get out of poetry. I've never been able to figure it out. There's obviously something, because some of them actually have said intelligent things about my poetry and other people's poetry, and so I know they do.

But at the same time, I think poets ought to center on, not just poetry, but, well, "community" is a good word. If you could make your own community, which you can't—there's no question about that—but if you could, that would be ideal. And the audience then, the people who are non-poets, who come in off the streets, that's fine. But, fundamentally, I don't think that non-poets like to read poetry, which is a hell of a thing to say.

I'll take one more question.

Q: Couldn't your position be clarified if you could tell us what you think the purpose of the poem is?

JS: Sure, I'll be very glad to.

I think poems are delivered very much like a message that's delivered over a radio and the poet is the radio. I don't think the poems come from the inside at all. Or at least the good ones don't. You get all sorts of static from the radio, the bad transistors and all of that. But I think fundamentally a poem comes from the Outside. I have no idea where, I have no theological or any other kind of notion of it. Green Martians was the thing I used before. It's obviously not Martians. But I do think poems are delivered, when they're good, from the Outside, and I think they give messages to the poet, to other poets. Maybe to the audience, the non-poets. But I'm not sure of anything except I know that, to my mind, a poem is not something that comes out of *me* unless it's a bad poem, which I've had plenty of.

When I suddenly want something, want to sleep with somebody or want to get some kind of job, and a poem comes out that way, it's almost invariably crap. I've been able to restrict it to two or three lines of the crap in recent years, but there's still that crap coming in. The question of the audience bothers me because the audience is, after all, people I know, the non-poets. I don't know what you do about that, but I don't think it's worthwhile worrying about it.

Q: Well, you know poetry has always been sung to people, going back to the days of *Beowulf*. I don't understand.

JS: Well, to begin with, *Beowulf* was a court poem, probably not sung, although it might have been. I taught the *Beowulf*s. I know something about it.

If there were some way that we could make a bridge between the two things, between the song as it is now, which is mainly just repeating some other tune and some other lyric, like "We Shall Overcome," and getting real songs, that would be great. I just don't see quite how we go about doing it. I've wanted to. If someone would start doing it, it would be fine.

Johnny Mercer is about the only one I know who, in song lyrics, has real poetic sense. Look at that "Knocked Out Moon" and "Blowing His Top" and "The Blue," "Never Saw the Likes of You," "Bye Bye Baby," and so forth. I mean, he's good.

Q: But I also meant in reading. Hopkins is like song. Even though you don't use a singing voice—it's a reading voice—but the poetry itself will make you sing when you read it. I meant using speaking as well as using singing.

JS: As you probably don't know, I have used songs in my poems all along. In *Language*, there are about five places where you have to sing the thing in order to get it, and anyone who doesn't know the fact that it's a song— since it's a popular song like "The Frog Went A-Courtin'"—well, doesn't belong there.

But certainly this appeals to me. Really, if there's any way of getting the poet, the individual, and society together, it would be the song. But I haven't yet been able to do it.[27]

I think that's all for now, and I thank you very much for the questions and so forth.

[Applause]

Notes

1. Professor Thomas Parkinson testified on behalf of Ginsberg in the *Howl* trial. While he spoke out in favor of the Free Speech Movement (discussed below) he didn't always agree with its methods. (See also Lecture I, note 43.)

2. See especially "Either/Or," where Luxemburg argues that political liberalism (as opposed to radical action) is the enemy of change. In the aftermath of World War I, she argues for transnational solidarity: even if German borders are secure, "what about the French, Belgian, Russian, and Serbian comrades who have the enemy in their country?" (339).

The line "the enemy is in your own country" appears in "The Book of Merlin" from *The Holy Grail* (HG, 204).

3. Spicer may be referring to the group of poets (including Stan Persky, Ebbe Borregaard, Bill Brodecky, Gail Chugg, James Alexander, and Larry Fagin) who worked at Merchandising Methods, a warehouse and printing business where *Open Space* (see note 6) was printed. The working conditions were such that they banded together to join a union, though it was not the IWW but the International Longshoremen's and Warehousemen's Union (ILWU). (See also Ellingham and Killian.)

4. Since 1942, University of California employees have been required to sign an oath swearing them to support the national and state constitutions and to "faithfully discharge the duties" of whatever their position entailed. In 1949 the oath was amended to include a patently anti-Communist clause, and beginning in June 1949 all University of California employees were required to sign the new Loyalty Oath or their paychecks would be withheld. The few faculty who refused to sign were dismissed in August 1950, among them Ernst Kantorowicz whose work on medieval and Renaissance history was a major influence on the thinking of the young Blaser, Duncan, and Spicer. (See especially *The King's Two Bodies*.) After several lawsuits, the new oath was repealed two years later. In 1949–1950 Spicer, then a graduate student at

Berkeley, was employed as a teaching assistant and would have been pressured to sign or lose his job. Refusing to sign, Spicer left Berkeley with an M.A. in June 1950 and taught at the University of Minnesota for two years. Spicer returned to Berkeley in 1952 to enter a doctoral program at about the same time that the California Supreme Court ruled against the amended oath, and it was repealed (Goines, Gardner, *passim*).

5. Spicer is referring to "The Long March," first published in October of 1935. Mao would have been forty-two.

6. A poetry monthly designed to exist only for the calendar year of 1964, *Open Space* provided a context for many of the figures of the North Beach scene: Jack Spicer, Robert Duncan, Robin Blaser, Stan Persky, Jess Collins, Helen Adam, Joanne Kyger, George Stanley, Ebbe Borregaard, Lew Ellingham, and Harold Dull.

7. Spicer did not reserve his critique of literary journals to "major" venues. In fact, he was outspoken on all forms of literary production, high and low. After receiving an unsolicited copy of the independent newsletter *Floating Bear*, for instance, Spicer responds by politely asking them not to send another issue and proceeds to critique their lack of either poetry or politics, signing the letter "Barely yours."

The second section of Spicer's *Book of Magazine Verse* is a series of "Six Poems for Poetry Chicago." Each section of the book was ostensibly written for a publication that was certain to reject it.

8. Ronnie Primack (b. 1937), a younger poet of Spicer's circle, was the author of *For the Late Major Horace Bell of the Los Angeles Rangers* published by White Rabbit Press in 1963.

9. Renowned literary critic Schorer was chairperson of the English department at Berkeley. During the *Howl* obscenity trial, Schorer was asked to explain the meaning of Ginsberg's lines for the prosecution. He refused on the grounds that poetry cannot be translated into prose. Like many Berkeley faculty, Schorer initially sided with the students involved in the Free Speech Movement but was later ambivalent about their methods.

10. David Bromige's (b. 1933) most recent books are *A Cast of Tens* (1994) and *The Harbormaster of Hong Kong* (1994).

In a recent correspondence with Bromige, he asked that I mention that Robert Duncan's reading of the poem "Uprising" was a vindication of the students' feeling that poetry has political power. He writes: "Let us not forget that many in that audience were active protesters of the Vietnam War. Consider how much they were inspired by [Duncan's] poem & strengthened in their resolve, and that ultimately, domestic protests shortened the war."

11. The Free Speech Movement developed on the UC Berkeley campus in the fall of 1964, when students were denied the right to practice political activism on campus, and for a time, the controversy focused almost entirely on the question of the precise boundary between the university and the city of Berkeley. Students traditionally occupied a strip of land at the edge of campus near Sather Gate with card tables and pickets, but when the university expanded, the location became problematically "on campus." An offshoot of the FSM—the "Filthy Speech Movement"—took precedence in the media when the focus of student action on campus began to turn in early 1965 to issues of censorship, which had lurked in the background of the controversial movement since the banning of Genet's film *Un Chant d'Amour* on campus in November 1964. Spicer's reference to "saying 'fuck' on campus" is not a flip reduction of the FSM's political agenda but a commentary on what the public image of the movement had degenerated to when student John Thompson was arrested for holding a sign that read "FUCK" in March 1965. (See Goines.)

12. The *Oakland Tribune* was notorious for its editorializing against the civil rights and Free Speech movements and as a result was a frequent target of student picketing. The *Tribune*'s owner and editor-in-chief, William F. Knowland, was a former state senator and the California director of Goldwater for President. (See Goines, 109 ff.)

13. As Spicer seems to suggest, Chancellor Edward Strong was in some ways the fall guy of the Free Speech Movement controversy. He was out of town when Assistant Chancellor Alex Sherriffs issued the initial ban on political action on campus, and when he returned he made significant concessions to the students though he ultimately toed the administrative line of disciplinary action against members of the FSM. In January 1965, he was replaced by Acting Chancellor Martin Meyerson, who met the movement's primary demands.

14. Both quotations are from Auden's poem "In Memory of W. B. Yeats." The first quotation should read: "the brokers are roaring like beasts on the floor of the Bourse" (Auden, 242).

15. The passage Spicer cites is from section IV of Yeats's poem "Nineteen Hundred and Nineteen." The person asking this question probably attended the third Vancouver Lecture (III, 136–37).

16. See Lecture 2, note 37.

17. See Lecture 1, note 39.

18. Mayakovsky shot himself in 1930 at the age of thirty-six. Shelley drowned in 1822 at the age of twenty-nine.

19. Mary Norbert Körte (b. 1934) is a poet who at the time of the lecture was a Dominican nun. Her publications include *Hymn to the Gentle Sun* (1967), *The Midnight Bridge* (1970), and *Mammals of Delight* (1978), among others. The next evening at the conference, Spicer had intended to read his new book *Language* but decided to read *The Holy Grail* instead. He introduced his reading by saying: "The nun isn't here tonight. She was the greatest thing yesterday that I ever saw and I was hoping that she'd be here because these are sacramental poems in my own twisted way of looking at the sacrament, and I wish she were here."

20. As a renegade populist poet whose work was distributed only through and by an underground community, Hill seems to figure for Spicer in a number of ways. One historian calls him an "Arthurian figure of the proletariat, who will return from the grave to help working men beat the boss." He is also described as tall and slender with "strikingly blond hair" like the voice from the grave in Spicer's "Imaginary Elegies." Hill was killed in Salt Lake City, in a set-up made to look as though he were shot by his girlfriend's jealous husband (see Renshaw, 190–91).

As the Ellingham and Killian biography notes, it is possible that Spicer's father was a Wobbly, though so far there is no evidence to support his claim and it may be a part of his imaginary autobiography that includes tracing his birth to the Berkeley Renaissance and claiming to be part Blackfoot Indian.

21. The piece Spicer sings is from Hill's song "The Preacher and the Slave" (IWW, 12).

22. "The New American Poets," *Harper's* 230, no. 1381 (June 1965): 65–71. Oblique references to the article appear elsewhere in the lectures.

23. Perhaps what Spicer refers to as the "best part" of the Agrarians was the interest of Ransom and others (the "Distributists," who eventually left the Agrarian movement) in such community-oriented projects as the Tennessee Valley Authority, which Paul Goodman praised for its de-privatized distribution of natural resources (see Conkin, 134).

In 1949 Spicer says about the New Critics: "The truth is that pure poetry bores everybody. It is even a bore to the poet. The only real contribution of the New Critics is that they have demonstrated this so well" (see Appendix). In 1954 he lampoons Ransom in a fake newsletter sent to Graham Mackintosh.

24. Lew Ellingham (b. 1933) was a young poet in the Spicer circle. Ellingham, along with Kevin Killian, co-authored the new biography of Spicer, *Poet Be Like God* (1998).

25. Stan Persky (b. 1941) is a poet, essayist, and editor who lives in Vancouver. He edited *Open Space* magazine. Persky moved to Vancouver with Robin Blaser in 1966. His *Lives of the French Symbolist Poets* was published by White Rabbit Press in 1967. His most recent books include *Buddies* (1991), *Then We Take Berlin* (1995), and *Autobiography of a Tattoo* (1997).

26. E.g., a model of heterogeneous social affinity which the physical form of a community has brought together; its elements are different but coexist in relation to each other, not in isolation. Spicer may have had in mind specifically Goodman's brief discussion of literary production in relation to the "intentional community" created by Black Mountain College: "Perhaps these communities are like those 'little magazines' and 'little theaters' that do not outlive their first few performances, yet from them comes all the vitality of the next generation of everybody's literature" (109). See also the dialogue with Goodman on the FSM in Miller.

27. This sentiment is reminiscent of Spicer's first public address in 1949. Speaking on a panel for UC Berkeley's *Occident* magazine, Spicer concludes by saying: "There is more of Orpheus in Sophie Tucker than in R. P. Blackmur; we have more to learn from George M. Cohan than from John Crowe Ransom" (see Appendix).

AFTERWORD

Jack Spicer and the Practice of Reading

> Mechanicly we move
> In God's universe
> —JACK SPICER

I. An Occult Circuitry

In the post-Desert Storm, Deep Space, X-Filed age of human and electronic viruses, chip architecture, information webs, and ether nets in which we live in the 1990s, it may finally be possible to imagine the extent to which Jack Spicer anticipated our poetic and political worlds and the extent to which he composed beyond or "outside" his own. The future, that is, has finally caught up with the dark vision of his poems, which in his time must have often seemed odd, anachronistic, paranoid, and as genuinely alien as his description of his writing practice. The recent increase of interest in Spicer's poetry substantiates his currency, but Spicer's poetic concerns have always been strikingly ahead of his time, as if he lived within the mechanistic and degraded future articulated in his poems, where computer stands in for God (BMV, 254), silicon inhabits the heart (L, 224), politics are informed by bombs (TP, 178; HG, 205; etc.), popular consciousness is preoccupied by outer space (L, 231; BMV, 253), the death of the author is an accepted trope of literary practice (AL, 34), and the social matrix of nation and community has collapsed into slums under the bosses of multinational self-interest. And with the advent of globalized electronic networks (the "information superhighway"), regional communities are finally being effaced. Truly "where we are is in a sentence" (TP, 175), as poets caught in a language game between marginality and pop-confessionalism and as political subjects facing the narrowing limits of democratic possibility.

While this book does not propose a prophetic Spicer, it takes as a given
Spicer's sophistication, self-awareness, and social and political understanding, all of which give his language games an added darkness and his
sampling of other texts an added seriousness and depth beyond their
comic or disruptive effects. Much useful work has been written about
Spicer in his historical context and about his practice of dictation and seriality.[1] But the significance of his various models of composition, the extent
of his visual imagination, the sophistication of his reading practice, his
program of intertextuality — the texts to which he refers as part of the available material or "furniture" of his assemblages — and its effect on the practice of reading Spicer's poems have yet to be elucidated.[2] Spicer's intertextuality plays itself out through his strategies of quoting and misquoting,
copying, punning, and the enactment of send-ups or jousts with other
poets. Spicer's extrapoetic texts — his letters and lectures — offer a glimpse
into his reading practice and the extent to which it informs, corresponds
with, and is reflected in his poems. In short, he is a "mirror maker" (A, 55).

Deeply embedded in these strategies is an imaginary reader who at
times shares in the various jokes and correspondences within the poems
and at times remains outside their oblique or hermetic meanings. Given
Spicer's view of the communal aspects of composition on every level — of
poems, magazines, cities, and finally some larger community of the
dead — it would be almost impossible to overestimate the importance of
reception within his practice, especially since for Spicer the traditional
roles are reversed: the poet is essentially a passive receiver of messages
from beyond, which he copies or translates. The reader, on the other
hand, is engaged intellectually and physically — even erotically — in the
creative act, and is the necessary supplement allowing the occult circuitry
of the poem to perform.

Ironically, Spicer's poems often play hard-to-get. Not only are they clas-

1. See, for instance, Robin Blaser's touchstone essay "The Practice of Outside" for both historical context and discussion of Spicer's work in terms of contemporary poetic theory and practice.
See Michael Davidson's *San Francisco Renaissance* for a broader discussion of Spicer's regional
context. See Lew Ellingham and Kevin Killian's biography, *Poet Be Like God*, for an in-depth account of Spicer's life and times. For further discussions of his poetics and various formal concerns, see especially the work of Joseph Conte, Maria Damon, Clayton Eshleman, Ross Feld,
Norman Finkelstein, Edward Foster, John Granger, Burton Hatlen, Stephanie Judy, Jerome Mc-
Gann, Miriam Nichols, Jed Rasula, Peter Riley, Ron Silliman, and Gilbert Sorrentino. *Acts*,
Boundary 2, *Caterpillar*, *Change*, and *Ironwood* have all devoted special issues to Spicer's poetics.
2. A list of Spicer's intertextual references would include Homer, Ovid, Dante, William Dun-
bar, Malory, Donne, Blake, Matthew Arnold, Lewis Carroll, Edward Lear, Yeats, Hawthorne,
Poe, Dickinson, Whitman, Rimbaud, Baudelaire, Lorca, Rilke, Cocteau, Jeffers, Stevens,
Pound, Eliot, Marianne Moore, W. C. Williams, Stein, Hart Crane, L. Frank Baum, Jessie We-
ston, Creeley, Blaser, Olson, Duncan, Kantorowicz, the King James Bible, Plato, Josephine
Miles, and Johnny Mercer, to name a few.

sically "difficult," but Spicer himself restricted their distribution during his lifetime. Yet this is part of the game that draws the serious reader into his work and fends off the casual heartbreaker; after all, he sees the relation between reader and writer as an amorous playing for keeps. No tourists allowed. And his insistence that poetry is for poets is a warning to the weak at heart as if to scare away the casual reader from the folly of poetry.

The "game" of the poem is expressed in terms of, but is not limited to, the discourse of love between poet and reader and the "games" of their amorous attachment: "It was a game. I shout to myself. A game," Spicer writes to Lorca (AL, 51). Dictation performs a serious and lasting entanglement of citizenship and eros; hence his earlier poems, which hint at but do not fully enact the multilogic (as opposed to dialogic) practice of dictation, become abandoned "one night stands" (A, 61). As Spicer suggests in Lecture 4, only poets are likely to care enough to cope with the absurd demands of the poem—particularly the long poem or serial poem. He is only interested in "serious" readers since they are the only ones whose commitment he understands, and he is anxious to provide for the future of his poems.

It is important to keep in mind that the issue of poetry's reception was not merely the concern of a discouraged, older poet. At his first public lecture in 1949, Jack Spicer (then twenty-four) was one of five poets, including Robert Duncan and William Everson, participating in a symposium for UC Berkeley's *Occident Magazine* (see Appendix). When it was his turn to speak, Spicer began by saying, "I can only ask an embarrassing question—why is nobody here? Who is listening to us?" The question rattles the most fundamental scaffolding of the art and is a pivotal question in Spicer's poetic development. His sense of the limits of an audience for poetry in the present prompts him to speculate about the curious atemporality of poetry and the need for continuity and tradition in order to sustain the art. Since poets write backward in response to their deceased poetic predecessors and forward to the eventual readers of their poems, they exist inevitably outside of their own time even as they reflect or embody it. Thus Spicer proposes that the poet is always posthumous in the act of composition—or outside of the present of the poems—since the "afterlife of the poem" (TP, 171) exists in a time beyond the life of the author.

By placing himself outside the poem, the poet creates a vacuum that draws into the poem both the textual predecessors of the poem's past and the readers of its future. The poet steps outside of his own work so that the Real—an unknown, X, an alterity Spicer calls the Outside—can flood in to occupy the poem. Within this model of composition, Spicer employs temporal distinctions between past, present, and future—which he then violates—rather than strict hierarchical roles (originality or "individual talent"). The past is inhabited by God and ghosts, but its master-narratives are subject to the poet's "taking them down" with a mixture of metaphors that bring them "across" into commerce and puns that confuse or deflect their power. The reader exists in the future—or "slums"—of the poet's imaginary city (TP, 175).

And here Spicer's description of the poet as a radio could not be more apt, since radio waves (the poem's messages) are produced by an oscillating frequency that transmits through—or "haunts"—the buildings, people, and things of the material world. The machinery of Spicer's poetry works by activating a variety of lines that jam any single origin or epistemological ground; the frequency oscillates so quickly from one text or texture to another that, like a hummingbird's wings, it appears to rest between materiality and invisibility, belonging to neither realm entirely. This model of radical openness creates poems that are empty at the center; instead of seeing poetry as a vessel for a poet's self-expression, it prefers the removal of self from the concerns of the poem. In light of Spicer's oppositional mind, dictation also works as a joust with culturally sanctioned myths of poetic authorship that were definitive in Spicer's time, from confessional poetry to the Beat aesthetic. The very process of dictation is one of vigilance, which is both spiritual practice and materialist tedium, placing Spicer closer to the sensibility of Samuel Beckett than to the automatic writing of the dadaists and surrealists, the first-thought-best-thought of the Beats, or any other form-driven mottoes of the New American Poetry. The indelible character arising out of Spicer's amalgam of dictated voices has a dark humor, sense of irony, and punning not unlike that of Beckett's *Waiting for Godot*. Like Beckett, Spicer writes during a period of resistance and his work is encoded with dense messages that signify to an underground community within a theater of war. Spicer's description of dictation in his lectures, particularly Lecture 3, curiously resonates with the opening of Beckett's late work *Company*: "A voice comes to one in the dark. Imagine" (5).

Aside from creating a practice, routine, or ritual for composition, dictation reduces the emphasis on originality, authenticity, and the individuality of authorship. This decentering liberates the poem into multiple systems of meaning and supplies it with a ground-level community beginning with the poet and the voice or voices that enter the poem. Instead of participating in the essentialist belief of a Romantically flamboyant poetic personality, Spicer's model poem and poet are likely to be so ordinary looking as to be invisible in the midst of commodity culture; they can be safely hidden in plain sight.

Spicer further de-emphasizes the superhuman specialness of the vatic poet by pointing out that he or she merely exists within a sequence of substitutions rather than in singular genius. Instead of being a "beautiful machine which manufactured the current for itself, did everything for itself— almost a perpetual motion machine of emotion until the poet's heart broke" (I, 5), the poet is virtually effaced in the reception of a transmission from elsewhere. The entire transaction exists within a post-original universe. Hence in *The Holy Grail*, Gwenivere's logic disrupts the romance of the Grail-quest by pointing out that what they're looking for is "Not Christ, but a substitute for Christ as Christ was a substitute"[3] (HG, 199).

At the same time that Spicer has the inversionary poetics and reputation of a *poet du mal*, his acknowledgment of the irretrievability of an original and his focus on substitution and reception lead him in lectures 2 and 3 to adopt the terms of a Judeo-Christian meditative tradition in which waiting becomes a spiritual exercise, the aim of which is to empty oneself so that something else can come through, and this transaction occurs through the mechanical tasks of the scribe: reading, waiting, and copying. Spicer describes dictation as a spiritual exercise with no assurance that what's coming through is an absolute good and with a constant wrestling to keep oneself out of the way of any "messages" that come (I, 15; III, 115). The act is not prophetic but contemplative, interpretive, and almost cabalistic in the sense that it reads within the texts of a particular group of scholars and practitioners of the art and looks at linguistic structures in order to create an adjacency to an Absolute. In fact, Spicer's work is filled with oblique references to a prime mover that can never really be named or that can be named in so many ways that it can never be located.[4] In "A Textbook of Poetry," which Spicer says is "analogous to [Dante's] *Paradiso*" (I, 18), it is clear that however this adjacency brushes

3. For another example of this kind of substitution, see Nichols's description of Eurydice as a "linguistic substitute" (32). Along a similar line, see Rasula's discussion of the shifting pronouns in Spicer's poems (51–100).

4. He writes: "I cannot proclaim him for he is not mine. . . . I cannot proclaim starlight for it is never in the same place. / I can write a poem about him a hundred times but he is not there. The mere numbers prevent his appearance as the names (Eros, Amor, feely love, Starlight) for his fame is as the fame of What. I have not words for him" (TP, 172). Obviously, his invocation of the "divine" is anything but traditional. Spicer thinks paradoxically, and he critiques the notion of belief at the same time he asserts it, as in section 8 of "A Textbook of Poetry." He purposefully translates his own poetic practice into multiple systems of correspondence in order to avoid creating a stable lexicon that would make his work easy prey to "embalmers" or systematizers.

against one, the expression of it in language is never one's own, never primary in itself: "we have it second-hand" (TP, 170). The presence of the divine can only be accommodated, invoked, and addressed through linguistic structures, and hermeticism only furthers the process: "the wires in the rose are beautiful" (TP, 170).

The identity of this ultimate Other is often mechanistic, just as dictation as a term implies a passive, mechanistic, even secretarial copying. Paul Valéry refers to the poem as a machine of language; Spicer borrows Poe's mechanical chess player—a machine with a man inside it—as a kind of *deus ex machina* model of composition; and Henry James, among others, enters the machine age by dictating his later novels to a typist.

Dictation as Copying

This is not to suggest that dictation or problems with the issue of originality and authorship in poetry are anything new. As far back as the ancient Greeks, poets have been seen as subject to derangement; and Plato famously placed them outside his city as Spicer reminds his audience in Lecture 4. In modern literary history, the originality of translation and the irretrievability of an authentic original became indelible with Ezra Pound. But Pound himself arose out of a rich tradition, from the mid-nineteenth century on, of displacing a stable poetic subject with something beyond his or her experience. Blake's poems; Browning's, Rossetti's, and Yeats's dramatic monologues; Pound's *Personae*; Eliot's *The Waste Land*; and H.D.'s *Trilogy* all essentially replace a unified subject with another presence that is intuited and transcribed from elsewhere. One of the declared aims of Spicer's first lecture is to construct a similar history of dictation via Yeats and Blake that leads through southern California to Spicer himself. Like Blake, Spicer is arguably more concerned with the continuation of a poetic tradition than with any claims to innovation.[5] In the midst of the translations, copies, and fake letters of *After Lorca*, he writes: "Invention is merely the enemy of poetry" (AL, 15).

While Spicer places himself within this genealogy, however, he takes

5. Kathleen Raine is responsible for discussing this issue in Blake. The demand for originality, it seems, is part of the mythology of those who experience some degree of artistic acceptance. For all his low dandyism and contrariness, Spicer, like Blake, is more concerned with establishing a context for his work than with distinguishing himself as an individual apart from his peers. Through the course of the lectures, it is remarkable the extent to which Spicer traces correspondences between his own work and the work of poets he critiques.

the practice of dictation, of emptying the self, to another level, one that is at the same time more literalist in its orphism and more cubist in its arrangement. Instead of channeling one frequency, one system of representation, one portrait, he displaces the personal content of the poet with a larger range of frequencies to bring the poem to a "higher level of abstraction" (I, 29) without a loss of humanity. This "channeling" of multiple narrative surfaces makes his work collage-like in structure, but without the pristine surface of a seamless fit: "it does not have to fit together. . . . Not because the pieces would not fit in time. But because this would be the only way to cause an alliance between the dead and the living" (TP, 176). Though he's capable of rendering the hypnagogic, fabled space of a Max Ernst collage, Spicer's work behaves materially more like the torn surfaces of a Kurt Schwitters piece, or the "California funk" aesthetic of his West Coast contemporaries Wallace Berman, George Herms, and Bruce Conner.

By 1957, with his discovery of seriality and correspondence in the writing of *After Lorca*, Spicer had constructed a poetics to account for the riddle of his initial concern in 1949 about "who is listening." But there are intimations of it in some of Spicer's earliest poems. In "The Song of the Bird in the Loins," for instance, the poet essentially copies the words whispered in his ear by a swallow. The poem makes clear, through the use of quotation marks to signify its shifts in speech, that the lines the poet receives are not meant for his pleasure but are something that the swallow (as an embodiment of the Outside) insists upon bringing into the world; the poet is merely the most available transmitter because he *listens*:

> A swallow whispers in my loins
> So I can neither lie or stand
> And I can never sleep again
> Unless I whisper you his song:
> (ONS, 41)

The physicality and erotic tension of the event—whispering in the loins rather than in the ear or the mind—is reminiscent of Lorca's *duende*, and the poem's manifestation of the discomfort of the poet begins a circuit that extends to Spicer's last book: "If this is dictation it is driving me wild" (BMV, 265). But the most striking aspect of the poem is the almost exact repetition of the first and last stanzas. What follows the first stanza is a report of what the swallow whispers, and the swallow explains that the song is whispered through the lips of the poet to a "you." The poem ends by the swallow (through the poet) beckoning this "you" to listen to the poet sing:

'A swallow whispers in my loins
So I can neither lie or stand
And I can never sleep again
Unless I whisper you this song.'
                              (ONS, 41)

The passive role of the poet is insisted upon almost to the point of brutality; he is merely the "cage" or "well of stone" through which the swallow
sings to the beloved, who is the source and object of the "song." The poet
is no dynamic genius but a clerk and a copyist whose power, like that of
Melville's Bartleby, is only through negation. In "A Textbook of Poetry,"
Spicer writes: "Boredom is part of the Logos too. You choose His word instead of someoneelse's because you are bored" (TP, 174). And he empha-
sizes in Lecture 2 that "there's no reason to be a poet. I mean it's the most
undignified thing in the world, other than the person who hands out towels in the Turkish bath" (II, 75). The fatigue of the copyist is a recurrent
theme for Spicer, embodied in the term "acedia," a form of spiritual tor-
por (III, 106). It is the "deadly sin" of sloth and was primarily an ailment of
monks who worked as scribes, repeatedly copying sacred texts. It is important to note that in Spicer's model of composition, the circuitry of copying
is reversed to the extent that the poet does not serve a stable belief system
but a machine that makes him "able to say anything," further amplifying
the groundlessness that causes the poet's chronic fatigue (AL, 46).

  The sacrificial quality of the transaction is further complicated elsewhere in *One Night Stand*, especially in "Psychoanalysis: An Elegy,"
"The Imaginary Elegies," "Song of Bird and Myself," and a Poe-like fable
called "The Scrollwork on the Casket." This last piece presents with horrifying calm the practical difficulties of engaging the dead in one's literary
routine in ways that seem consciously to mimic not only the isolation of
the poet but also the experience of gay lovers in the 1950s—a love that had
no public space in the larger social world of American life. Since it would
be dangerous to be seen on the street together, the two are relegated to a
fiction—a short story—which is "narrower than a room in a cheap hotel."
And in order for the writer to fit his dead companion within this structure,
he must brutalize him:

One must maim him to fit him in the coffin of the short story. Then when success is
achieved, and the sweating author has managed to get shut his casket of paragraphs
. . . [he ends up with] a casket, a small regular box with a corpse inside it. And he can
sell it on the market where such boxes are sold. (36)

  Beyond its sexual overtones, this "market" applies in part to the commercial world of conventional literature that uses human experience as "material," and to the "selling out" that Spicer warned young poets about in Lecture 4—a betrayal of one's origins, personal tragedies, sources, and so on, by using them for one's own gain. The result is marketable but inert. The terminology of the writing is classically Spicerian in its sexual and literary ambiguities; Spicer always favored small, devoted communities over any larger cultural order that might compromise the specificity of one's values, and this manifests itself throughout Spicer's poetry on the level of vocabulary in the form of subcultural meanings and encrypted messages or puns that are evident to the initiate but hidden to the culture at large.[6]

But coexisting with this hermeticism is an openness in his terms. If, as Gertrude Stein writes, "poetry is essentially vocabulary" (231), Spicer's diction is sufficiently ambiguous to draw his reader in to create his or her own system of meaning. He uses almost exclusively a populist, often folkloric, and widely accessible vocabulary and frames of reference: ghost stories, murder mysteries, baseball, Martians, romantic love, popular outlaw heroes like Billy the Kid and Joe Hill, and war stories. Even at his most literary he quotes a text that has been so extensively renovated as to have a popular life outside of the matrix of an original author—the Holy Grail. And here Spicer's initial attraction to Lorca as a Virgilesque poetic predecessor is clear: they share a fascination with the folkloric, not only as an "authentic" texture in their work but as a sophisticated model of intertextuality.

In his lecture on dictation, Spicer describes the insistence on literary conventions of form as equivalent to putting on a straitjacket in order not to scratch one's nose. And in "The Scrollwork on the Casket," this kind of composition has the hallucinatory quality of a crime, though it is hard to distinguish between perpetrator and victim: "Whenever I hammer a nail into the outside of the casket, I can hear someone, on the inside, also hammering a nail. That's the trouble with this burial business; it's hard to know who's on the outside, whether the living bury the dead or the dead bury the living" (37). The confusion is due partly to the notion that the poet is already posthumous in the act of composition, so there is no way of knowing if by nailing the dead into place he or she has merely been drawn into the underworld in order to be trapped there.[7] Spicer echoes

6. As an example of Spicer's blending of the erotic and the macabre, he writes from Boston to Allen Joyce: "As I said New Years Eve to a bewildered trick, 'It's like having a picnic in a graveyard.' He thought I meant the town was like a graveyard" (149). For further discussion of Spicer's encrypting of a specifically gay male vocabulary, see Damon.

7. The nineteenth-century American gothic qualities of Spicer's work, especially his early work, may have been heightened by the research he and Robin Blaser did in the late 1940s for

this dilemma in "A Textbook of Poetry," where "the ghosts the poems are written for are the ghosts of the poems. We have it second-hand. They cannot hear the noise they have been making" (TP, 170). The poem cannot be gotten at a glimpse; it must be lived in—and at the risk of never emerging.[8]

Because of the disruption in the "time" and "timing" of Spicer's lines, his poems create a space that both the living and the dead share in the act of reading. What Spicer calls time mechanics is essentially a kind of quantum poetics through which different poets are patiently writing the same poem in different times and places. Hence the poem is always in the present; its time is outside time. The poem is not immortal because it endures through the ages but because it exists in all ages at once. For Spicer this constitutes "tradition" as he describes it in *After Lorca*. In such a construction, the "anxiety of influence" is beside the point because it is based in linearity and as a result embalms poetry into museum pieces. Spicer's model keeps poetry contemporaneous and thus always news without subscribing to the annihilating progress of "the new." Thus in *After Lorca*, in spite of the intervening span of several years and an ocean, Spicer and Lorca are lovers within the rooms of their shared text. In this space there can be no discreet, unified author; but, as Spicer says, these are "our poems"—his and Lorca's.

Since, in Spicer's terms, the scrollwork on the casket is where the dead speak, it is appropriate that he opens *After Lorca* with Lorca's posthumous address. But he's less interested in a dialogue with the dead than in inhabiting the same space with them, as in a poem, a room in a pub, or on a baseball diamond. That is to say, he's more interested in sharing this space with

---

Roy Harvey Pearce's book on the "savage" in American literary history. Spicer even wrote a play adaptation of "Young Goodman Brown," which unfortunately exists now only as an incomplete manuscript. The influence of nineteenth-century New England authors would initially seem to violate Spicer's California regionalism, but since books house their own ghosts and regions are defined in part by the ghosts that haunt them, one's regionalism is also informed by one's reading practice. But as Spicer quotes or copies from nineteenth-century literature, the sense of the quoted line will be different in a California context, sometimes to humorous effect. Hence the echo of Poe's "Cask of Amontillado" has the atmosphere of a Hollywood B-movie in "The Scrollwork on the Casket." Likewise, when Spicer quotes Yeats—"Everything a man needs can be found in Berkeley"—the pun is entirely dependent upon its shift in regional context.

8. Again, this sense of poetry as an underworld leads Spicer to discourage anyone from entering it unless absolutely necessary. In a letter to his former lover Gary Bottone, Spicer describes bohemia as "a hell full of windows to heaven," and acknowledges "it would be wrong of me to drag a person I love into such a place against his will. Unless you walk into it freely, and with open despairing eyes, you can't even see the windows. And yet I can't leave Bohemia myself to come to you—Bohemia is inside of me, in a sense is me, was the price I paid, the oath I signed to write poetry. . . . We can still love each other although we cannot see each other. . . . And we can continue to love each other, by letter, from alien worlds."

others, putting it into play—making it public. If one opens the circuitry between the living and the dead, one has to be willing to surrender the notion of social acceptability, of clearly delineated public and private realms, of property.

Instead of being a private artifact, the dictated poem is a shared place. As collaborators, the poet and the poem's ghost-texts create a community to inhabit their own posthumous future and in this way, the poem remains a commerce between the living and the dead even after the death of the author. Though *After Lorca* was written more than thirty years ago, we as readers inhabit the poem now with Spicer and Lorca, and the rest of the cast they initially brought with them. Whitman, Keaton, and Creeley, from whom Spicer steals the book's title, as well as the individuals to whom each "translation" is dedicated, all become "our" community.[9]

As the consummate readerly text, *After Lorca* offers a template for reading Spicer's other books. In it, he places himself in the position of the reader who exists in Lorca's future. To read the intimacy of this text correctly, I think, we have to enact a similar procedure on Spicer's later books: to get caught with Spicer himself in the machinery of his poems as they become shared in the act of reading, to fall for his lines, so to speak, just as he is caught up with Lorca in the sheets of "their" poems. If one were to enact Spicer's practice of dictation as he suggests (in Lecture 1) all poets, particularly young ones, should do, it would create a vacuum of words to draw back the poets of the past, like Eurydice, into the world of light and speech, out of their godlike, ghostly priorness into the future poems of others.

And we need not worry about our ghosts' disappointment with the digs. Spicer foresaw that "futurity" is by nature degraded—what he called "slums" (I, 22). The imaginary city exists for the poet in the moment of making the poem, when he or she is irrevocably outside it—or, at best, at its gates. As Blaser writes in "The Practice of Outside": "Jack's voice remained . . . outside the paradise or city of its concern because such a city is outside our time or at the edge of it" (CB, 286). His loneliness at that moment of composition is structural. "Loneliness is necessary for pure poetry," Spicer writes (AL, 48). He even goes so far as to say in Lecture 2 that if the poet does enter the poem, the poem is bound to fail. A poet's role, as Spicer puts it in Lecture 1, is merely to put his furniture at the disposal of the poem's (or city's) alien guests. The machine of the poem may allow the poet to "say anything," but he can only imagine its "rooms" from a distance:

9. For a useful discussion of the "community" of *After Lorca*, see Hatlen.

FRIDAY THE 13TH

At the base of the throat is a little machine
Which makes us able to say anything.
Below it are carpets
Red, blue, and green-colored.
I say the flesh is not grass.
It is an empty house
In which there is nothing
But a little machine
And big, dark carpets.

(AL, 46)

Here, in a word game with Whitman, Dickinson, and the Bible, Spicer connects the book and the body, not as organic entities but as architectural structures—as empty houses. Contesting Whitman's metaphorical connection between flesh and grass in "Leaves of Grass" and the Biblical "All flesh is grass" of Isaiah, the poem's sentiment closely resembles Dickinson's "Nature is a Haunted House—but Art—a house that tries to be haunted" (Dickinson, vol. 2, 554). The flesh is an empty house, the poem is an empty house, and subject to ghostly inhabitants. While this emptying—this negation—is an essential move of Spicer's poetic practice, at the same time the poem wants to "spook" its readers with its superstitious title and its ghost-story tableau, combining the classic haunted house with a futuristic "little machine" that, by making us "able to say anything," might seduce the ghosts into speech or the Faustian visitor of the present into the timeless rooms of the poem.[10]

By avowing the practice of dictation, Spicer clearly created something more than a dialogue or duality of two lovers; he made something other, something multiple. Otherwise, Spicer and Lorca's "affair" would be over, relegated to the coffined past, which it evidently is not. In this way the poem can go beyond the narratives of either human or divine love (a fundamental duality) which Spicer critiques in "A Textbook of Poetry":

—A human love object is untrue.
Screw you
—A divine love object is unfair

Define the air
It walks in
Imagine this as lyric poetry.
(TP, 177)

10. To further complicate the haunting of this house, "Friday the 13th," labeled as a "translation" after Lorca, is actually an original Spicer poem. For a thorough accounting of what is and what isn't Lorca in *After Lorca*, see Eshleman.

Since human and divine love fail the poet, it is the poet who must provide an erotic and social identity outside of those constructs. When Spicer writes "imagine this as lyric poetry," he is both critiquing the personal content of the lyric and insisting on the empty space that moves from line to line, thereby allowing a larger discursive community to be dictated, what he calls "An argument with the dead. That is what these pauses are mainly about" (TP, 174). The poem is the ground not for private revelation but for a social epiphany. Seriality provides the linkage to a space where the dead and the living perform and enact their community, a community that is not limited by either the personal content of the lyric or the false delineation between past, present, and future bodies created by conventional narrative. Now imagine *this* as lyric poetry.

Poet and Machine: The Mechanical Chess Player

How does Spicer connect the poem's past and future—its ghosts and its readers? First, as he explains in his Vancouver lectures, he'll often wait hours between lines, casting off the lines he "wants" (I, 8, 13; II, 76). That pause between lines creates an interruption in the temporality of the poem; it creates a space. Secondly, "Metaphors are not for humans," Spicer writes, but to bear across "the ghosts the poems were written for" (TP, 170). It would seem that in the actual moment of dictation, at the most illegible moment in the creation of the poem, linguistic devices such as metaphors and puns create an outrageous figure of speech for Spicer's personification of the Outside: the Martian, the incarnate Christ (I, 21), and the mechanical chess player. Through the use of poetic devices which he allows to play out against each other, one line creates the symbolic, metaphorical, or literal meaning which another line will successfully jam with a pun. In fact, he puns on the very term "metaphor" by making its "bearing across" into "bearing a cross" and calling the incarnation of Jesus a metaphor for poetry, whose function as a metaphor is also jammed by Spicer's Logos/Lowghost pun.[11]

Though he is intrigued by the system of verticality inherent in a linguistic structure such as a metaphor, Spicer is less interested in metaphor than he is in puns (I, 31, 36, 39). For instance, "tanks" occur in "Homage to Creeley" as military tanks, tanks in which crawdads are kept, and

---

11. See Davidson's discussion of this metaphor in his excellent chapter on Spicer, "The City Redefined."

"thanks" pronounced as "tanks." While metaphor as a linguistic device can create symbolic meaning, it tends to reinstate the master narratives of the past—the "unfair" domain of divine love—while puns disturb the hierarchical frequencies set up by metaphor. A pun deforms the machinery that makes language appear transparent; in an abstract sense, it incarnates.

While the metaphor of incarnation works as a model for bringing across a body from the past (say, that of a dead poet) into the vanishing point of the future, the ironies and ambiguities of Spicer's choice of metaphor are almost endless: the availability of the Lowghost/Logos pun makes conscious both the scientific and religious aspects of language at the same time that it debunks them with wordplay; it eroticizes the act of translation by insisting on the physical coming across of the dead; it puns on the pathetic cliché of "having a cross to bear," used to address physical abnormality (with which Spicer, according to the Ellingham and Killian biography, was preoccupied); and for a poet—especially one who is also a linguist—the cross one bears is less likely to be Christ's than Roman Jakobson's X of metaphor and metonymy. In Spicer's practice, the horizontal axis is manipulated on many levels, from lines (assemblage) to the arrangement of poems (seriality). In this way, contiguity and contingency replace metaphor as the organizing principle of his poetic architecture (Jakobson, 109–114).

Language itself can be a cross—if not a double cross—which we bear (endure) as we are irresistibly drawn to it as a ground of recovery at the same time we experience it as a loss of ground. It is where we meet an "other"; it is where Spicer meets Lorca in "a game"—and we in turn meet them. It is also where one meets oneself, as in the ambiguous mirroring in the poem "Narcissus": "I'm in the rose myself" (AL, 38).

How we, as readers of Spicer's poems, are transported here is, from the standpoint of the poet writing, something of a sleight of hand in the serious game of language. Dictation comes from outside, but its source is no less physical. While Lorca whispered in Spicer's ear (AL, 51), his presence was inexplicable and real, just as Spicer's seems inexplicable and real in the moment of reading his poems. If in the act of composition poets are writing into existence their future readers, they are also creating a community of readers which they are ultimately inside—voting for their own incarnation, so to speak, to be borne across through the devices of the poem into human relation—a city. "Poe's mechanical chessplayer was not the less a miracle for having a man inside it, and when the man departed, the games were no less beautiful" (AL, 51). We don't have to ignore the man behind the curtain; in fact, the Oz of the poem is more profound for its humanity.

How does Spicer embody poetically this move from the game between lovers to the language game that creates community, the plurality of "beings" (TP, 177)? To begin with, he destabilizes the metaphorical neatness of a one-to-one correspondence by establishing parallel vocabularies to describe his poetic practice. Each of these primary vocabularies—radio, Martians, and baseball—introduce a multiplicity and an alterity into the traditional concept of poetic voice. Just as Rilke wrote that poets translate objects into the invisible, Spicer proposes a writing that translates a city into language. The presence behind the surface of the poems is not exactly the poet but the multiple sources with which the poet has become affiliated in the act of composition by dictation. We can "see them in the distance not understanding their destiny as we do not understand ours" (TP, 174). The poem's community comes through to us, and reading Spicer we are reminded that "every city that is formed collects its ghosts" (TP, 175). It would seem that within this practice the self, other, companion, and community all collapse or enfold into the space of the poem and become an oscillating frequency that blurs temporality and physicality, creating a location and a history of its own, a lyric history.

II. Figures and Ground

Radio Telepathy and Talking Furniture

Radio offers the simplest analogy for Spicer's practice of dictation as it literalizes the actual transmission of words from elsewhere through technology and reinforces the notion that language itself is an alien medium. Like "Poe's mechanical chessplayer" Spicer's radio is an inhuman machine that is "no less beautiful" for its human content (AL, 51). As a model for poetic dictation, it suggests that composition begins with listening and not self-expression, with emptiness and not an overflow of autobiographical content.

For decades radio was a fixture of the modern living room, a piece of "talking furniture" that engaged its listener with a community of public readers and private listeners. It shaped the public imagination of everything from political elections to racial and sexual stereotypes to dish soap. Popular radio shows of the thirties—serials like *The Shadow* and regular programs like Orson Welles's Mercury Theater productions of *The Hitchhiker* and the famous *War of the Worlds* broadcast—often involved the supernatural. Heightening the dramatic experience of listeners who received their "messages" (commercial and otherwise) out of thin air, such programs engaged the public in an imaginary relationship with the invisible.

As a powerful and mysterious transmitter of information, radio was used as a metaphor for extrasensory perception relatively early in its history. In the wake of the Society for Psychical Research's popularity, early twentieth-century American interest in the paranormal shifted from spirit rappings and table tiltings to telepathic experience.[12] As Americans became increasingly interested in the scientific rather than the religious study of psychical phenomena, extrasensory experience seemed to suggest a previously ignored source of energy and information. During the great Depression of the thirties, there was a resurgence of interest and faith in "mental energy," and the metaphors of psychical phenomena shifted from apparitions to telegraphs to wireless radio.

In the 1930s, Upton Sinclair's treatise on his experiments with ESP, entitled *Mental Radio*, and J. B. Rhine's account of the Duke experiments to which Spicer refers in Lecture 1, both make use of the radio as a model for sending and receiving mental transmissions. It was argued that, just as radio waves could travel through objects at the speed of light, brain waves were sent and received almost simultaneously, but that transmitted thoughts had a periodicity that often provided better reception the farther they were from the source. In Spicer's terms, the more distant the source, the more likely it would be to survive the poet's interference.

The supernatural aspects of radio are perhaps most alluring in Jean Cocteau's underground camp classic *Orphée* (1949), which came to have a profound effect on Spicer's visualization of poetic transmission. In many ways *Orphée* is the ultimate art film: a seductive combination of ancient mythology, popular psychology, avant-garde aesthetics, and poetry. In *Orphée*, the poet begins to receive messages—from a dead poet, no less—through a car radio; he is not a Romantic genius but a scribe, taking down what this machine of sound transmits. But unlike the upscale Orphée (played by Cocteau's lover Jean Marais), who remains eminently photogenic throughout his bid for poetic immortality and his descent into the grimy ruins of Hell, for Spicer the poet's circuitry is still primitive—a "crystal set at best" (I, 17). He becomes not merely baffled by his engagement with the invisible and entrapped by its mirrors but visibly battered by its contradictory messages.

12. See Lecture 1, note 3.

Ultimately, Spicer's poems explain, dictation is not "a simple process like a mirror or a radio," but these are the devices through which the ghosts of the poem "try to give us circuits to see them, to hear them" (TP, 170). Not that such transmissions in any way benefit the poet; on the contrary, "words turn mysteriously against those who use them" (I, 16; HC, 125). In the act of composition the poet becomes a "counterpunching radio," "punch drunk" from the blows of the messages received from a ghostly sparring partner; and, in spite of the odds, the poet "thinks continually of strategies, of how he can win out against the poem" (L, 218; TP, 171). As Spicer writes in "Sporting Life": "The trouble with comparing a poet with a radio is that radios don't develop scar-tissue" (L, 218).

Radio is also a model for the dehumanizing speed with which human information and error can be disseminated over large territories—it can be virtually everywhere at once. In this way, radio might prefigure Spicer's own interest in computers and the ways in which they accelerate the course of human events and language acts, making the poet's tasks of listening and waiting—not to mention being heard—even more of a battle in the onslaught of the information age. From the advent of radio to the present, the earth has been literally encircled by a band of disembodied sound hovering in its atmosphere, so it's appropriate that the book that most bears the mark of *Orphée*'s ghostly transmission is *Heads of the Town Up to the Aether*, in which Spicer develops his Logos/Lowghost pun to describe a space between the human and divine. Just as this pun brilliantly deforms theological conceits, the "aether," no longer restricted to the metaphysical world of religion, becomes an invisible empire of commerce as the "heads of the town" translate into the CEOs of ABC, AOL, CBS, NBC, TBS, and so on. It's as though, in reading the politics and technologies of his own time, Spicer anticipated other violent repercussions of the media, as the "aether" was already becoming increasingly regulated and controlled.

Our Favorite Martian

> Might be somebody up that way tapping the wires. Or back that way listening to us like we're listening to him . . . And sometimes you think that the wind gets in the wires and hums and listens and talks, just like what we're hearing now.   —*It Came from Outerspace*

> I feel like a stranger in my own country.
> —*Invasion of the Body Snatchers*

If radio supplies the schematic diagram of Spicer's poetic practice, then "aliens" offers it a vocabulary of otherness. The 1950s saw McCarthyism, the "red threat," the Iron Curtain, blacklisting, increases in the power of the FBI, the enlistment of American citizens in spotting undercover spies, the development of atomically generated power, the Soviet Union's first hydrogen bomb, Einstein's "General Field Theory," Sputnik, beatniks, the establishment of NASA, the mass production of antibiotics, the civil rights movement, crackdowns on illegal aliens, and a continuous stream of alien invasion films that narrated the rise of cold-war paranoia and the pressure for cultural homogeneity.

Spicer's sense of the Outside is clearly influenced by—or provoked into exaggeration by—the 1950s fear of difference, of Communists, of "sexual deviation," and of outer space, a context within which virtually any independent community would be considered a potential menace to "national security." In contrast, Spicer writes that his ideal world would contain hundreds of thousands of smaller independent nations, so that even San Francisco and Oakland could be independent from each other and one's allegiances would be clear and absolute ("Letters to Graham Mackintosh," 96).

While the popular spy dramas and alien invasion movies of the time generally promoted the idea that horror descends to us from outside our world, the threat was seen as even more dangerous when the enemy's expert disguise could in fact resemble your next-door neighbor and live in your world. In three of the most popular science fiction movies of the early fifties—*It Came from Mars, Invaders from Mars,* and *Invasion of the Body Snatchers*—the aliens take over human forms. Often these films involve a metaphorical connection between the alien Outside and disease, and many of them involve doctor-heroes who describe the crisis as a parasitical plague—a social and political menace that manifests itself as a physical threat. In a nation that had only recently begun to use antibiotics, connecting these aliens with plague offered ample subtextual justification for scientific and military intervention. Sometimes the amorphous aliens of these films physically engulf their human victims in a cloud of low-tech smoke, but they always prey on their American hosts psychologically and materially.

A few of these films (most notably *Invaders from Mars*) blatantly place the Martians underground, where mutants—primitive replicas of humans —carry out the wishes of Martian intelligence.[13] The trope reinforced the

13. *Flight to Mars* (1952) shows American astronauts, including a lonely writer, crash-landing on Mars only to discover that the Martians, who have a sophisticated underground society, have been listening to earthly radio broadcasts for years without the technology to respond. While Martians help them repair their ship, they teach the Martians how to play bridge. In *Invasion of the Body Snatchers*, this underground is metaphorical as the story takes place in an orphic Hell

McCarthyist drive to smoke out both political and gay "undergrounds" as threats to democracy, since homosexuality was often misunderstood even within the psychiatric profession as either a genetic aberration or a moral weakness; by associating homosexuality with perversion and addiction, military recruitment and training films argued that gay citizens were more vulnerable to enemy propaganda, and thus less "American."[14]

At the same time, Martians and other aliens were repeatedly represented as having a form so ugly that image-conscious America would only see them as evil. Hence the audience was left with a complex combination of moral messages: paranoia is justified but is often misdirected; the equation of beauty and goodness is naïve, yet we pursue it; America is wrong-headed and trigger happy but does after all have a manifest destiny to control the planet, violently if necessary; and we are willing to learn at anyone's expense but our own.

As a gay anarchist poet son of a Wobbly,[15] Spicer was less likely to embrace the popular imagery of his time than to employ it as a kind of armor. He uses the vocabulary of Martians hypothetically and duplicitously, pushing it to reveal its own contradictions. In many ways, the notion of Martians dictating poems from the Outside, the sense of the poet as a dead man, and poetry as an (underground) community of the dead are all literalist manifestations of McCarthyism's ultimate paranoid fantasy: its underlying fear that the enemy has already invaded from elsewhere and that innocent-looking American citizens are the unwitting hosts to a parasitical alien culture. Spicer extends and distorts the deep-seated distrust of his time through an elaborate mirroring designed to expose the poem's reader.[16] The poems are designed to reveal the reader, but they also produce a "frightening hall of mirrors in a fun house" (A, 55). In this way the dictated poem baffles both poet and reader. As the writer-astronomer in *It Came from Outer Space* puts it, there's no way for anyone to know whether he's telling the truth or is "something come here from another world to give you a lot of false leads."

---

disguised as the small town of Santa Mira (gaze or mirror), and the network of aliens, disguised as humans, conduct their work in plain sight.

14. See the recent documentary *Coming Out Under Fire*.

15. Spicer claims his father was a "Wobbly" in Lecture 4. He establishes a "Committee for Anarchist Unity" as well as an "Unpopular Front" while an undergraduate at Berkeley (CB, 376).

16. See especially *Admonitions*, in which each poem or letter is a mirror designed especially for the person to whom he dedicates it. Within the first letter in the book, Spicer obliquely compares his poems to Rorschach blots, which were used like mirrors to reveal and bar gays from admission into the military: "Are not these poems all things to all men, like Rorschach ink blots or whores? Are they anything better than a kind of mirror?" (A, 55).

One of his bridge partners of the time recalled Spicer as a highly constructed William Burroughsesque character who for years wore the same brown suit week after week to their Friday night bridge game.[17] While there were worlds between them aesthetically, socially, and economically, Spicer, like Burroughs, is a low dandy. Both writers drew from popular culture and popular science for their models of composition, and both discussed the obsessional aspects of writing in terms of addiction (II, 76; III, 126). But for Burroughs "language is a virus from outer space," and for Spicer what is alien—what is dictated from Outside, the parasite that is invading the host-poet—is not exactly the material but the arrangement of a composition (I, 9, 13). The material is composed of the poet's own reading practice and experience, but it is selected and arranged like "furniture" by the dictating source.

By the late 1950s, Martians were more frequently seen as benign, highly evolved creatures whose mission was peaceful. And by the mid-1960s, within Spicer's lifetime, space had been conquered to the extent that astronauts were often seen as popular adventurers rather than soldiers, and while alien horror thrived in venues like *The Outer Limits*, a few aliens made their way from B-horror films to more tongue-in-cheek presentations such as the popular television comedy *My Favorite Martian* (I, 34).

Enter the Diamond

> Let us go forth awhile and get better air in our lungs. Let us leave our close rooms. The game of ball is glorious.
> —WALT WHITMAN, *Brooklyn Eagle* (1834)

> Writing is exciting / and baseball is like writing.
> —MARIANNE MOORE

> But is not baseball more than like writing? Is not baseball a form of writing?   —A. BARTLETT GIAMATTI

While Spicer's other poetic models—Martians and radio—emphasize the alien and mechanistic aspects of the "muse" in his dictated poetry, baseball represents a complex system that reflects and materially embodies its humanity, geometry, and sociality. Clearly his use of baseball as a model for poetry is part of Spicer's larger attempt to degrade the high tone of critical discourse. The social function and intricacies of baseball are

17. Author's interview with John Halverson (July 1996).

significant elements of this endeavor. Spicer was a master gamesman and was known for taking games seriously, particularly bridge and baseball. He makes clear in Lecture 2 that, like poetry or music, games have a function and significance beyond entertainment (II, 86–87). Baseball was, above all, a sport Spicer loved; and as with most of his interests, he found ways of translating it into a poetic construction: as a metaphor within his poetry and as a kind of architectural allegory *for* poetry in the building of his imaginary city.

As radio identifies one model of the circuitry of dictation, baseball represents its practical embodiment, ritualized enactment, and communal structure. For Spicer, both models represent the adjacency of the Outside, as the poet receives barroom punches from the radio (L, 218) and catches the fast balls, curves, and junk of the dictating pitcher who is haunted by the ghosts that supply the lines of a poem (BMV, 257; III, 128). The repetitive narrative enactment of baseball and its division into serial units—innings and series—make it a model of both isolated events (poems) and larger arrangement (books). The arrangement of Spicer's serial poems is also dictated, so the unpredictability of content and the rigidity of sequence correspond to the formal elements of a ball game.

Since its early days, baseball has been promoted as an embodiment of democratic values. Every player must take a turn at bat, and yet winning is entirely dependent upon teamwork. It offers a framework within which one could transcend one's class, much in the way that war heroes obtained a status beyond class considerations. Franklin D. Roosevelt, "the radio President," who often used baseball to explain national and international conditions, was particularly keen on equating the two for the purposes of World War II recruitment. He kept the decimated major leagues in business during the war because he felt it would promote patriotism at home. Every major-league game ever played in America has, after all, begun with the national anthem. Although it announces heroism, one's own team is no more likely to win than to lose, sustaining a pattern of perpetual hope and disappointment that, Spicer seems to suggest, poets know better than anyone.[18]

Although still used rhetorically to reinforce the democratic paradigm, baseball is an independent cooperative community that is extraconstitutional: it is literally above and beyond the law.[19] As such, the game consti-

18. "I can't stand to see them shimmering in the impossible music of the Star Spangled Banner. No / One accepts this system better than poets. Their hurts healed for a few dollars" (BMV, 265).
19. In 1922, when the Federal League charged that baseball's major leagues were a monopoly in violation of antitrust laws, the Supreme Court ruled that antitrust laws applied for other sports but that baseball could rule itself. Justice Oliver Wendell Holmes wrote that although baseball

tutes its own imaginary civilization with its own rules, history, and ruins, a parallel to the culture of poets who occupy the same space and time with American popular culture but exist irrevocably outside it. As a fraternity committed to teamwork in the face of absurd repetition, baseball, like poetry, suggests a kind of impossible Grail quest[20] with a deep subculture, folklore, and civic function. In Lecture 3, and especially in his "Poems for the Vancouver Festival," Spicer uses the vocabulary of baseball in a larger sense to embody or incarnate a city. The diamond at its center creates a permeable ground (or "Open Space") for individual and social identity.

Baseball as an enterprise of community building gets literalized in *Book of Magazine Verse* as the building of a city through the societies created by magazines, a comparison that Spicer develops further in Lecture 4 (IV, 157). It is the embodiment of Spicer's sense of composition as cross-temporal teamwork. Good poets, like good players, divest themselves of the mythology of specialness and individual talent in favor of a shared goal.

In addition to its appeal as a populist form—a game, a common American text—baseball provides a ground for Spicer's gamesmanship with ready puns and wordplaying critiques that put him in play with the vocabulary of other poets. The fact that Spicer actually sings about athletes links him with Pindar and indirectly with Robert Duncan, another one of Spicer's local team players. As Duncan's muse can be irreverently understood to be a Martian, Olsonian field theory is translated by Spicer into a brawling, noisy, beer-drinking field of everyday heroism.[21] Through baseball, Spicer rewrites the Polis, unseating Olson's authoritative poetic agency by grounding it in a populist, even athletic origin. In Lecture 3, he describes the shift from "A Textbook of Poetry" to *Book of Magazine Verse* as a move from celebrating a city toward "building the city" (III, 110), and the process is literalized in the imaginary construction of Vancouver from the baselines of a baseball diamond. His first of the "Seven Poems for the Vancouver Festival," in which this projected construction begins, mimics Olsonian syntax:

was a profit-making enterprise, baseball games were not commerce in the common use of the term. Baseball players were governed by a "reserve clause" which bound them legally to their team until the team chose to sell or trade them; their constitutional rights and freedoms were secondary to their obligations to baseball, and no government agency would be permitted to intervene in disputes between players and management.

20. "The Giants / Winning 93 games / Is as impossible / In spirit / As the grass we might walk on" (L, 225).

21. See Herndon's contrasting descriptions of Spicer and Olson: "Olson, for ex. even with all that talk about America, strikes me often as 'read about' america, wouldn't recognize ball game or common bars (like Days in SF) or rooting sections for himself. I mean, might recognize them

> We shall build our city backwards from each baseline
>   extending like a square ray from each distance—you from
>   the first-base line, you from behind the second baseman,
>   you from behind the shortstop, you from the third-baseline.
> We shall clear the trees back, the lumber of our pasts and
>   futures back, because we are on a diamond, because it is our
>   diamond
> Pushed forward from.
> And our city shall stand as the lumber rots and Runcible
>   mountain crumbles, and the ocean, eating all of islands,
>   comes to meet us.
>
> (BMV, 259)

Later in the poem the city becomes located specifically as Vancouver, the antipodal coastal extreme of Olson's Gloucester, yet Spicer also sets the entire poem in the "Runcible" mountains, the landscape of Edward Lear's nonsense poem "The Owl and the Pussycat." Spicer's geographical imagination places nonsense as the overarching condition of even the most serious games, but the heroism within such an architecture is no less meaningful for its absurdity.

The diamond works particularly well as a frame for Spicer's poetic community as it combines white and black magic. It heretically corresponds to the writings of Saint Theresa of Avila, whose crystal palace Robin Blaser uses to discuss Spicer ("My Vocabulary," 103) and whose "bejeweled" cross is a trace of poetic mediumship to André Breton.[22] The diamond as a suit in playing cards is represented by the pentacle in the tarot deck, and in a letter to Graham Mackintosh, Spicer writes that a good magus can trap spirit demons in a pentacle (105); effectively, it creates a daimon, a confluence of poetry and magic. Here the supernatural mythologies of pitching and of poetry intersect. So the transposition of the pentacle into a (baseball) diamond makes sense both in terms of Spicer's account of dictation and in his sense that the pitcher is haunted. But it is not just the pitcher who is affected. In Spicer's construction, poets are catchers; their position behind home plate is adjacent to both the field of

---

as images or beauties or whatever, but not just to go to like everyone else. Beauty of Jack—double thing with ball game etc.—I mean, used it in poetry, of course, but didn't go for that reason only. I mean, what other poet sings 'Cardinals Be Damned Boys' at Big Game night? year after year?" (CB, 378).

22. "By the sole fact that she sees her wooden cross become transformed into a bejeweled crucifix and maintains this as a vision both imaginary and sensory, Theresa of Avila can be said to command that line which poets and mediums straddle. Unfortunately, she is still only a saint" (Breton, 153).

In *Mansions*, Theresa of Avila describes the soul as a spiritual castle "composed of a single diamond, or very clear crystal, containing many apartments, just as there are many mansions in heaven" (Dicken, 188).

play (the diamond) and to the quotidian life of the stands. Like Orpheus, they move from a mortal existence into a supernatural architecture from which they may not be able to emerge.

The model of dictation coming from Spicer's baseball diamond corresponds both figuratively and homophonically to Yeats's "daimon." Spicer's friend and colleague Thomas Parkinson describes Yeats's daimon as a "spiritual coven" of his "most deeply affiliated friends and enemies" who exist in relation to each other (Parkinson, 46), a configuration akin to a field of opposing ballplayers. Spicer accepts and to a certain extent adopts Yeats's methods in *A Vision*, but in his lowghost mishearing of Yeats, Spicer translates daimon into diamond and again uses it figurally to transform duality into multiplicity.[23]

Baseball would have appealed to Spicer as an embodiment of poetic composition for a number of reasons:

1) Like poetry, baseball is a game in which stealing counts and is even considered fair play. The legitimate capturing of bases and borrowing of another player's style offer a kind of sanctioned transgression akin to quotation and collage within a poem. As in poetry, copying or learning from another player's moves is common, allowing a player's stylistic innovations to be felt long after he or she retires from the game. In Lecture 2, Spicer quotes René Char as suggesting that rules of composition were meant to be broken (II, 57). As evidenced in the 1919 Black Sox series, baseball is a game that can even survive large-scale cheating, although the game temporarily suffers for it. Spicer makes the distinction between legitimate stealing and wholesale corruption in his poem "October 1, 1962," in which he appropriates Ginsberg's syntax: "I have seen the best poets and baseball players of our generation caught in the complete and contemptible whoredom of capitalist society." But this permissible steal contrasts with the poem's refrain—"Say it isn't true Joe"—implying that, like the Black Sox star player Shoeless Joe Jackson, certain poets of the San Francisco team had committed the unspeakable crime of selling out the game for personal gain (ONS, 87).[24]

2) With no clock to mark playing time, a baseball game continues as long as there are good hits, so it is potentially endless. It creates a myth-

23. A related example Spicer might have found of interest: in H. L. Mencken's *The American Language*, "diamond" and "poem" are two of the five terms he uses to illustrate the dropping of a vowel sound in vulgar usage, so that "diamond" becomes "dimon" and "poem" becomes "pome" (341).

24.The poem's date-title marks the day the Giants beat the Dodgers in the first game of the 1962 National League playoffs. San Francisco would win the pennant, as Spicer's poem predicts, but would lose the world series to New York.

ology of immortality and heroism. Spicer's lines, too, are effective by virtue of their timing, which is non-normative and almost spastic in its un-predictability, just as curve balls, screw balls, change-ups and other pitches can appear to warp space magnetically or magically in the hands of a good pitcher. It is virtually impossible not to make mistakes in read-ing his lines aloud, and Spicer himself often stumbles in his recorded public readings. The unpredictable sequence of long lines, short lines, and even broken words corresponds to the variation of pitches in a pitch-ing cycle. The sequence interferes with the timing of the lines and the transparency of the "messages" they contain in order to keep the reader off balance, disoriented from the everyday, and more available to the imaginary realm of the poem.[25]

3) Allegedly (but not actually) founded by a theosophist (Abner Dou-bleday), baseball would appeal to Spicer's heretical mysticism and sense of correspondence. To play the game the poet has to learn the black magic of the underworld. Good pitches are supernatural because in Spicer's model the pitcher is full of the "ghosts" that inhabit the center of the diamond (or daimon). The poet is also a catcher who, in order to ap-pear in the poem, has to descend into Hell (or "Dis-appear"): he "must be dead, because he wouldn't appear in the poem otherwise" (III, 128). In this empyrean field where dead poets play with the living, they literally play God, who turns up in the equation as a figure of chance, the baseball (BMV, 258). The construction is also a twist on baseball history, since the first official baseball field was the Elysian Fields in Hoboken, New Jersey, where players would literally have to cross the river from Manhattan in order to play.

4) Baseball is a form of, and substitution for, religion, and has often been in direct conflict with it both in terms of its schedule and its moral influence. The field is designed as a play between threes and fours, circles and squares, a numerology consistent with the geometrical play between heaven and earth in devotional structures such as the cathedral at Chartres. At the center of this geometry is Spicer's baseball pitcher, a sac-rificial figure who is "obviously not human" himself and who delivers God (the baseball) to the poet (catcher): "The pitcher, in his sudden hu-manness looks toward the dugout in either agony or triumph" (BMV,

25. This notion of Spicer as a supernatural pitcher within his own poems is indebted in part to Bill Gregoire, who wrote about Spicer and pitching in a graduate seminar I taught at Brown University in 1993–1994. Spicer himself claims that "a poet is a catcher more than a pitcher, but the poet likes to think of himself as a pitcher more than a catcher" (III, 117).

257). Baseball is a game in which God (the "big white baseball") is captured geometrically, having "nothing to do but go in a curve or straight line" (BMV, 258).

5) Baseball is a game as much talked about as it is watched. Since no major sport is more traditionally linked with radio reporting or with verbal conflict between players and umpire, fans and umpires, or fans and players, baseball is also a venue of informal debate and must have appealed to Spicer's love for argument. It connects with a world of alcohol and bar talk. It is a possible topic of conversation with virtually anyone in that space; baseball's effect is relational and communal. The *St. Louis Sporting News*, for which Spicer wrote a series of poems in *Book of Magazine Verse*, called baseball "the national tonic."

6) For the avid fan it is organized, ritualized derangement. Baseball scholar Richard Crepeau writes that baseball provides a social matrix within which anyone "could now belong to a strong clan without being accused of being a cultist or a fanatic. One could be as avid as one wished over baseball, nothing being more American and less deviant" (50). Hence, it provides the coverage of the ordinary. Spicer uses it to "hide in plain sight."

7) Baseball embodies a Spicerian combination of the esoteric, the profane, and the populist. The rich correspondences of baseball's vocabulary of "pitching," "catching," and "base hits" translate readily between the vocabularies of sexuality, poetry, and politics. Besides Spicer's beloved bridge, baseball is the only sport that has "rubbers" and "grand slams."

8) Baseball is both poetic and narrative in its action. It is an activity grounded in a quest for home. Home is the game's beginning and end; its movement is both Grail-like and Odyssean, presenting repeated disappointment and failed heroism like "Telemachus sad over his father's shortcomings" (BMV, 252).

9) Baseball is grounded in and promoted through regionalism to such an extent that any change in location — like the forced migration of the Dodgers and the Giants from New York to California — is extremely disruptive and economically risky. Spicer's outspoken commitment to the California landscape and to the Bay Area in particular as a poetic ground created an intense sense of team identity and allegiance which was often disappointed. The nicknaming of stadiums according to the star players that filled them with fans (for example, Yankee Stadium as "the house that Ruth built") is both a poetic and a regionalist gesture, the way one might think of sonnets as the "houses" of Petrarch and Shakespeare. In

Spicer's poetics, "the house that Jack built," baseball produces a complex architecture in which "a poem can go on forever" (L, 233; ONS, 39).

Landscape and Seriality: A California Tor

Spicer's sense of regional identity is all-inclusive: it informed his poetry, his relationships, his bar life, and his work as a linguist. It was a major factor in the eventual rift between him and Robert Duncan; it deepened and in part explained his commitment to baseball; it was the basis of his only published paper in linguistics; it was the focus of his work on the "Linguistic Atlas of the Pacific Coast" at UC Berkeley; it defined and circumscribed his social life in North Beach, at Gino & Carlo's, The Place, Aquatic Park, and elsewhere; it informed his publications with White Rabbit Press and *Open Space* magazine, and was the source of specific rules such as that they were to be distributed only within the San Francisco Bay Area; it was the social and political basis of his belief that magazines are societies; it provided materials for his writing practice as he inscribed and recontextualized the California landscape within his poems, bringing across material from one context to another to create a new field of multiple meanings, puns, and correspondences; and it shaped his poetic allegiances. It may have informed his understanding of Emily Dickinson as a poet of location and frontier. And it sustained his appreciation of Charles Olson and the California modernist Robinson Jeffers.

Formally, Spicer's regionalism argues for his theory of correspondence—that the fables, jokes, and songs of one region don't connect but correspond to those of another. The linguistic atlas he worked on aimed to show the movement of speech patterns and the differences in pronunciation from region to region and town to town, tracking the most minutely perceptible shifts in sound. Such concern for the sublinguistic minutiae of expression was, for Spicer, anything but trivial. Throughout the lectures he invokes his training as a linguist when it seems that his audience is not following him poetically. In his discussion of rhyme and puns in Lecture 1 (I, 35–39), he mentions that because rhymes depend upon pronunciation for their meaning they may be lost through time or through a shift in region, that is, they are site-specific. Puns are also site-specific but are more stable, more translatable. In Lecture 3 Spicer offers the example of the first poem from "Six Poems for Poetry Chicago," in which he uses popular song (the "lemon tree" song) and pronunciation

("limon" instead of "lemon") to reveal regional identity and difference
(BMV, 248). While the "limon" tree is used to discuss southern Californian pronunciation, it also corresponds with Lorca's Spanish lemon (AL,
34) and with his correspondence with Lorca.

In this way Spicer reinvents the principle inherited from the orphic
and troubadour traditions of defining boundaries through song.[26] But for
Spicer it also shows the extreme authority of a single vowel sound in
defining boundaries, in mapping one's territory, in establishing regional
identity through language. In this sense Spicer is less like Orpheus, who
emotionally "moves" rocks and trees, and more like Amphion, a figure
often associated with Orpheus, who supernaturally builds a city out of
sound. If poetic tradition for Spicer means that poets in different regions
and times are "patiently writing the same poem," then the only way for
poets to define the boundaries of their own region is to transpose or translate traditional music into the music of their own instrument and location. So in *Language*, the poem "Transformations II" traces the series of
substitutions and syntactical ("transformational" or transpositional) changes
that make a song work regionally:

> "In Scarlet Town where I was born
> There was a fair maid dwelling."
> We make up a different language for poetry
> And for the heart—ungrammatical.
> It is not that the name of the town changes
> (Scarlet becomes Charlotte or even in Gold City I once heard a
> good Western singer make it Tonopah. . . .
> But that the syntax changes. This is older than towns.
>
>   (L, 233)

The significance for Spicer of this act of community building through
song leads him to an imaginary association with Charlie Parker—the
"bird" of Spicer's "Song for Bird and Myself"—whom Spicer again invokes in *Language* as dancing "now in some brief kingdom (Oz)" that is
created through its unique pairing of the phonemes /ä/ and /z/, "two
phonemes / That were never paired before in the language" (L, 237).
While the "brief kingdom" could be an afterlife for the posthumous
Parker, the kingdom's "briefness" and the reference to Oz suggest that it is
an imaginary world created and entered only in the act of song. In Lecture 4, Spicer extends this notion of territories and allegiances to the
larger sense of poetic community in which even literary magazines establish boundaries (IV, 157).

26. Hence Spicer's claim that there is "more of Orpheus in Sophie Tucker than in R. P.
Blackmur." (See Appendix.)

Spicer's commitment to California as his poetic context and ground is well documented. He was devoted to California writers like Ambrose Bierce, who defined poetry as "a form of expression peculiar to the Land beyond the Magazines" (Bierce, 258). The California landscape recurs within Spicer's work as a backdrop that is almost literally a theatrical backdrop; the Pacific Ocean often functions as punctuation, as a façade, and at times as a character within his poems; and the proximity of the ocean like the "dark at the sides of our fires" provides a palpably inhuman scale beyond the limits or lines of his poems, which by contrast only serves to make the lines themselves more humanly real.[27]

As a major agro-industrial empire as well as an empire of the moving image, California is both Kansas and Oz. In *The Holy Grail*, for instance, the landscape appears complete with classically northern California crops (oranges, pumpkins, artichokes, cabbages, and so on). It resembles the normalcy and homogeneity of Kansas mixed with over-the-rainbow surreality and estrangement. California contains the quotidian pace of small towns and the big magic of films in which such communities were visited by Martians, body-snatching seed pods, and various atomic threats. For Spicer, California is America *in extremis*. It combines and locates his frontier mentality, his sense of limit in poetry, his questioning of "grand narratives," and his sense of living out a posthumous existence in a post-apocalyptic, image-making, border culture. When Spicer was growing up in the 1930s, California was the promised land for dust bowl farmers. When he died in the mid-sixties, it was the home of various communal semi-agricultural groups. He uses farming metaphors three times in his lectures as a model of composition: in Lecture 1 his agricultural imagery is a tongue-in-cheek correspondence to Yeats—"We have come to bring fertilizer for your fields"; in Lecture 3 he talks about plowing the fields to prepare for poems; and in Lecture 4 he compares poets to peach farmers who must learn how to manage themselves, knowing when to "sell out," if they are to survive as poets. Spicer's sense of the necessity of self-management is not necessarily anti-utopian though he repeatedly proposes that narratives of liberation—like Christianity, domestic happiness, agape or eros, the American dream, the flower children, the King of the May—are traps for poets. As soon as liberation is made to fit any single, unified narrative, it has been falsified; it becomes a lie or "line" one falls for.

As a manifestation of futurity, California in 1965 already showed signs of an American empire in decline—an empire that can be understood as "ruins," a beautiful failure that ghosts inhabit. Part of Spicer's commitment

27. For more on Spicer's use of the ocean as ending or punctuation, see Granger.

to the California scene and California landscape is possibly its status as a failure, a de-promised land, like a run-down farm out of which arise Oz-like imaginary communities. It corresponds to the wasteland of Grail legend in part because historically what has been sought in California has been based on a false belief that prosperity is the just reward of western expansionism, greed, and the American spirit of adventure. Californian identity from the Gold Rush of 1849 to *Escape from L.A.* (1996) has been shaped by improbabilities and (mostly failed) promises which only serve to prove its capacity for endurance, its tenacity, and its frontier know-how.

Thus Spicer characterizes California as wiser than the East, having already seen through civilization into nonsense and having experienced the mental and emotional extremity of land's end. He writes to Allen Joyce from New York in 1955: "I had hoped [New York] would be frightening and it just isn't. The people seem so damnably innocent—like the Americans that Henry James writes about. I hadn't realized how old California was. . . . Like most primitive cultures, New York has no feeling for nonsense. Wit is as far as they can go. . . . No one speaks Martian, no one insults people arbitrarily, there is, to put it simply and leave it, no violence of the mind and of the heart, no one screams in the elevator" ("Letters to Allen Joyce," 142).

In fact, the year Spicer spends in the East, first in New York and then in Boston, creates a turning point in his poetics. It galvanizes his western identity, aesthetics, and personal allegiances, and is important in his mapping of California as antipodal to the East. In an essay Spicer writes on John Donne in graduate school, he uses a geographical vocabulary to describe the poetic tension between the imaginary and the real. Pointing out the significance of the antipodes (the sense that if the earth is round, then no matter where one is on the globe, there are people upside down under one's feet, a mirror world), Spicer represents the concept of this alien reflection of a "distant race" as being so contrary that it could only be conceived in contemporary terms as "Martian," or like the notion in childhood that one might dig a hole through which one might "fall to China." To Donne, savage America was antipodal to England.[28] For Spicer, the American East Coast was the ground of normalcy that one couldn't help but want to escape. Spicer saw Alice's fall into Wonderland and Orpheus's fall into Hell as corresponding with an imaginary fall through the world into a "savage" realm that is actually more complex and sophisticated than the ground of Western civilization. When things "disappear" within

---

28. One of the central theological debates of his time was the question of whether or not such "savages" were saved. Donne ruled in the affirmative.

Spicer's poems, they have fallen through a mirror into Hell (or "Dis"), the backward, counterclockwise, antipodal world. Hence, Spicer's breaking of the word "dis-appear" in "Lament for the Makers":

A distant race
With the seawater
Between them. Beating
Great clouds of smoke. A worm
In the whole visible world held still. To whom? As we define them they dis-
appear.   (LM, 112)

In Spicer's imaginary geography, where you land when you fall through reality is the imaginary realm of California, "the seacoast of bohemia" (L, 233), which Spicer describes in his last interview in August 1965 as "the other end of the rabbit hole." In the same interview he claims to be part Blackfoot Indian, hence a "savage" belonging to the West Coast, which he hopes will one day become an independent commonwealth (see Appendix).

California is both older (still inhabited by first-growth forests) and younger (more fallen, more futuristic, and geologically newer and more changeable) than the East. In this way the California landscape mimics or corresponds with the mysterious echo and return of writing itself, the primariness and doubling back of the Orphic experience as well as its terrifying force. It represents a limit: the geographical limit of the West, the ocean, the sunset, The End. As this extremity is a defining narrative of American geographical conquest and media-expansionism, it is a narrative based in repetition. This narrative of the edge becomes caught in its own echoes and the reiteration of temporary endings: the repeated projection of cultural icons, the crash of the surf, the fade-out, etc.

In Spicer's view, California is stylistically and materially a negative of Whitman's eastern landscape. While Whitman is clearly part of Spicer's poetic imagination and is a significant voice in the writing of *After Lorca*, in the first poem of the "Book of Galahad," Spicer invokes Whitman in order to critique an eastern, transcendentalist view of America and especially the American West. Within the poem, "Contemplating America from Long Island Sound," an apparent reversal of Whitman's poem "Facing West from California's Shores," is as "foolish" as contemplating the Grail from the standpoint of purity.[29] The distance invoked in Whitman's vision of the West romanticizes America's grand narrative since he

29. Presumably, the Grail cannot be achieved by someone who has not been stained with it; while Percival, the innocent, fails, Galahad, the illegitimate son, "wins" it. Galahad is no better off personally for having achieved his goal—he literally disappears into the sunset, though it's more of an annihilating loss than a victory—but poetically his position is more supportable than Percival's. See also Lecture II, 64.

doesn't see that the real Indians "who still walked the Plains were dead," killed off in the name of civilized exploration (HG, 206).[30] As an ultimate manifestation of American conquest, California could not be understood from a safely civilized intellectual East. From the standpoint of a frontier imagination, Long Island Sound was no match for the Pacific Ocean, and neither purity nor Puritanism could compete with the mobilized violence of the "wild west."[31]

In contrast, the seeing-through of the California poet was embodied, for Spicer, in Robinson Jeffers. In one of his last public statements, Spicer tells the *San Francisco Chronicle* in the summer of 1965 that Jeffers was "'a real California poet,' with the 'same association with the Pacific Coast, as a far shore of the continent and a treacherous sea coast, that the San Francisco poets have had'" (see Appendix). And in the "Poetry as Magic" workshop, Spicer distributed copies of two poems by Jeffers, "Local Legend" and "Skunks."[32] Both poems are Spicerian in the sense that they debunk grand narratives: "Local Legend" tells of a good deed that becomes an instance of horror, and in "Skunks," Jeffers clarifies his "inhumanist" position by showing how the distancing effect of grand narratives turns war into romance—a view Spicer seems to share in *The Holy Grail* and in his letter to the *San Francisco Chronicle* about its biased reporting of the Vietnam War. Whitman's distance from the West makes possible a vision of unsullied beauty and infinite opportunity, but in Jeffers's poem that very perspective becomes insupportable. The fact that from a distance skunks almost smell pleasant corresponds to the fact that from a distance "The corruptions of war and peace . . . soften into romance" (Jeffers, 406), a perspective Whitman would clearly have concurred with in his "local" experience as a wound dresser, but which is lost whenever regional perspective is sacrificed to global observation.

Like Jeffers, Spicer writes an inhuman landscape of real cliff faces, surf, seagulls, and an ocean that is "tougher than anything" (L, 217). The line and narrative structure of Jeffers's mature work of the 1950s are also comparable to Spicer's, particularly in *The Holy Grail*—Spicer's most Californian poem. Formally it resembles Jeffers's serial compositions and verse novels, and Spicer even wrote in a letter to Charles Olson that his

30. The passage also echoes Spicer's letter to Harris Schiff, in which he writes that even the trees that can be seen from a highway are not real but fiberglass replicas; the "real" trees grow five miles in any direction beyond the road ("Letter to Harris Schiff," 22).

31. In typical Spicerian fashion, even something as stable as the proper noun "Whitman" can produce multiple meanings. The Whitman in this poem may also refer to the nineteenth-century American pioneer and missionary Marcus Whitman, who was eventually killed by the "Indians" he tried to convert.

32. See Ellingham and Killian (84).

serial poems should be read novelistically. *The Holy Grail* more than any other poem reflects and renovates Jeffers's inhuman landscape. The failed romance of conquest is reiterated in *The Holy Grail* with the Australian soldiers singing "We're off to see the Wizard" and with the correspondence of Grail and bomb in "The Book of Merlin." The correspondence between the failure to reach the Grail and the failure of western conquest is reiterated in "The Book of the Death of Arthur," in which Spicer swaps "Avalon" for "California," echoing Ginsberg's send-up of Whitman in "A Supermarket in California" (HG, 212). And Spicer's purposeful misspelling of Australians as "Austrailians" (or Oz-trail-ians) reinforces his underlying assertion that, as Avalon, Oz, and Wonderland, California is the site of great and absurd battles, a war-torn and imaginary Promised Land (HG, 207).

Jeffers's poems too are interspersed with a critique of militarism and the only landscape he writes about in his enormous opus other than California is Grail territory. Jeffers's Grail poem is composed as a series and has the orphic title "Descent to the Dead."[33] The first poem in Spicer's "Book of Merlin" also contains a reference to Hengest and Horsa, two leaders of a fifth-century Germanic invasion of Britain, to whom Jeffers addresses one of his last poems. Jeffers even goes so far as to take on Grail-period architecture, building and living most of his life in a stone "tor" on the California coast near Carmel, an anachronism reflected in the third poem of the "Book of Merlin": "The tower he built himself . . . / He pretended that he was a radio station and listened to grail-music all day and all night every day and every night. / Shut up there by a treachery that was not quite his own" (HG, 203).

In *A Book of Magazine Verse*, Spicer invokes, echoes, and critiques Jeffers's poem "Quia Absurdum,"[34] even breaking his line to emphasize the correspondence:

33. Jeffers's sensibility that as a political subject, "I am not dead, I have only become inhuman," is echoed in at least one strand of Spicer's apocryphal view of humanity, inhumanity, and orphism.

34.   Quia Absurdum

Guard yourself from the terrible empty light of
    space, the bottomless
Pool of the stars. (Expose yourself to it: you might learn
    something.)

Guard yourself from perceiving the inherent nastiness of
    man and woman.
(Expose your mind to it: you might learn something.)

Faith, as they now confess, is preposterous, an act of will.
    Choose the Christian sheep-cote
Or the Communist rat-fight: faith will cover your head
    from the man-devouring stars.

Get those words out of your mouth and into your heart. If there isn't
A God don't believe in Him. "Credo
Quia absurdum," creates wars and pointless loves and was even in
      Tertullian's time a heresy.

(BMV, 253)

And in "A Textbook of Poetry," Spicer mirrors the "Communist rat-fight"
of Jeffers's poem: "It is so absurd that the rats calling, 'Credo quia absurdum' or the cats or the mountain lions become a singular procession of
metaphors" (TP, 180). Jeffers's poem in fact looks and sounds very much
like one of Spicer's own poems, and the poem's tone can be read as either
a severe self-critique or a railing against the hypocrisy of an institution that
can use the radical power of Tertullian's heresy to justify its own ends. In
Spicer's poem the phrase "credo quia absurdum" (I believe because it is
absurd) is taken as a truism but one which, like the "little machine" in
"Friday the 13th," can make you "able to say anything." Clearly Jeffers is
part of Spicer's own Grail landscape—an Eliotic "waste land" on "the sea
coast of bohemia" (L, 223).

A Poetics of Presence: Spicer's Letters

> We should write out our thoughts in as nearly as possible the language we
> thought them in, as though in a letter to an intimate friend.
> —WILLIAM BUTLER YEATS, *Autobiography*

> The letters will continue after both of us are dead.
> —JACK SPICER, Letter to James Alexander

In 1956 Spicer wrote an article on the then-recent edition of Dickinson's
poems and letters for the Boston Public Library's newsletter (see Appendix). This period represents a turning point for Spicer between his abandoned early work and his mature work, which began with the publication
of *After Lorca* in 1957. Not only does Spicer's review show his capacity for
meticulous textual scholarship, but it is significant in Spicer's recognition
of the literary importance of Dickinson's letters and the poetic possibility
of letters as a form, as his own conflation of letters and poems becomes
more complex.

   In his article, Spicer also notes that Dickinson's letters are her only surviving prose—and even these are so often embedded with poetry that it is
impossible to distinguish poetry from letter with absolute confidence.[35] Increasingly, this becomes true for Spicer as well, and the Dickinson article

---

35. This gesture, along with Spicer's recognition of the difference between the printed texts
and Dickinson's manuscript versions, is later developed through the scholarship of Susan Howe
and Marta Werner.

is itself one of his last pieces of prose outside of his own letters. In 1958, when the young poet George Stanley asked him to write the program notes for his reading, he insisted on responding only in the form of a letter of "apology" in which he nevertheless discussed Stanley's work and which he gave Stanley permission to print in the program.

In Lecture 3, Spicer talks about dictation taking over his poetic practice during the writing of *After Lorca*, a book formally composed of real and "fake" translations and letters (III, 135). This is also the beginning of seriality for Spicer, which partly manifests itself in the form of letters as serial compositions with an openness at their center: the physical distance between sender and receiver. This mixture of a heightened address with intentional distances or gaps even between his lines gives Spicer's most abstract poems a kind of epistolary intimacy.

In *After Lorca*, the use of italics transmits and transforms Baudelaire's term "correspondence" into a co-respondence (printed with an italic *r* as "cor*r*espondence"), proposing that poetry and translation operate like an exchange of letters—a correspondence in which neither writer's words are more original or more "real" than the other's. Lorca is no longer the distant predecessor or source for Spicer's work since in their poem/letters they exist contemporaneously.

Spicer's "personal" letters are often provocative, begging response, jousting, and punning. He signs a letter to *Floating Bear* magazine "Barely yours," puns on Ebbe Borregaard in a letter to the same, and prods Creeley by sending a copy of *After Lorca* with a note to the effect that he "stole more than the title" from him. The letters of *Admonitions*, among others, were sent as personal letters which stated that they would be included in a book of poems or publicly read.[36]

For Spicer the seemingly ephemeral form of letters has a staying power beyond any immediate context. Like poems, letters are built to last, even beyond their writers. The sense of letters as documents meant to endure and eventually be overheard even by strangers persists in Spicer's own

36. See Spicer's letter to Robin Blaser in *Admonitions* (A, 60):

> Halfway through After Lorca I discovered that I was writing a book instead of a series of poems and individual criticism by anyone suddenly became less important. This is true of my Admonitions which I will send you when complete. (I have eight of them already and there will probably be fourteen including, of course, this letter.)

And in a private letter to James Alexander, he writes:

> So it is (the violence of the impatient artist) that I keep trying to draw the form of these letters to a close merely because I am going to read them to an audience of boobies and one or two poets. Ridiculous attempt to break the glass! The letters will continue. The letters will continue. The letters will continue after both of us are dead. (170)

poem/letters. In his introduction to *After Lorca*, Spicer has Lorca notice that even what appears to be a simple exchange between the two poets is triangulated, as one poet writes to another:

> . . . not in any effort to communicate with him, but rather as a young man whispers his secrets to a scarecrow, knowing that his young lady is in the distance listening. The young lady in this case may be a Muse, but the scarecrow nevertheless quite naturally resents the confidences. The reader, who is not a party to this singular tryst, may be amused by what he overhears. (AL, 11–12)

This mirroring is accentuated by the further complication of Spicer writing *as* Lorca.[37]

Spicer's letters defy the traditional limits of their form by focusing less on conveying information than on bringing a number of possible readings into play through pun, innuendo, and riposte. By virtue of the intimacy of their form, letters also create a conspiratorial bond within which every reference and pun can indelibly mean something, and the stakes are real. If, as Spicer's *Troilus* suggests, war is a permanent condition which informs our living, letters might form a counter to it. His letters to Graham Mackintosh, his close friend and publisher who was drafted into the Korean War, are beautiful and complex, sometimes funny, sometimes declaring love, not unlike Whitman's letters to the young men he tended during the Civil War. Within them he elucidates his own poetic practice and often shares the texts he reads as powerful imaginary counters to the meaninglessness of war.

In one of Spicer's most important letters, which prefigures the letters in *After Lorca*, he writes to Mackintosh in the army in 1954 to help assuage the young soldier's boredom and fear. In it, he evolves one of his most potent tropes of the poet as a time mechanic and poetic composition as a vehicle that defies time and place. Out of a matrix of love, amusement, thoughtfulness, and resistance, he creates a politically salient argument for what he sees as one of the great purposes of reading—to free someone from the tyranny of war:

> Dear Mac,
>   . . . I am rereading Proust for the umteenth time and am more than considerably impressed. The whole book consists not only of what he is able to remember but actually to *evoke* from the past and the process of this evocation leads the reader to do likewise with his own past so that the reader is soon not only reading a novel but (in a

37. The introduction to *After Lorca* itself can be read as a reflection of another imaginary document from a posthumous poet, Charles Olson's 1946 essay "This is Yeats Speaking," written as an imaginary radio-broadcast-style message from a posthumous Yeats to America on behalf of Ezra Pound (*Collected Prose*, 141–44). Olson's essay also mirrors the form of Pound's notorious broadcasts.

passive way) writing a novel and for every page he reads there is a ghostly page the reader recovers from his own life. It is the nearest thing to a time machine that I am likely to see.

Proust's method for summoning up absolutely forgotten fragments of the past (or rather almost literally revisiting them) is to concentrate on some sight, some smell, some taste in the present and let it ride him back on its similarity to something forgotten. It is a time machine with no controls on it unfortunately—one cannot tell if one is going to go back a day or fifteen years, whether one is going to arrive in a meadow or a jungle—but it is an exciting trip. Such a vast majority of our lives we have never once remembered; it sits like an iceberg under the surface of our minds and only the small cap of the tip rises above the surface. Perhaps, in these last tortuous days of basic training, you might like to try this time machine in moments of boredom, exhaustion, or terror. When you are marching, for example, let the smell of the dust send you back to a section of the past you have never visited (it was present when you were there before); in bayonet drill let the sharpness of the light on the bayonet's edge send you back to another place in the past. This may be the only certain way to defeat the army. They can't draft you from ten years ago.

Past, present, or future, don't forget that I'm thinking about you and am

Yours
Jack (101)

In another letter to Mackintosh, he explains a seventeenth-century Portuguese poem he is reading, the "Lusiads" by Camoëns, which combines reportage of Portuguese exploration with narratives of the Roman gods. The form of the letter itself evokes an unmapped world through which one can escape the horrors of territorial disputes. Spicer writes:

Imagine the magnificence of such voyages—not to know how big the world is and how many islands it has. . . . A world like that would be worth fighting for, a world that had no maps. . . . It is not the Army I object to but the kind of army, not killing I object to but the kind of killing. They have given us danger without adventure, labor without reward, pain without dignity. They have wiped out the treacherous Mohammedans with their H-bombs and killed the unicorns with flame-throwers. They have made maps of every square inch of the world and imprisoned us inside those maps. Let's escape. (100)

And a few weeks later (December 15, 1954), in a letter that is enormously telling and illustrative of Spicer's later practice, he gives advice on the practical and poetic applications of fear:

A good example of how a fear can be, not overcome but imprisoned in a pentacle, is my fear of the supernatural. Even up to my early adolescence I used to be afraid to go to sleep because I would dream about ghosts—chasing me and singing in weird voices, things like that. I think that at the time if I answered honestly what I was the most afraid of it would have been ghosts rather than death. But I discovered that fear of the supernatural could be used in poetry and magic (if these things are different) and could give me a kind of contact with things outside of myself. Now, when a ghost comes into a dream I am still afraid, but I use that fear to force the ghost to tell me something. (105)

Yeats writes that "our lives give our letters force as the lives of people in plays give force to their words" (*Memoirs*, 62). Spicer's letters likewise are dramatic utterances that are intensified by their form. As he puts it, they are often constructed formally as mirrors to reveal not their sender but their recipient, and mirrors are often their subject as well. In a letter to James Alexander, he writes: "these letters are our mirrors and we imprisoned singly in the depths of them." To be successful prisons, of course, the letters must capture an enduring and infinitely patient presence. Their content is beside the point: "The mirror does not break easily regardless of what is reflected in it, regardless of whether there are blue apples, Rimbaud, or even angry white light belonging in it, imprisoned, one might say, in the death of its surface. It is the oblique patience of an Alice who plays with her cat and waits for something between her and the image to melt away. It is the oblique patience of children" (170).

III. From Orphic Cubism to California Funk

A *Color Wheel for Sounds*

In the mid-1950s, Spicer's demand that poetry go beyond self-expression led him to rethink his poetic ground and search for corresponding systems of meaning through which to describe his practice. He wrote to Robert Duncan that "the best way to get a method for a new description of poetics is to look at the failures and successes of such things in other arts. Color theory for painting gives, I think, the most exact analogy. What we need is a color wheel for sounds" (*Acts*, 20–22). The letter provides a useful frame of reference for this critical period in Spicer's poetic development when his practice was about to shift from one-night stands into dictated books.

The vocabulary and sentiment of Spicer's letter corresponds closely to the thinking of the cubist painter Robert Delaunay, whose work led Apollinaire to coin the terms "orphism" and "orphic cubism" in his essay "The Cubist Painters," published in translation in Robert Motherwell's "Aesthetic Meditations" series in 1944. Delaunay was interested in using color as an abstract language, capable of producing depth without relying on traditional laws of perspective or representation. In Spicer's terms, Delaunay's new color wheel was essentially a system of "correspondence," a theory of poetic transmission which Spicer would articulate in *After Lorca*.

The use of color rather than images as the material of composition was

a means to push the limits of abstraction, while the viewer's experience of
an art work would be even more immediate and arguably more "human,"
despite the fact that the work is less descriptive of the conventional scenes
of the human world. In effect, it created a readerly experience of painting
without giving it an overall structure of either narrative or image. For Delaunay the experience of both painter and viewer was essentially a poetic
one, and his process bears obvious similarities to Spicer's: he was concerned with effect rather than expression, he painted primarily in serial
format, he described his experiments with color wheels as a "blow with a
fist," and his metaphors of composition are architectural in their ambition. As Delaunay writes:

> The colors are arranged according to intensity, number, and measure . . . This is
> where time is introduced into the picture structure . . . This art combines perfectly
> with architecture, indeed it is architecture, for it is based on architectonic color laws.
> (Vriesen, 85)

The idea of building materially through abstraction corresponds closely
to Spicer's practice of textual mirroring as well as his use of phonemes
and narrative fragments to create imaginary kingdoms and intertextual
cities, like Charlie Parker's "brief Kingdom (Oz)" (L, 237).

Delaunay's cubism was diagrammatic and—like the work of his fellow
"orphic cubists" Leger, Picabia, and Duchamp—his work is at times mechanical in appearance. His paintings often represent multiple perspec-
tives within a single canvas, using color to create visual depth without the
expected perspectival cues. They evoke movement. His paintings show
such careful attention to the disparate parts of things that matter itself begins to seem porous, and the sum of any set of parts seems greater than
any imaginable whole. An airplane, for instance, might be composed of
ten to twelve rectangles of different colors, without any clear line separating plane from sky. So the basic distinction between figure and ground is
disturbed, placed in motion, as both are merely the effects of Delaunay's
arrangement of color fragments. At the height of his mature work, Delaunay produced serial variations of windows, circles, sporting events, the city
of Paris, and an Eiffel Tower series in which the famous radio tower is re-
fracted and reconstructed. A critical description of the series sounds very
much like an account of Spicer's later practice: the painting's "increasingly complex and contradictory readings make the pictorial structure
denser and remove it further from the source. . . . The painting thus becomes a structure composed of conflicting movements which jostle
across the surface or melt into indefinite depth. Such movements are dis-
continuous, so that one has to choose how one shall read them" (Spate,

173). As the same critic notes, the Orphists were deeply engaged with the "materiality of creation . . . which seemed to develop a life that was separate from theirs even as they themselves formed it" (341).

Similarly, Spicer's orphism is a gamble between the visible and invisible, things and nothingness. He explicitly composed poems that were separate from himself, animated from outside: "Hello says the apple" (TP, 125). And by the early sixties, Spicer's poems begin to feel more "assembled." Each element is used within a poem like a color fragment brought up from depth; it represents some piece of a shattered mirror that is then assembled into a kind of cubist portraiture: "Empty fragments, like the shards of pots found in some / Mesopotamian expedition. Found but not put together. The unstable / Universe has distance but not much else" (L, 236). Part of the trick of poetic abstraction is that language also conveys meaning; so it must be made abstract before it can enact other meanings or effects beyond the everyday transmission of data.[38] The act is essentially gestural and thereby resists any overarching concerns of a unified narrative. It is an aesthetic strategy that narrates the process of making; what emerges is not a coherent structure but a way of reading. Narrative is simply deployed as a gesture, as traditional representation may be enacted or quoted within the context of abstraction—the way a newspaper clipping might be used within a cubist collage, the way Delaunay uses the Eiffel Tower, or the way Wallace Berman repeats the image of a radio in a serial composition.

Like the voice on the radio in Cocteau's *Orphée*, Spicer's mirroring fragments create a sense of immediacy and insistence so that taking down the messages becomes a theater of life and death, a disappearing chamber. Spicer's orphism is more than "deep song"; the depth of his lines is ultimately neither *duende* nor Rilkean angel. The play between surface (cubism) and depth (orphism) within his work creates the distortion built in to Spicer's visual and auditory mirroring, like "the faint call of drums" that becomes "the faint call of . . . the faint call of / Me" in "The Book of the Death of Arthur" (HG, 211). It is responsible in part for the transformative "magic" of Spicer's practice. There is of course no guarantee that the messages will tell the poet anything useful, but in a world in which gods have been replaced by computers and human beings are vaporized into graphemes, they present a kind of last hope for meaning within dada.

38. Ashbery's experimentation in the early sixties offers another point of correspondence. In the jacket copy for *The Tennis Court Oath,* he writes: "I attempt to use words abstractly, as an abstract painter would use paint. . . . My aim is to give the meaning free play and the fullest possible range. As with the abstract painters, my abstraction is an attempt to get a greater, more complete kind of realism."

Orphism is in its mythic sense the poet's power to rescue even the dead (Eurydice). For the materialist Spicer this can also mean the recovery of whatever the poet values that is "dead" to the culture at large. In the process, the act of assembling poems from disparate voices (sources) becomes meaningful when seen as rescue. In an early poem, "Orpheus in Hell," Spicer anticipates this shift when he writes, "Later he would remember all those dead voices / And call them Eurydice" (ONS, 21). This transference between people and sounds is addressed in his version of *Troilus*, in which Cressida the "girl" is not really the thing sought after but a substitution for it. Spicer proposes that any coherent historical reclamation would be impossible, and that even if it were possible it would only result in something that was "some nice furniture to work with, but no more than furniture, as history is" (I, 29). Instead he replaces historicity with correspondence, a construct within which history may be used abstractly, like color. For example, the war-torn landscape in *The Holy Grail* is composed as "not lost battles or even defeated people / But blackness alive with itself / At the sides of our fires. . . . / a simple hole running from one thing to another" (HG, 212).

The transmission of this orphic depth comes in fragments that create an illusory or illusional hole-ness—like the pixels of a TV screen or the "electrical impulses" on a telephone—yet what has been brought across through the poem is "real." "Your voice / consisted of sounds that I had / To route to phonemes, then to bound and free morphemes, then / to syntactic structures" (L, 237). The process reveals the porosity not only of the material world but of perception itself. Recalling Orpheus's ability to make "trees and stones dance," Spicer compares the special effects of poetry to "telekinesis, which I know very well on a pinball machine is perfectly possible" (I, 11; L, 237). Through his practice of dictation and waiting, Spicer creates orphic gaps in the surface of his poems, and every time we read a gap we fall, like Orpheus, into the poem's underworld. When we fall through and into the poem, we enact our struggle to make meaning. We light up with various potential meanings, like pinball machines.

Narrative Assemblages

As a form of composition, dictation consists not only of orphic depth but of lateral movement on the surface of a poem through the arrangement of the poet's already existing "furniture" which often takes the form of fragmented narratives (I, 29 ff.). As he asserts in Lecture 1: "It seems to me that, essentially, you arrange" (I, 9). In his work from *Heads of the Town Up to the Aether* on, Spicer clearly activates and combines a wide range of narratives in his poems — *Morte d'Arthur, The Wizard of Oz*, the Kennedy saga, *Alice in Wonderland*, the history of magic, baseball, "The Hunting of the Snark," the crucifixion, the Fool-Killer, the dropping of the Bomb, and so on — each engaged for a line or two at a time, or mixed within the same sentence, or superimposed where their vocabularies coincide. In the second poem in "The Book of the Death of Arthur" in *The Holy Grail*, we find:

> Marilyn Monroe being attacked by a bottle of sleeping pills
> Like a bottle of angry hornets
> Lance me, she said
> Lance her, I did
> I don't work there anymore.
> The answer-question always the same. I cannot remember when
>   I was not a king. The sword in the rock is like a children's
>   story told by my mother.
> He took her life. And when she floated in on the barge or joined
> the nunnery or appeared dead in all the newspapers it was
>   his shame not mine
>   I was king.
>
> (HG, 210)

While lines 1–2 invoke the real life and death of Marilyn Monroe, lines 3–5 quote the bawdy "I used to work in Chicago" song (II, n.32), emphasizing Monroe's role as a sexual icon. Lines 6–8 reference Grail legend from its various corrupt sources, including a fragmented monologue from King Arthur and the sword in the stone quoted as children's literature; and lines 9–12 recall the death of Ophelia in *Hamlet* and the Lady of Shalott. The subtext that activates all these figures and gives them an added immediacy is the fact that the book was written in the context of Kennedy's Camelot presidency, at the same time the popular musical was running. The paratactic construction of the poem is not unlike Pound's subject rhyme, conveying a deep sense of loss for the inevitable oppression of history on its subjects. The frequency of the poem oscillates so quickly between its variant (corrupt) sources that the transmission has the tinny reception of the degraded life of figures as they get caught in the repeated cycle of figural law.

The effect of such an assemblage is one of intense conversation and mutual critique, creating a tension between populism, literary tropes, utopia, and espionage — a particularly American combination of concerns. When the narratives quoted are master narratives that form the basis of cultural judgment (democracy, free speech, the American dream, Christianity, heterosexual love, the bomb, and so on) Spicer tends to mix them in such a way as to display their emptiness, to show where they "lie," as, for instance, the first poem in "The Book of the Death of Arthur":

> "He who sells what isn't hisn
> Must pay it back or go to prison,"
> Jay Gould, Cornelius Vanderbilt, or some other imaginary American millionaire
> —Selling short.
> The heart is short too
> Beats at one and a quarter beats a second or something like that. Fools everyone.
> (HG, 210)

While the doggerel quality of the first two lines is set in tension with the legitimacy of ownership, it simultaneously exposes the thievery of the "imaginary American millionaires" who would invest in such a moralism to maintain their property while "selling short" the public. And it further disrupts the economic focus of American well-being, undermining the narrative of industrialism and upward mobility by shifting the scale from the grandiose and judgmental to the personal and homely scale of the heart as a human motor ("beats at one and a quarter beats a second") that short-changes and "fools" everyone. Because of the dramatic shifts in perspective and by its placement in the poem, the "sincerity" of the heart is undermined; it is implicated as an instrument of greed.

Instead of being determining superstructures, these narrative fragments form the cultural "rubble" from which the poem is made. Spicer was always testing the waters and discovering that master narratives inevitably betray themselves and those who believe in them. As a student at Berkeley, he was convinced enough of the value of democracy and dissent to get involved in student activities—but only to the extent that he used the forum to expose its own hypocrisy. (See Herndon's colorful reminiscence in CB, 375–78.)

Of course, the grandest narratives for America are democracy itself, the right to free speech, and the mythology of individual voice, a narrative that was rediscovering its power in the 1960s with the civil rights movement, anti-Vietnam War protests, and, in Berkeley, the Free Speech Movement.[39] As Paul Goodman points out in his collection of editorials, *The Society I Live in Is Mine*, this was a moment when individuals were testing their powers of self-expression and social critique in a way that was ultimately disappointing. In Spicer's terms, freedom of expression is meaningless in a culture in which no one is listening. He reiterates in the first poem of *Language* that "No one listens to poetry" (L, 217). The sentiment also informs

---

39. It is important to remember that Spicer is dead by 1965, so he doesn't live to see the results of these various movements.

the *Book of Magazine Verse*, in which, as a serious joke, the poems are ostensibly written for magazines that would reject them; and it forms the basis of his last lecture, in which he warns young poets against the delusion that "political poetry" has political effect. With his sense of the "big lie of the personal," which is countered by the practice of dictation, Spicer further evolves and exposes the notion of democratic self-expression, since what is voiced in a poem is not necessarily one's own in the first place.

But Spicer's contrary poetics also reflects the rhetorical energy and duplicity of the political system he implicitly critiques.[40] He sets up corresponding dualities—such as the tension between belief and disbelief, or the human and divine love object—in order to show the arbitrariness of culturally sanctioned narratives or belief systems. He makes it clear we can't escape the tyranny of whatever system we propose. Spicer writes in *Language*: "'If you don't believe in a god, don't quote him,' Valéry once said when he was about ready to give up poetry. The purposefull suspension of disbelief has about the chance of a snowball in hell" (L, 226). Logic is often corrupted and countered in Spicer's poems by non sequiturs and false assertions, "which explains poetry. Distances impossible to be measured or walked over" (L, 227). To assert meaninglessness as a universal construct is, in contrast, not to be disappointed by the apparent arbitrariness of meaning, and Spicer's poems make us aware of the infinite and even constructive possibility of misunderstanding.

In addition to collaging narrative fragments, Spicer purposefully intrudes antinarrative bits into existing grand narratives, like adding false verses to existing "authentic" folksongs in his KPFA radio show of 1948, or later making King Arthur sing "Rex Quondam et futurus with a banjo on my knee" (HG, 211).[41] He also delights in taking our memory of the known American theological and folkloric discourses into cul-de-sacs and wrong turns on the road of a shared text like the Bible. He purposefully foils the declared origins of our communities to show their arbitrariness, their "false" origins and etymologies. In this way, the capacity of language to convey a coherent story is thwarted as an artificial system of sign-making which we must undo in order to expose the ultimate randomness of his-

40. See the letter to the *Chronicle*, Lecture I, note 24.

41. In his account of the Berkeley days, Jim Herndon writes that Spicer, Herndon, and Dave Fredericksons produced a radio show Spicer called the "Most Educational Folk-Song Program West of the Pecos." Spicer wanted "'American' 20th century versions of songs" and he would persuade Fredericksons to "make terrible changes in some revered 'authentic' version, so it would go along with a statement Jack planned to make to the effect that Dave had learned it on the Santa Monica pier from an old bus-driver fishing for shiners . . . (Only after reading *After Lorca* could I understand why Jack wanted to do this)" (CB, 375).

tory, perception, or even the intimate ground of love. This is a difficult if not desperate course through language, as it seeks to unseat the transmission of cultural codes through time.

Spicer often blends the quaint, the folkloric, the populist, and the esoteric within the space of a single poem—like "God is a big white baseball" or "Where is the poet? A-keeping the sheep" (BMV, 258; L, 230). This technique corresponds to the California funk aesthetic developing in the fifties in San Francisco and Los Angeles and marks a divergence for Spicer away from the predominantly vatic tendencies of the period.[42] Spicer foregrounds the special effects of assemblage rather than a "special view of history." His lines create a curious blend of homily, grief, blasphemy, and critique. In a 1967 exhibition catalog, Peter Selz writes that when the elements of a funk assemblage are examined closely "they do not read in a traditional or recognizable manner and are open to a multiplicity of interpretations. Like the dialogue in a play by Ionesco or Beckett, the juxtaposition of unexpected things seems to make no apparent sense. Funk is visual double-talk, it makes fun of itself although often (though by no means all the time) it is dead serious" (3).

One aspect of Spicer's arrangement of his material is that, coming

42. California "junk" or "funk" art, sometimes called "neo-dada," was officially dubbed "assemblage" by the 1961 exhibition "The Art of Assemblage" at the Museum of Modern Art in New York. For most art viewers, including the national arts magazines, this constituted an introduction to little known West Coast artists like Jess Collins, Bruce Conner, and George Herms. But California assemblage had been thriving in L.A. for well over a decade; Simon Rodia worked essentially in isolation on the Watts Towers (1921–1954), and by the early fifties artists like Berman and Herms began to gather at small galleries like Syndell Studio and Ferus. In San Francisco, Jay De Feo and Wally Hedrick were practicing a similar aesthetic, and Hedrick and Spicer were two of the original "Six" of the Six Gallery, a poetry and assemblage-oriented gallery, which opened in September 1954 as an extension of a class Spicer had been teaching at the San Francisco Art Institute. By the late fifties Bruce Conner had made his way to San Francisco via Kansas, Colorado, and New York; and Berman and Herms had moved up the coast to join the Bay Area scene.

Like Berman, Herms, and Conner, Spicer had roots in Dada, and the mix of poetry and art at the Six Gallery created an environment of experimentation and genre-bending similar to that of the Dadaists. As evidenced in his early "Unvert Manifesto," Dada was an important component of Spicer's poetic ground, and it becomes used as an assembled texture in *After Lorca, Heads of the Town*, and *The Holy Grail*. In fact, a number of Spicer's books, especially *Language* and *Book of Magazine Verse* are in themselves art objects. In the manner of Duchamp, they are copies of other "original" documents (*Language* journal and *Poetry* magazine); they announce themselves as not merely functional objects but as sculptural assemblages in themselves.

In spite of the almost immediate shift in national attention to pop art in the early 1960s, California assemblage continued to find an audience out west, where it became more commonly known as "funk"—a term taken from hot jazz—perhaps to distinguish itself from the more visible east-coast junk artists like John Chamberlain whose car-crash assemblages appeared in the pages of *Life* magazine. As an assemblage term, "funk" has been attributed to Wallace Berman, who loved jazz and who, like Spicer, was particularly influenced and impressed by Charlie Parker (Hopkins, 15–16; Solnit, 5, 47–49; Kane, 63).

through from multiple sources, its structure is basically dramatic (dynamic). From his early days at Berkeley, Spicer, like Duncan, was interested in drama. Spicer wrote a dramatization of *Young Goodman Brown*, *Pentheus Among the Dancers*, and a version of *Troilus*. As the recordings of his public readings show, he's interested in voicings, in the dramatic potential of voices, rather than in a unified personal voice; he also introduces repetition and interruption through the use of a chorus.[43] In an early letter he discusses the importance of stress patterns in reading, and he even claims in Lecture 4 that parts of his poems need to be sung in order to be understood (*Acts*, 18–19; IV, 169). This performative element connects him with the dramatic qualities of Browning, Pound, and Eliot, who appear as part of the ghostly backdrop of his poems. He even writes to Pound at St. Elizabeth's specifically to ask how much Pound owed his sense of the dramatic to Browning.[44]

Spicer's quoting, misquoting, copying, and translating of the work of fellow poets sustain these dramatic qualities. Not only does he echo Pound's address to Browning in the "damn it all, Robert Duncan" passage in the original draft of *Lament for the Makers*, but with a dadaist gesture, he further dramatizes the publication with scandal by replacing his own acknowledgments with an exact copy of the acknowledgments page of Duncan's *Opening of the Field*.

Textual Mirroring

> Mirror makers know the secret—one does not make a mirror to resemble a person, one brings a person to the mirror.
> —JACK SPICER, *Admonitions*

Mirroring is the most pervasive device of Spicer's poetic practice, from the early poems of *One Night Stand* to the last line of his last poem. The mirroring properties of "The Song of the Bird in the Loins," with its reiterated stanza, heighten the drama of composition, as does the terrifying

43. See *The Exact Change Yearbook #1* for a recording of Spicer's lively reading of his "Imaginary Elegies" in 1957.

44. He ends his irreverently breezy letter from Berkeley: "All this reportage can be paid for by the answering of one question seriously. What relation does Browning (the poet not the perversion) have to your Cantos? In your critical works (or those I can get hold of) there is almost nothing to indicate that Browning meant more to you at any time than, say Francis Thompson. The Sordello business in the Cantos and the earlier version of same, however, indicate what I suspect—that the inner dramatic of Browning's later work—those long arguments that he monologs against dead influences (people, that is)—was the primary source of the infinitely better dramatic method of the Cantos. Am I crazy?"

amplification and reversal of "The Scrollwork on the Casket" in which the hammering on one side of a casket is echoed with a hammering on the other side. This mirroring enacts a play—a drama—between materiality and invisibility, the lines and what's between them. Reversal is all that distinguishes a reflected image from a "real" one, and Spicer's dedications further complicate this mirroring, as for instance the "Ode for Walt Whitman" reflects Whitman through Lorca to Stephen Jonas, and the poem becomes almost funhouse-like in its structure as it enacts the shared experience of a dark game of reversals. Mirroring is the central trope of *After Lorca*, and *Admonitions* is a book whose declared aim is mirror-making (A, 55). In both books, each poem is a mirror or "translation" meant to implicate, capture, or seduce a particular reader. As Spicer writes in Lorca's fake introduction to the book, the poems mimic or mirror Lorca's early style, so the mirror is already double. "Homage to Creeley" contains a number of repeated lines, one poem that is repeated in its entirety, as well as a double text which provides contradictory and provocative "explanatory notes" on the text above it. Spicer's last book, the *Book of Magazine Verse*, contains both a repeated poem ("Pieces of the past arising out of the rubble . . ." [BMV, 247, 248]) and repeated lines ("People are starving" [BMV, 256, 267]).

Spicer's mirroring of other texts occurs as a narrative gesture throughout his books and is not limited to a process of mere repetition. The distancing, reversals, and intimacy of mirrors inform many of his most significant letters, provide much of his "critical" vocabulary, and reiterate his view of poetry as a tradition based in copying. Spicer writes from his reading as a way of engaging in discourse with what is otherwise isolated, keeping poetry in play by simultaneously borrowing, copying, critiquing, and adoring the living, the dead, peers, and legends. This process is evident in his bending of terms like "correspondence" from Baudelaire and his reversal of sentiments like "a map is not the territory" from Alfred Korzybski's *Science and Sanity: an Introduction to Non-Aristotelian Systems and General Semantics*. On a larger scale, it informs the naming of each of Spicer's books: *After Lorca* borrows from Creeley; *Admonitions* echoes a letter to Spicer from Olson; *A Book of Music* is a variation on a theme by Poe; *Fifteen False Propositions Against God* refers to Pound; *Red Wheelbarrow* mirrors Williams; *Lament for the Makers* reflects William Dunbar, and the major poem of that book borrows from Matthew Arnold's "Dover Beach"; "Homage to Creeley" reflects Creeley and Cocteau; "The Fake Novel" mirrors Rimbaud; *The Holy Grail* and *Billy the Kid* mirror popular legend; and his last two books mimic covers of the journals *Language* (in which his only professional publication in linguistics appeared) and *Poetry*, just to list a few. To further complicate the process, none of these books presents a unified image or reading of any of the texts they mirror; instead, they are faceted, difficult, diamond-like, refracting each text against many others, activating them within a larger poetic tradition, recontextualizing them all within a Spicerian funhouse.

When Spicer invokes, quotes, or critiques other poets within his work it is because he sees them as worthy opponents—since, as he quotes Olson in Lecture 1, poetry is "what we have to do": a task and a necessity. Part of the absurd labor of poets is to parry with each other as well as with the invisible power structures of the "enemy," which Spicer defines as anything that gets in the way of making poems, including other poets (IV, 153). So Percival's plea for a worthy sparring partner in *The Holy Grail* ("If someone doesn't fight me I'll have to wear this armor all my life") sounds curiously like the Spicer who in his lectures repeatedly asks for verbal battle ("Won't somebody argue with me?") (HG, 192; II, 76). The act requires stamina, as the poem goes on to say with formality and exhaustion: "I am, sir, a knight."

Spicer's use and explanation of mirrors is extensive and contradictory. Within his work at least two kinds of mirrors appear, or each mirror performs one of two functions, depending upon who is looking into it. The orphic mirror is a literal passage between life and underworld or real and imaginary. But for Spicer, mirrors are not purely transportive; they also reflect, deflect, cover, hide, and baffle. In the "Explanatory Notes" of "Homage to Creeley," a poem in which Orpheus and Eurydice appear and disappear, Spicer writes with a mixture of nostalgia and punk: "Alice's mirror no longer reflects storybook knights. They reflect the Thirty Years wars and the automobiles people rode in during them." This shift from Alice's mirror to the knights as mirrors ("they" reflect the Thirty Years wars) amplifies and distorts what at first appears to be a single reflection. As the poem goes on to say, "Cocteau invented mirrors as things to move through. I invent mirrors as obstacles" (HC, 126). And in "Apollo Sends Seven Nursery Rhymes to James Alexander," Spicer claims for himself the regeneration and terrible repetition of mirrors: "I died again and was reborn last night / That is the way with we mirror people / Forgive me, I am a child of the mirror and not a child of the door" (ASSNR, 98). The lines proclaim and enact Spicer's sleight-of-hand by which things appear and disappear within his poems. At the same time these lines may also be a response to Creeley's poem for Duncan, entitled "The Door," which celebrates the notion of "the Lady" as muse.

A poem that is a mirror is both a seduction and a warning to its reader, a kind of admonition; the reflective, two-dimensional mirrors of *Admonitions* are meant to reveal the reader to whom each poem is dedicated by drawing each one into the poem in the same way that Narcissus is drawn into his pool. Any poem that contains a quotation or reflection of someone functions in this way for that individual; readers are purposefully drawn in by the echoes or reflections they recognize. Ideally this mirroring attracts the poem's most serious readers, those poets who share the poem's textual references and whose lines or syntactical gestures have been quoted, sampled, or transposed.

In this way, Marianne Moore (who would later write about the Eliotic qualities of Spicer's "Imaginary Elegies" in her review of Donald Allen's anthology *The New American Poetry*) becomes both a sampled voice and a mirrored reader throughout *After Lorca*, in which her poem "Poetry" is reflected and fragmented. Spicer's letter to Lorca about wanting the real to appear in the poem—"Live moons, live lemons, live boys in bathing suits" (AL, 34)—echoes Moore's sense of poetry as a "place for the genuine. Hands that can grasp, eyes that can dilate, hair that can rise, if it must" (40). As if insisting that his poems fulfill Moore's famous demand that poems provide "imaginary gardens with real toads in them" (I, 31; Moore, 41), Spicer breaks the mirroring surface separating life and art with a turbulence repeatedly declared by the intrusion of frogs and splashes within the mirroring surface of a pool, particularly in "Narcissus": "How wide awake the frogs are. They won't stay out of the surface in which my madness and your madness mirrors itself" (AL, 35). The transformational figure of the frog (transposed from "toad") creates a continuity between the work of different poets, a trace of the act of transposition itself. The poem ends with "My sorrow / Self of my sorrow," which is echoed again in the book's final poem dedicated to Moore, "Radar": "I crawled into bed with sorrow that night / Couldn't touch his fingers. See the splash / Of the water" (AL, 52). Spicer's affinity with Moore is both structural and tonal. Both poets assemble poems from textual fragments, and, like Spicer, Moore writes with precision and patience about love and its disappointments, and about the solitary nature of being a recorder of human relations.

Robert Creeley is the only poet to whom Spicer pays the dubious honor of writing an "Homage," a serial poem full of intertextual dialogue, echoes of Creeley, or reflections that correspond with Creeley's own echoes. Spicer gets a particular Creeley. He identifies with his darkness, reflexivity, bitter wit, the fatigue of the voice, and the acedia within its repetitions and reflections, the way "hello" can register anything from surprise to friendship to a call for help echoing within a "well of sound." In "Homage to Creeley," Spicer responds poetically to Creeley's music, his use of the everyday, his humor and self-mockery in the midst of paranoia (see Creeley's "The Dishonest Mailmen"), and his sense of poetic transmission in a poem like "Heroes."

But the title is also a false lead, using Creeley in the way *After Lorca* uses Lorca, as a kind of scarecrow. Even in the most minute ways, Spicer folds into his homage a poem that appears to be a transposition of a poet whose influence they share: Pound's "In a Station of the Metro." For Pound's "apparition," Spicer replaces "ghosts"; for "petals on a wet black bough," we find "Wet shadows on a stick" (HC, 131). In the poem "Ferlinghetti" the musical crossing between bebop and beat has the compression of a joke shared between Creeley and Spicer: "Be bop de beep / They are all asleep / They're all asleep." Meanwhile the car—presumably Cocteau's orphic car *and* the car in Creeley's poem "I Know a Man," itself a parodic echo of the Beat image—careens through the poem's Explanatory Notes: "The car is still travelling. It runs through the kingdoms of the dead picking up millions of passengers" (HC, 133). The car's wild ride further deemphasizes the significance of individual poets to the processes of Poetry since, as a further joke, the promising young poet Cegeste is killed in a traffic accident within the first few minutes of *Orphée*.

Spicer's intertextual mirroring is also a way of engaging and distorting the dominant discursive modes of his time. In a society that survived economic depression only by means of a war economy, the mirroring between concept and commodity, between image and idea, became intensified and encoded within poetic practice. Mid-twentieth-century America was a time and place of particularly intense mirroring and portraiture; an early example is Wallace Stevens's "Man with a Blue Guitar," followed later by one of the most canonical poems of the New American Poets: Ashbery's "Self-Portrait in a Convex Mirror." With the advent of photojournalism—*Life* magazine and television—more than ever America was being reflected back to itself. Spicer explodes this snapshot mentality with the ultimate grafitti in the age of nuclear holocaust: the vaporization of a human body into a linguistic trope in "Graphemics":

> You flicker,
> If I move my finger through a candleflame, I know that there
>   is nothing there. But if I hold my finger there a few minutes
>   longer,
> It blisters.
> This is an act of will and the flame is is not really there for the
>   candle, I
> Am writing of my own will.
> Or does the flame cast shadows?
>   At Hiroshima, I hear, the shadows of the victims were as if
>   photographed into concrete building blocks.
> Or does it flicker? Or are we both candles and fingers?
> Or do they both point us to the grapheme on the concrete
>   wall—
> The space between it
> Where the shadow and the flame are one?

(L, 241)

As "words turn mysteriously against those who use them" bodies are turned again to language, turned to stone in the poem's flickering between the pronouns "you" and "I." The poem's gestural pointing toward the end becomes a horrific literalization of what a culture can do with its hands.

The End

With an expanding commodity culture in the 1950s and the rise of pop art in the early 1960s, aesthetic time became inhabited by advertising and commerce. Like the California funk artists, Spicer saw that commercialism was making its human subjects into objects and tabloid commodities: "The Beatles, devoid of form and color" or "Marilyn Monroe being attacked by a bottle of sleeping pills" (BMV, 261; HG, 210). He realized that literary history too could be collapsed into commodity culture, like Ginsberg caught in his role as "King of the May" (BMV, 267).[45] By blurring the frequencies of the sacred and profane, he was capable of showing the degraded space of sacred practice in terms of the commercial object, for instance in his conflation of technology and God. In this way, the space of the eternal has become toy—junk—something that can be abandoned. And once abandoned, such objects inhabit the slums that his linguistic architectures become through time (TP, 175).

The architecture of his poetics is immanent *and* antitranscendent,

45. In a review of Henry Miller for *Occident* magazine, reprinted in the Appendix, Spicer writes that criticism has become something of a futures market, in which the critic finds himself on the floor of the stock exchange, anxiously watching the ticker tape as he writes.

materialist *and* metaphysical. The assembled fragments themselves disrupt each other, like the lines in a cubist portrait, sufficiently abstracting the content so that they produce an overall effect of poetic composition, but not an effect of representation. This dynamic accounts in part for the incredible sadness and freedom of Spicer's work. It has cast off the "anxiety of influence," and it lives in "slums." The fact that "no one listens to poetry" gives the material of his compositions an abandoned and reconstructed quality not unlike the work of Wallace Berman, Bruce Conner, and George Herms. His poems imply a negative liberation of material; at the same time that they display no hope for the cultural status of the art in the present, Spicer insists that they act not as museum pieces but as time machines so that they can find those artists and poets who exist in the slums of their future.

Like Spicer's poems, Conner's films play with narrativity and sequence. In "A Movie," Conner collages narrative textures much as Spicer does, using pop movie build-up music while showing cowboys racing through the desert spliced with footage of bombs being dropped. The caption "THE END" is repeated throughout the film and becomes the film's subject and a formal device to disrupt the film's narrative surface, in the same way Spicer describes the "tip-tap of the branches in *Finnegans Wake*" or the use of obscenity in *Admonitions*: it creates a rhythm.[46] One might add that Spicer's and Conner's problematizing of the "end" may signal a postapocalyptic world; but rather than subscribing to the significance of the end and the ironizing power of a "post-" society, it deflates the narrative curve toward finality and presents instead a film loop of Western civilization's failure to end its own wars. In this way, the repeated last line of Spicer's last book, "People are starving," is a trace of history's own echo chamber (BMV, 267). To a certain extent this also parallels his theory of correspondence and tradition: "generations of different poets in different countries patiently telling the same story, writing the same poem" (AL, 15). Given the grim prospect of recording such repetitions, the acedia of the scribe seems a rational defense against business as usual. For Spicer the end appears as an inconclusive, bloody, and bureaucratic finale without any actual progress or ultimate achievement; even "death is not final. Only parking lots" (L, 221).

46. "In these poems the obscene (in word and concept) is not used, as is common, for the sake of intensity, but rather as a kind of rhythm as the tip-tap of the branches throughout the dream of *Finnegans Wake* or, to make the analogy even more mysterious to you, a cheering section at a particularly exciting football game. It is precisely because the obscenity is unnecessary that I use it, as I could have used any disturbance, as I could have used anything (remember the beat in jazz) which is regular and beside the point" (A, 55).

Seeing Spicer as an assemblage artist further clarifies his program of dictation as composition. Within his constructivist aesthetic, to insist on originality or newness in a poem is as absurd as to insist that every object in an assemblage be made from scratch by the artist. Assemblage offers a way to understand Spicer's insistence on poetic renovation, since assemblage itself represents an ultimate posthumous life of objects, a place both within and outside the dominant culture. It is a vehicle for the return of whatever the culture has excluded or lost, a way for the past to continually haunt the present. One might argue that the absence of salvation in Spicer's poetry makes room for a kind of salvage yard of lost songs and stories—like the fisherman who "has done what he can do to protect home and mother" (HG, 212). The terms are not only metaphorical but material. Like all material, "things decay, reason argues. Real things become garbage," and "as things decay they bring their equivalents into being" (AL, 34). So the conflated images of a "boy" and a "tree" in *After Lorca*, both "caught forever in the structure of words," are then darkly translated in *Language*, where the "real" redwoods of Jeffers's California end in "real" parking lots (AL, 34; L, 221).

In its use of familiar and cast-off material, an assemblage violates the boundary between life and art; it exists in both worlds. In this way the art object (the assembled poem) becomes a "new Eurydice" which the orphic reader must rescue from oblivion, as the circuit of the poet's orphic vocation is reversed and mirrored in the reading process. For both poet and reader, "stepping up to poetry demands hands" (HC, 121). In a postindustrial society, poetic assemblage represents the ultimate in recycling, by turning the detritus of culture—its literal garbage—into art. But from the perspective of the 1990s, when books are becoming more and more virtual and poetry more and more marginal, what gets salvaged in the process is often significant: histories that have been cast off, failed kingdoms, lost vistas, magical worlds no longer believed in, and works of literature no longer read—the "imaginary gardens" of poetry itself.

Uncollected Prose and A Final Interview

MILLER: REMEMBER TO REMEMBER

from *Occident Magazine*, Fall 1947

It is slightly embarrassing to review Henry Miller. He has recently ceased to be an important force of emancipation to young writers and he is suffi-ciently alive not to have yet become a prerequisite on the reading list of sophomore English classes. This is the bear-market that comes at some time to the reputation of every important experimental writer of recent years and a reviewer, not sitting very high off the floor of the exchange finds himself casting down worried glances at the tape and hoping fer-vently that he is ahead of the trends of the trading. Criticism cannot be honestly written under such circumstances. (The reader should keep this pious apology in mind during the ensuing four hundred words.)

One assumes that the reader of this review will have read at least one of Henry Miller's three works of prose fiction. In these Miller has taken the novel of sentimental pornography (previously a sub-literary form) and has made it a vehicle of serious fiction. *Black Spring*, the best of these, is prob-ably the best work of prose written by an American in the last ten years. (The reviewer, shivering, glances down again to the floor of the stock-market.) Since the war started Miller has been far less successful. He has been writing violently occasional (almost momentary) prose of the type that D. H. Lawrence made familiar to us, articles about anything which are written on the unusual theory that everything that a good novelist thinks about everything is of great interest to everybody. New Directions has just issued another collection of such articles (*Remember to Remember*, New Directions, $3.75) and the public that is still legally unable to buy the books that brought Miller his reputation will have a chance to buy this book and to wonder again why on earth Miller is known throughout most of Europe as the greatest living American writer.

Approximately one-half of the book consists of Miller's art criticism. (What an unhappy day it was when someone convinced Lawrence that he could paint! The avant-garde has not yet recovered from the effects of that fatal bit of malice!) Miller's pattern of art criticism is inflexible. The title of the essay is always something like, "The Cosmic Effulgency of Ephriz Tdreck," or, as an alternative, "Looking Through Buddha's Navel with Graatian W. Follicle." The body of the article will tell how Mr. Tdreck or Mr. Follicle are men of great ("almost mystic") genius, how well they are able to boil abalones in great dinners on the beach ("with the finesse of a St. Francis or a Lao Tse") and reveals just a few choice selections of their metaphysics (combined at times with vague suggestions that their potency is more than human). The article generally concludes with a disturbing warning to the reader that "all saints are not in monasteries."

The balance of the book is far better stuff. There is an excellent short-story, "The Astrological Fricassee" which reminds us (if we had ever forgotten it after reading *The Tropic of Capricorn*) that Miller can be uproariously humorous—and intentionally, too. The book also reprints the long pamphlet, "Murder the Murderer," which was a courageous and clear anti-war document published at a time when most American writers were passive or active collaborators with a brutal war. But whatever the humor or the moral force (or the combination of the two in the essay on bread), the contents of this volume are essentially occasional and looked far better and less pretentious in the magazines and pamphlets in which they first appeared. To reprint them between stiff covers is presumptuous.

None of this, of course, is pertinent to any discussion of Miller's importance as a writer. I simply would like to protest the attitude which causes the occasional writings of a good writer to be collected in a volume and to be hawked down the streets like Mohammed's bath-water. Take out again your old paper covered Capricorn, reread it, and leave this book to Miller's dismal friends and his equally dismal enemies.

Jack Spicer

THE POET AND POETRY—A SYMPOSIUM
from *Occident Magazine*, Fall 1949

The opinions of several poets as to the most interesting problems in writing poetry. In-
cluded in this symposium are: Robert Duncan, William Everson, Rosalie Moore, Jack
Spicer, Leonard Wolf.

Jack Spicer:

Here we are, holding a ghostly symposium—five poets holding forth on
their peculiar problems. One will say magic; one will say God; one will
say form. When my turn comes I can only ask an embarrassing question—"Why is nobody here? Who is listening to us?"

Most of us are rather good poets. If we were actors or singers or car-
toonists of the same relative talent, a sizable percentage of the students of
this University would recognize our names and be familiar with our work.
As it now stands, I doubt if there is a reader of this magazine (including
the editorial staff and the pacts themselves) who is familiar with the work
of all five poets. Yet, I repeat, there is not one of us that has not been recognized as a good poet by critics, magazines, or publishers.

The usual answer to this complaint, given, to use a home-grown example, in the letter column of the *Daily Californian* every time a new issue
of *Occident* comes out, is so much hog-wash: "Modern poetry does not
make sense," the letter-writer will passionately exclaim, "Nobody reads it
because nobody understands it."

That is just not true. If a lack of intelligibility makes a work unpopular
with the public, why is it that there is always at least one song with nonsense lyrics near the top of the Hit Parade? "Chickery Chick" was far less
capable of prose analysis than *Finnegans Wake* and no one can claim that
its bare, monotonous tune was responsible for its popular favor.

As a matter of fact recently some of the same people that condemn
modern poetry as unintelligible express (weirdly enough) admiration for
Edith Sitwell and Gertrude Stein. The phonograph records of "Façade"
and "Four Saints In Three Acts" have made two writers (who are hardly
paragons of intelligibility) perfectly acceptable to a large audience. What

this audience has found is not the intelligibility that it had modestly asked for, but that greater boon that it did not dare to ask — entertainment.

The truth is that pure poetry bores everybody. It is even a bore to the poet. The only real contribution of the New Critics is that they have demonstrated this so well. They have taken poetry (already removed from its main source of interest — the human voice) and have completed the job of denuding it of any remaining connection with person, place and time. What is left is proudly exhibited in their essays — the dull horror of naked, pure poetry.

Live poetry is a kind of singing. It differs from prose, as song does, in its complexity of stress and intonation. Poetry demands a human voice to sing it and demands an audience to hear it. Without these it is naked, pure, and incomplete — a bore.

If plays were only printed and never acted, who would read them? If songs were only printed on song sheets, who would read them? It would be like playing a football game on paper. Do you wonder where the audience is?

It affects the nature of the poetry too. There was a time in the middle ages when music was mainly written and not sung. It was a time when crab canons were composed, complicated puzzles made of notes that no ear would think of hearing. Poetry, when it is removed from a living audience, loses its living form, becomes puzzling. It becomes blind like the salamanders that live in dark caves. It atrophies.

Orpheus was a singer. The proudest boast made about Orpheus was not that his poems were beautiful in and of themselves. There were no New Critics then. The proudest boast was that he, the singer with the songs, moved impossible audiences — trees, wild animals, the king of hell himself.

Today we are not singers. We would rather publish poetry in a little magazine than read it in a large hall. If we do read in a hall, we do not take the most elementary steps to make our poetry vivid and entertaining. We are not singers. We do not use our bodies. We *recite* from a printed page.

Thirty years ago Vachel Lindsay saw that poetry must connect itself to vaudeville if it was to regain its voice. (Shakespeare, Webster, and Marlowe had discovered this three centuries before him.) Our problem today is to make this connection, to regain our voices.

We must become singers, become entertainers. We must stop sitting on the pot of culture. There is more of Orpheus in Sophie Tucker than in R. P. Blackmur; we have more to learn from George M. Cohan than from John Crowe Ransom.

Jack Spicer

THE POEMS OF EMILY DICKINSON
from the *Boston Public Library Quarterly*, vol. 8, 1956

One of the most important publications in the field of American literature in recent years has been the handsome, three-volume edition of *The
Poems of Emily Dickinson*, edited by Thomas H. Johnson and issued by
the Belknap Press of Harvard University Press. Critics have agreed that
this long-awaited *variorum* has equaled, indeed surpassed, all expectations. The Boston Public which, as a gift from Thomas Wentworth Higginson, owns the manuscript of one version or another of some eighty of
the poems, is especially pleased with the acclaim. One wishes the work a
success similar to that of the thin green volume in which Emily Dickinson's poetry was first offered to a presumably hostile world by Mabel
Loomis Todd and Colonel Higginson. The Library has Higginson's own
copy in which he noted on the inside cover: ". . . it sold 10,000 copies
without especial effort, to the utter amazement of the editors, who would
gladly have accepted a guarantee of 400!"

Perhaps for no other modern poet would a *variorum* edition be so necessary. Early or rejected versions of printed poems are usually of interest
only to the specialized scholar; however, since Emily Dickinson had only
seven of her poems published in her lifetime—and even these were al-
tered by timid or careless editors—the printed text cannot be used as a test
of her wishes. It is difficult to tell which of the existing versions is the earlier, and it is usually impossible to decide which version, if any, she rejected. One is confronted with a number of forms of the same poem—fair
copies, draft copies, work copies, and even copies written as prose in the
bodies of letters. They differ from each other in varying degrees, and often
it is apparent that the poet had never made up her mind as to which version she preferred. The reader has to choose for himself. With the aid of
the present edition this is, for the first time, possible.

No edition can be perfect. Just as the new edition has had to take advantage of the efforts of earlier Dickinson students, so the work of many
others will be needed to correct its minor inexactitudes and omissions. The
excellent use which the editor has made of the Higginson manuscripts in

this edition is an incentive for a first attempt at such a contribution — solely from the examination of these manuscripts.

One of the most difficult problems of the editor has been the separation of prose from poetry. This may come as a surprise to some readers. The only surviving prose Emily Dickinson wrote occurs in her letters, and, in their published form, the poetry in them is always neatly set off from the prose. In her manuscripts, however, things are not so simple. She would often spread out her poetry on the page as if it were prose and even, at times, indent her prose as poetry. Mrs. Todd, who intended her collection of *Letters*[1] to be a popular edition, could not have been expected to reproduce this orthographic chaos. She was obliged to decide for herself what lines Emily regarded as poetry and what lines she did not.

On the whole, Mrs. Todd did very well in her selection. Some lines which she printed as prose occur as poetry in other places, and some lines she printed as poetry were almost certainly meant to be prose; but the general reader could ignore these small blemishes. In a *variorum* edition the task is more exacting. Assuming that what Emily meant as poetry must be taken out of her letters, how does one go about it? Should one only print variants of lines which she has used somewhere else in her poems? Should one set up a standard for indentation, rhyme, or meter? Or should one merely do again what Mrs. Todd tried to do and divide the poetry from the prose by guessing the poet's intentions? Mr. Johnson seems to have chosen this last solution.[2] But there is an added difficulty. When the *Letters* prints something as a poem which is not one, the reader can disregard it; or if the prose suddenly begins to rhyme, he can do his own indenting. In the new edition he has to depend on the editor's notes, which rarely contain the rest of the letter.[3]

An example is the letter to Colonel Higginson in which the poems numbered 1648 and 1647 appear in that order. The note to 1648 states: "Preceding the quatrain, and introducing it, in both drafts is the sentence, 'There is no Trumpet like the Tomb.'"[4] However, in the letter, following

1. *Letters of Emily Dickinson* (New York, 1931).

2. In his note to poem 1637 Mr. Johnson writes: "It is impossible in such a *jeu d'esprit* to be sure where the prose leaves off and the poetry begins, a situation that in many instances ED seems to have intended." True, yet not all the eighty-six poems which are known solely from their occurrence in letters are of that nature.

3. Among the poems for which key prose passages are not included in the notes are 1600, 1602, 1390, 1294, and 1259. One of the poems, 1390, is not a complete sentence in the letter; yet the remainder, "is Sunset's perhaps only," is omitted from the notes, and there is no mention that the sentence is incomplete.

4. The other draft referred to is the first trial draft of this letter. It was published in *Letters*,

and not preceding the quatrain, the lines read, "The sweet Acclamation of Death divulges it. There is no Trumpet like the Tomb." After that, without a break in form or sense, comes what the edition prints as 1647. In other words, what had been a single unit for the poet has been split into two poems, plus one line in the notes and one line omitted.

There are also problems of inclusion. Two-lined unrhymed sentences like 684 and 685 have little excuse for being presented as poems, although they were so printed in the *Letters*. Even more, 1161 is indistinguishable in indentation and capitalization from the other lines of the letter; but while

> Truth adjusts her "Peradventure"—
> Phantoms entered "and not you."

is offered as if it were a complete poem, the succeeding lines, printed here as they occur in a letter to Higginson, are not included in the new edition:

> How luscious is the dripping of February eaves!
> It makes our thinking pink—
> It antedates the Robin—
> Bereaving in prospective
> that February leaves—[5]

Not much of a poem, perhaps, when taken out of its context, but more so than many included under similar conditions.

The existence of other copies indented as poetry in the cases of 1069, 1208, and 1399 has necessitated the inclusion of passages which Mrs. Todd had printed as prose. One may mention that, in his notes to 1399, the main text of which derives from a worksheet draft, the editor prints the version included in the letter to Higginson as poetry, although Emily had actually indented and capitalized it as prose.

The new edition excludes the following passage from a letter to Higginson:

> Would you with the Bee return,
> what a Firm of Noon!
> Death obtains the Rose, but
> the news of Dying goes
> no further than the Breeze.[6]

Mrs. Todd had printed this as a poem in the *Letters*, starting the fourth line with "but" and adding capitals at the beginning of this, the second, and the fifth line. Except for these changes, one must agree with her.

---

p. 391. In reproducing the draft Mrs. Todd prints "There is no trumpet like a tomb" as part of the poem, although on p. 321 she prints the finished letter with the line as prose.

    5. *Letters*, pp. 297–298; transcribed here from the letter.

    6. *Letters*, p. 306.

The reason for the difficulty of drawing a line between the poetry and prose in Emily Dickinson's letters may be that she did not wish such a line to be drawn. If large portions of her correspondence are considered not as mere letters—and, indeed, they seldom communicate information, or have much to do with the person to whom they were written—but as experiments in a heightened prose combined with poetry, a new approach to both her letters and her poetry opens up. The new edition of her letters which Mr. Johnson promises for the future may provide evidence on this point.

A sizable number of the surviving poems—133 of those included in the new edition—have no known autograph copy, and derive from transcripts or a later printed source. Often as well different versions of a poem have been copied out from manuscripts that no longer exist. One of the merits of the new edition is that it prints all of these. However, several versions which occur among the Library's Higginson Manuscripts seem to have been overlooked. Thus a letter from Mrs. Todd to Colonel Higginson written during the time they were editing the second series of the poems, contained two versions of poem 228 and one of these differs from anything printed by Mr. Johnson. The other is probably a copy of the version referred to in Millicent Todd Bingham's *Ancestors' Brocades* (New York, 1945), p. 140, from which it was copied in the notes of the new edition. However, it varies in punctuation in four places from the manuscript in the Library.

Another transcript of interest, which may be the one which the new edition refers to as "lost" is a version of poem 824, probably in Mrs. Todd's handwriting. It varies from all the other versions printed by Mr. Johnson (including the one published in *Poems Second Series* that it may be the lost copy of) in punctuation, capitalization, and in that "livid Claw" of line 12 is rendered "Vivid Claw."

The note to poem 409 maintains:

The transcript, made by Mrs. Todd, from which the published version derives, is among the T. W. Higginson papers at BPL. It is an accurate script, but penciled editing in the handwriting of Higginson regularized the first stanza into a quatrain by combining lines 1 and 2, and effects a rhyme for lines 6 and 8 by altering the word order of the last two lines to read;

> But God on his repealless list
> Can summon every face.

The text is so printed.

The nearest thing among the Higginson Manuscripts to what this note describes is a manuscript in Mrs. Todd's handwriting, which, however, has no editing on it and varies in punctuation and capitals from the text in the new edition. No other transcript of poem 409 exists among the papers, and there are no lacunae in this part of their numbering to suggest that there might have been one.

Several other letters from Mrs. Todd to Colonel Higginson contain information which might have been included in the notes. For example, in a letter of July 22, 1891 (printed in *Ancestors' Brocades*, pp. 143–144) discussing poem 389, Mrs. Todd affirmed: ". . . the dog's belated feet *'were'* like intermittent *plush* — she wrote the word unmistakably, every letter distinct and separate."

Emily Dickinson's punctuation is difficult to follow. As Mr. Johnson writes, "Her use of the dash is especially capricious. Often it substitutes for a period and may in fact have been a hasty, lengthened dot intended for one. On occasion her dashes and commas are indistinguishable."[7] However, in the Library's manuscripts the pattern is fairly consistent. Her dashes slant downward to the right; her periods, even if lengthened, do not slant; her commas slant downward to the left. Her use of the dash certainly seems over-frequent, even for an age when writers tended to employ a great many dashes. But she usually used them as a sign of stress and tempo stronger than a comma and weaker than a period. There seem to be variations in the reproduction of the punctuation of the manuscripts of seventeen poems belonging to the Library[8] — although none of the differences change the meaning.

In the case of only three poems are there variations between the manuscripts and the printed text in matters of capitalization.[9] This is an excellent record, for, as Mr. Johnson points out, a number of Emily Dickinson's capitals can only be distinguished from their lower-case counterparts by their size. In spelling only two minor differences occur: poem 319 has "teazes" in the manuscript instead of "teases"; and 1487, "Fellow men" instead of "Fellowmen."

In what may have been the haste of inspiration, Emily Dickinson would often divide her lines in erratic places. The new edition is laudably conservative in correcting these slips, and usually it reports them. There are exceptions in five cases,[10] where the change was introduced without notice. In only one does the omission seem to matter. In his note to poem 1209, Mr. Johnson states, "ED ran lines 17 and 18 together; they are here

7. *Poems*, I, p. lxiii.
8. Poems 1564, 322, 325, 321, 815, 1183, 1260, 1256, 1255, 1364, 1463, 1602, 409, 1138, 686, 1360 [Spicer only listed sixteen].
9. Poems 228, 409, and 1399.
10. Poems 1399, 86, 815, 1209, and 1210.

separated, as she probably intended them to be, with 'but' capitalized."
However, the edition has made the same change with lines 1 and 2 which
Emily Dickinson also "ran together" in the Library's manuscript! It seems
considerably less likely that the poet combined the opening lines of both
the first and last stanza without definite intention.

The new edition makes excellent use of supplementary evidence in its
notes. Envelopes have been carefully examined for signs of date; the floral
gifts that Emily often sent with poems have been when possible, reported.
It might be mentioned, however, that three of the latter—a flower, a leaf,
and a rose for poems 86, 1257, and 1364 respectively—are still preserved
among the Higginson Manuscripts, although their existence is merely
speculated upon in the notes.

Finally, an addition should be made to the note to poem 986 and, for
that matter, to the bibliography of Emily Dickinson. Mr. Johnson rightly
conjectures that Emily had "evidently enclosed a clipping" of the poem
"from the *Republican*," with a letter in which she complains of the punctuation of its third and fourth lines. This clipping still exists among the
Higginson papers. But it is not, as the note suggests, from the February 14,
1866 issue of the Springfield *Daily Republican*, but from the February 17,
1866 issue of the Springfield *Weekly Republican*, although the poem appeared in both papers. There are a number of differences in punctuation
between the two printings, and also one word-change—"but" to "yet" in
line 21. Lines 3 and 4, of which Emily wrote to Higginson: "defeated too of
the third line by the punctuation. The third and fourth were one—" reads

> You may have met him—did you not?
> His notice instant is,

instead of

> You may have met him—did you not,
> His notice instant is.

as it appeared in the *Daily Republican* and is cited in the notes. This
makes her complaint easier to understand.

The pleasures of the new edition are many. One may observe the poet
at work, mark all her revisions and hesitations, and even discover new
facts about her life. Best of all, it enables one to enjoy the whole of Emily
Dickinson's poetry in exactly the form she wrote it.

John L. Spicer

A CORRECTION

from the *Boston Public Library Quarterly*, vol. 9, 1957

I made an error in my review of Mr. Thomas H. Johnson's new edition of Emily Dickinson's poems in the July 1956 issue of the *Boston Public Library Quarterly*. The Library's transcript of poem 409, in the handwriting of Mabel Loomis Todd, does have editing on it, as Mr. Johnson stated in his note to the poem. Time has turned invisible the lightly penciled circles, except when seen in a strong light. Close inspection reveals all of the corrections that Mr. Johnson mentions—and, in addition, the encircling of the words "the place" in line seven. The latter mark, whatever its intention, was not followed in *Poems, Second Series*, nor was the punctuation of the transcript.

John L. Spicer

WIMPFELING'S ADOLESCENTIA, 1505
from the *Boston Public Library Quarterly*, vol. 9, 1957

The Library has recently acquired a copy of the first revised edition of Jacob Wimpfeling's *Adolescentia*, published by Johann Knoblauch at Strassburg in 1505. This handsome quarto consists of eighty-four numbered and four unnumbered leaves and is illustrated with three woodcuts, each three-quarters of a page in size.

The work was first published, also at Strassburg, five years earlier by Martin Flach, whose widow married Knoblauch who thus obtained a part of his press. The revisions and additions were made by Johann Gallanarius, a former student of Wimpfeling and a teacher of rhetoric in a church school of the city, which used the *Adolescentia* as a text-book. In the next ten years the book was reprinted seven times.

Jacob Wimpfeling (1450–1528) was, along with Sebastian Brant, mainly responsible for Strassburg's becoming, in the words of Erasmus, "a guild of muses and of graces" in the early sixteenth century. In few cities of Northern Europe did humanism reach such a complete flowering. According to one writer, nearly half of the books published at Strassburg between 1500 and 1520 dealt with the "new learning," and Wimpfeling's were among the most famous of them. A violent controversialist, he was equally at home in an argument about "pagan poetry," the history of the Germans, or church matters. But he was primarily a teacher, and it is for his books on education that he is remembered today.

Adolescentia was written at Heidelberg in 1498 while the author was lecturing at the University there. It is a collection of extracts from both Christian and pagan writers, including Virgil, Horace, and even Ovid, arranged and edited to inculcate the principles of morality in the young. It was written for Wolfgang, son of Count Ludwig von Löwenstein, who however died in a fire before he could experience the benefits of its moral. Wimpfeling, a radical for his day, believed that good conduct could be taught from selected Roman and Greek writers as well as from Christian tracts, and proposed that a secular secondary school be set up at Strassburg to teach classical Latin to the young men of the city. His suggestion was rejected, and he had to content himself with the success of his text-book in the local cathedral school.

The woodcuts excellently fit the tone of the work. The first shows Death, represented as a skeleton armed with a sickle, standing in a grave-yard; the second depicts a young nobleman on promenade with his dog; and the third represents a young man, perhaps the same one, on his death-bed comforted by his family and two monks. These illustrations, all on the last few leaves, have the air of being an afterthought.

The printer's mark of Knoblauch includes a griffin above an initialed shield. This is the first known example of his use of it.

John L. Spicer

THE LEGEND OF ST. MEINRAD, 1567

from the *Boston Public Library Quarterly*, vol. 9, 1957

Among the Library's recently-acquired books is a copy of *Sanct Meyn-rhats Läben* printed at Freiburg im Breisgau in 1567. It is a quarto of forty leaves illustrated with thirty-two large woodcuts, each occupying two-thirds of a page. The edition is not listed by Brunet or mentioned by Hind or Muther. The first edition, with text in Latin, was published at Basel in 1496 by Michael Furter, who followed this with three editions in German before the turn of the century. However, parts of the book existed long before in manuscript, and from these a block-book was compiled, perhaps the first of its kind south of the Rhine.

Albrecht von Bonstellen, a Swiss humanist who lived for a time at Einsiedeln, the Benedictine monastery that was built around St. Meinrad's hermit's cell, has been called the author. However, the work is a collection of separate narratives of various dates and styles, dealing not only with the life of Meinrad but also with the history and miracles associated with his shrine. The edition of 1567 has, in addition, a long preface by Huldrich Wytwyler, who became later abbot of Einsiedeln.

Meinrad, Count of Sulgen, was born in 797 at his mother's castle of Sülich. As a child he entered the famous convent school of Reichenau, from where he wandered from cloister to cloister, seeking a spiritual home. Finally, as an *Einsiedler*, a hermit, he retired to a small hut on the Etzelberg built for him by a pious lady. His reputation for holiness was already great, and the hut was soon crowded with people asking him for advice or blessings. He finally moved into the wild forests of the Finsterwald, and made his cell where the chapel of the monastery of Einsiedeln now stands. Here he received from Hildegarde, abbess of the nearby Zurich convent, an image of the Virgin and Child.

Meinrad lived in his retreat for many years, with only the company of a pair of pet ravens. In 861 two thieves came to his hut; and he gave them food and drink. However, they demanded gold and, when Meinrad told them that he had none, murdered him. The ravens followed the thieves all the way into Zurich, screeching over their heads until they were apprehended. Here the legend presents a parallel to the classical story of the cranes which followed the robbers who had murdered the poet Ibycus, until they were brought to justice.

The book goes on to tell of the miracles wrought at Einsiedeln. Perhaps the greatest of these happened in 948 when the Bishop of Constance, about to consecrate the new chapel which enclosed Meinrad's hut and contained the image of the Virgin, was stopped by an angelic voice: "Leave off, brother. This church has already been consecrated by Heaven."

The woodcuts are picturesque. They detail the life of St. Meinrad, his murder and the punishment of the evildoers, and some of the later history of Einsiedeln. The ravens are not forgotten. They appear in seven of the woodcuts, hovering over the heads of the escaping thieves and attacking the Devil himself as he tries to tempt Meinrad. Several of the woodcuts, based on the block-book, are taken from Furter's first edition. The volume was intended for a popular audience, and it is likely that copies were sold at Einsiedeln, then as now one of the most frequented places of pilgrimage in Europe.

John L. Spicer

IMPRESSIONS FROM AN 'ESTRANGED' POET
from the *San Francisco Chronicle*, August 29, 1965

Jack Spicer, one of the most widely known North Beach poets, died at the age of 40 earlier this month. He died from multiple causes, one of which his friends described as "estrangement." The free-lance writer Tove Neville, who interviewed the poet shortly before his death, reports that this "estrangement" was not from individuals, for he kept in constant touch with others. "It was a deeply felt collective estrangement from a society that has sold out its real values."

When I tried to obtain interviews with some of the poets before the first Berkeley Poetry Conference in July, one asked why I wanted to do that, and recommended that I just come and attend. Another promised me the material, but was too busy. When I asked Jack Spicer, I suggested he choose a time it would be convenient for him, but he said, "We can do it right now; it's all right," and we did.

The strongest impressions of him in those first moments were, first, his kindness and gentleness, then, as he began to talk and answer questions, his brilliance of mind. My first thought was that here undoubtedly was the most intellectual of all the San Francisco poets, past or present. His answers were unique and original, well-considered, not off the top of his head, yet they came instantly to my questions. And when I read my interview back to him, he remembered everything he had said, verbatim. Such a man died at the age of 40, largely from despair.

His friends later testified to this, but you will realize it from his own words. Asked how it all happened in poetry in the San Francisco area—two revivals, first the San Francisco renaissance of which he was a part, and then the so-called Beat movement—he said:

"It is impossible to say what really happened in San Francisco (poetry), but it is like Alice In Wonderland. It gets curiouser and curiouser, is the key to how it happened. California is the other side of the rabbit hole. It is because we are so far away from the East Coast that the new American poetry is able to survive.

"What has happened to poetry is even the H-bomb and the Beatles records. It hurts because you are not able to take the sounds that these things make. A poet almost has to invent his own land and then has to defend it."

Coast Association

He called Robinson Jeffers a real California poet and added, as an aside, that during a time when you had to be a Stalinist to be a poet, Jeffers was anti-Stalin. However, "he had a rich wife and could afford it." He said Jeffers had the same association with the Pacific Coast, as a far shore of the continent and a treacherous sea coast, that the San Francisco poets have had. That association John Steinbeck had in his "Pastures of Heaven" and "In Dubious Battle"; and the early William Saroyan in his "Darling Young Man on a Flying Trapeze."

A Bierce Tradition

"This," he said, "represents a continued tradition from Ambrose Bierce, that the sea coast of California is so different from the rest of the U.S., (in climate, or economic or political interest) that it isn't really part of the rest of the U.S."

When I asked him what could be done about it, Spicer said he would like to see a Pacific British Commonwealth formed from the Tehachapi mountains near Bakersfield and all the way up to northern Canada and perhaps even Alaska. He would not include Los Angeles, although he was born in Southern California, as he said it did not belong to the rest of the seacoast in interest and natural environment.

Jack Spicer's concern for his native State was as genuine as it was devoted. He was extremely well-versed in its history, and vitally, almost desperately interested in its survival. He had received two degrees at the University of California, one in philosophy and one in English but his concern was mainly for the people of his State, from which sprang his keen interest in politics, and in the young, from where he saw the only hope for the future. He himself was one-eighth Blackfoot Indian and had seen what could happen to minority groups from within his own family.

His next remarks divulged his concern for his native State. "San Francisco needs trade with all countries, including Red China," he said. "You would find few Californians with money who would not want to admit

Red China to the U.N. Washington is so far back East that there is often
the feeling that the interest of the West is not considered back there, or in
New York."

Stream of Objections

He said his father had also had this feeling of remoteness from the East,
that China was as close as the East Coast. You could send goods either to
New York or to China. It seemed equally far away. However, he said:

"We were not estranged from everything until the railroad took over
California between 1870 and 1906. The Babbitts of this time don't like to
sell their redwoods—unless they get a hell of a price for it." I asked if they
do sell, and he said, "Yes, they sell and then they join the Sierra Club and
pay their dues."

He added, "You can't save anything, but you can defend it. It isn't
much good to have property in Marin county and have three sons killed
in Korea and Vietnam and then sell out to real estate. You can't keep a
ranch with no one to ranch it. It is demoralizing for poets to see what happens." All this came out as a steady stream of objections to what he saw
happening.

At last he reiterated, "I would like to be in a separate country; I would
like our logs and grain to be sent to people who need them."

As an end to our interview he added, "Nothing else I can say, but a
kookie vision."

                                                        Tove Neville

BIBLIOGRAPHY AND WORKS CITED
IN LECTURES, NOTES, AND AFTERWORD

By Jack Spicer

"Miller: Remember to Remember." Review. *Occident* (Fall 1947): 44–45.
"The Poet and Poetry: A Symposium." *Occident* (Fall 1949): 43–45.
Troilus. Unpublished play, 1955.
"Impressions from an 'Estranged' Poet." Interview with Tove Neville. *The San Francisco Chronicle,* 29 August 1965: 33.
"Letters to Graham Mackintosh." *Caterpillar* 12 (1970): 83–114.
"Letters to Jim Alexander." *Caterpillar* 12 (1970): 162–74.
"An Arcadia for Dick Brown." *An Ode and Arcadia.* Berkeley: Ark Press, 1974.
Collected Books of Jack Spicer. Edited and with commentary by Robin Blaser. Santa Rosa, Calif.: Black Sparrow Press, 1975.
One Night Stand & Other Poems. Edited by Donald Allen, with an introduction by Robert Duncan. San Francisco: Grey Fox Press, 1980.
"Letters to Allen Joyce." *Sulfur* 10 (1987): 140–53.
"Letters to Robert Duncan." *Acts* 6 (1987): 5–30.
"Letter to Harris Schiff." *o.blek* 10 (1991): 22.
"Imaginary Elegies." Sound recording. *Exact Change Yearbook* 1 (1995).
"Donne's Use of Mediaeval Geographical Lore." Unpublished essay.
Unpublished letters. Cited in text by name of recipient.

About Jack Spicer

Blaser, Robin. "The Practice of Outside." In *The Collected Books of Jack Spicer*, edited by Robin Blaser, 271–326. Santa Rosa, Calif.: Black Sparrow, 1975.
———. "My Vocabulary Did This To Me." *Acts* 6 (1987): 98–105.
Boone, Bruce. "Spicer's Writing in Context." *Ironwood* 14, no. 2 (1986): 202–5.
Conte, Joseph M. "The Dark House: Jack Spicer's Book of *Language*." In *Unending Design: The Forms of Postmodern Poetry*, 105–20. Ithaca: Cornell University Press, 1991.
Damon, Maria. "Dirty Jokes and Angels: Jack Spicer and Robert Duncan Writing Gay Community." In *The Dark End of the Street: Margins in American Vanguard Poetry*, 142–201. Minneapolis: University of Minnesota Press, 1993.
Davidson, Michael. "'The City Redefined': Community and Dialogue in Jack Spicer." In *The San Francisco Renaissance: Poetics and Community at Mid-Century*, 150–70. Cambridge: Cambridge University Press, 1989.

Ellingham, Lew, and Kevin Killian. *Poet Be Like God*. Middletown, Conn.: Wesleyan University Press, 1998.

Eshleman, Clayton. "The Lorca Working." *Boundary 2* 7, no. 1 (1977): 31–50.

Feld, Ross. "The Apostle's Grudge at the Persistence of Poetry." *Ironwood* 14, no. 2 (1986): 188–94.

Finkelstein, Norman. "Jack Spicer's Ghosts and the Gnosis of History." *Boundary 2* 9, no. 2 (1981): 81–99.

Foster, Edward. *Jack Spicer*. Boise: Boise State University Western Writers Series, 1991.

Granger, John. From "The Idea of the Alien in Four Dictated Books." *Ironwood* 14, no. 2 (1986): 165–86.

Halverson, John. Interview with author. Santa Cruz, Calif. June 1996.

Hatlen, Burton. "Crawling Into Bed with Sorrow: Jack Spicer's *After Lorca*." *Ironwood* 14, no. 2 (1986): 118–35.

Herndon, Jim. Letter about Spicer. In *The Collected Books of Jack Spicer*. Edited by Robin Blaser, 375–78. Santa Rosa, Calif.: Black Sparrow, 1975.

Judy, Stephanie A. "The Grand Concord of What." *Boundary 2* 7, no. 1 (1977): 267–85.

McGann, Jerome. "Composition as Explanation." In *Black Riders: The Visible Language of Moderism*, 76–118. Princeton: Princeton University Press, 1993.

Nichols, Miriam. "The Poetry of Hell: Jack Spicer, Robin Blaser, Robert Duncan." *Line* 12 (1988): 14–41.

Rasula, Jed. "Spicer's Orpheus and the Emancipation of Pronouns." *Boundary 2* 7, no. 1 (1977): 51–102.

Riley, Peter. "The Narratives of the *Holy Grail*." *Boundary 2* 7, no. 1 (1977): 163–90.

Silliman, Ron. "Spicer's Language." *The New Sentence*. New York: Roof, 1989. 147–66.

Sorrentino, Gilbert. "Jack Spicer." In *Something Said*, 49–67. San Francisco: North Point, 1984.

Additonal Works Cited in the Lectures, Notes, and Afterword

Alexander, James. *The Jack Rabbit Poem*. San Francisco: White Rabbit, 1966.

Allen, Donald M., and Warren Tallman. *The Poetics of the New American Poetry*. New York: Grove Press, 1973.

Apollinaire, Guillaume. *The Cubist Painters (1913)*. Translated by Lionel Abel. The Documents of Modern Art, edited by Robert Motherwell, no. 1. New York: Wittenborn, 1944.

Arnold, Jack, dir. *It Came From Outer Space*. Universal Studios. 1953.

Ashbery, John. *The Tennis Court Oath*. Middletown, Conn.: Wesleyan University Press, 1962.

———. "Frank O'Hara's Question." *Book Week* 4, no. 33 (1966): 6.

Auden, W. H. *The English Auden*. London: Faber, 1977.

Baum, L. Frank. *The Wizard of Oz*. 1899. Reprint. Edited by Michael Patrick Hearn. New York: Schocken Books, 1983.

Beckett, Samuel. *Company*. London: John Calder, 1980.

Bierce, Ambrose. *The Devil's Dictionary*. 1911. Reprint. Cleveland: World, 1941.

Blake, William. *The Complete Poetry & Prose of William Blake*. Edited by David V. Erdman. Rev. ed. Garden City, N.Y.: Anchor / Doubleday, 1982.

Blaser, Robin. *The Moth Poem*. San Francisco: Open Space, 1964.

———. *The Holy Forest*. Toronto: Coach House Press, 1993.

Borregaard, Ebbe. *Sketches for 13 Sonnets* [by Gerard Boar]. Berkeley: Oyez, 1969.

Breton, André. "The Automatic Message." Translated by Michael Palmer and Norma Cole. In *The Surrealists Look at Art*, edited by Pontus Hulten, 135–55. Venice, Calif.: Lapis, 1990.

Burns, Ken, dir. *Baseball: A Documentary History*. Turner/PBS, 1994.

Butler, E. M. *The Myth of the Magus*. Cambridge: Cambridge University Press / New York: Macmillan, 1948.

Carroll, Lewis. *The Complete Works of Lewis Carroll*. New York: Modern Library, 1936.

Churchill, Winston S. *Their Finest Hour*. Cambridge: The Riverside Press, 1949.

Conkin, Paul K. *The Southern Agrarians*. Knoxville: University of Tennessee Press, 1988.

Crane, Hart. *The Complete Poems and Selected Letters and Prose*. Garden City, N.Y.: Doubleday Anchor, 1966.

Creeley, Robert. "Letter to the Editor." *Contact* (Toronto), no. 6 (1953).

———. *For Love: Poems 1950–1960*. New York: Scribner's, 1962.

———. *A Quick Graph: Collected Notes and Essays*. Edited by Donald Allen. San Francisco: Four Seasons Foundation, 1970.

———. *Collected Poems 1945–1975*. Berkeley: University California Press, 1982.

Crepeau, Richard C. *Baseball: America's Diamond Mind 1919–1941*. Orlando: University of Florida Press, 1980.

Dark, Alvin, and John Underwood. *When In Doubt, Fire the Manager: My Life & Times in Baseball*. New York: Dutton, 1980.

Davey, Frank. Introduction to *Tish 1–19*. Vancouver: Talonbooks, 1975.

Dicken, E. W. Trueman. *The Crucible of Love: A Study of the Mysticism of St. Teresa of Jesus and St. John of the Cross*. New York: Sheed and Ward, 1963.

Dickens, Charles. *The Posthumous Papers of the Pickwick Club*. 1837. Reprint. New York: Modern Library, 1937.

Dickinson, Emily. *Letters*. 3 vols. Boston: Belknap Press, 1986.

Dong, Arthur, dir. *Coming Out Under Fire*. Zeitgeist Films. 1995.

Dunbar, William. *Poems*. Oxford: Clarendon, 1958.

Duncan, Robert. *The Opening of the Field*. New York: Grove Press, 1960.

———. *Roots and Branches*. New York: Scribner's, 1964.

———. *The First Decade: Selected Poems 1940–1950*. London: Fulcrum Press, 1968.

———. *Bending the Bow*. New York: New Directions, 1968.

———. *Fictive Certainties*. New York: New Directions, 1985.

Eliot, T. S. "Tradition and the Individual Talent." *Selected Essays 1917–1932*. New York: Harcourt Brace, 1932. 3–11.

Eustis, Helen. *The Fool Killer*. Garden City, N.Y.: Doubleday, 1954.

Faas, Ekbert. *Young Robert Duncan: Portrait of the Poet as Homosexual in Society*. Santa Barbara, Calif.: Black Sparrow, 1983.

Fitzgerald, F. Scott. *The Great Gatsby*. New York: Scribner's, 1925.

Frisch, Frank. *Frankie Frisch: The Fordham Flash*. Garden City, N.Y.: Doubleday, 1962.

Gardner, David P. *The California Oath Controversy*. Berkeley: University of California Press, 1967.

Gauld, Alan. *The Founders of Psychical Research*. New York: Schocken Books, 1968.

Giamatti, A. Bartlett. *Take Time for Paradise: Americans and Their Games*. New York: Summit, 1989.

Goines, David Lance. *The Free Speech Movement: Coming of Age in the 1960s*. Berkeley: Ten Speed Press, 1993.

Goodman, Paul. *The Society I Live in Is Mine*. New York: Horizon, 1962.

Goodman, Paul and Percival. *Communitas: Means of Livelihood and Ways of Life.* New York: Vintage, 1960.

Harper, George Mills, ed. *Yeats's Vision Papers.* 3 vols. London: Macmillan, 1992.

Holzel, Tom, and Audrey Salkeld. *First on Everest: The Mystery of Mallory and Irvine.* New York: Holt, 1986.

Hopkins, Gerard Manley. *The Correspondence of Gerard Manley Hopkins and Richard Watson Dixon.* Edited by C. C. Abbott. London: Oxford University Press, 1935.

Hopkins, Henry. "Recollecting the Beginnings." *Forty Years of California Assemblage.* Exhibition catalog. Los Angeles: Wight Art Gallery, UCLA, 1989. 15–16.

Industrial Workers of the World. *IWW Songs.* N.p.: IWW, n.d.

Jakobson, Roman. "Two Aspects of Language and Two Types of Aphasic Disturbances." *Language in Literature.* Cambridge: Harvard University Press, 1987.

Jeffers, Robinson. *The Collected Poetry of Robinson Jeffers.* 3 vols. Edited by Tim Hunt. Stanford: Stanford University Press, 1991.

Jonas, Hans. *The Gnostic Religion.* Boston: Beacon Press, 1963.

Joyce, James. *Finnegans Wake.* New York: Viking Press, 1945.

Kane, Art. "Art Crashes Through the Junk Pile." *Life,* 24 Nov. 1961: 63–66.

Kantorowicz, Ernst. *The Fundamental Issue.* San Francisco: Parker Printing Co., 1950.

Korzybski, Alfred. *Science and Sanity: An Introduction to Non-Aristotelian Systems and General Semantics.* Lakeville, Conn.: Institute of General Semantics, 1933.

Lear, Edward. *Nonsense Books.* 1843. Reprint. Boston: Little, Brown, 1888.

Levertov, Denise. *O Taste and See.* New York: New Directions, 1964.

Loewinsohn, Ron. *Meat Air: Poems 1957–1969.* New York: Harcourt, Brace, 1970.

Lorca, Federico Garcia. *Deep Song and Other Prose.* Edited and translated by Christopher Maurer. New York: New Directions, 1975.

Luxemburg, Rosa. "Either/Or." *Selected Political Writings.* Edited and introduced by Dick Howard. New York: Monthly Review Press, 1971.

Malory, Sir Thomas. *Morte d'Arthur.* Translated by Keith Baines, with an introduction by Robert Graves. New York: New American Library, 1962.

Mao Tse Tung. *The Poems of Mao Tse Tung.* Translated by Willis Barnstone. New York: Harper & Row, 1972.

McGann, Jerome. *A Critique of Modern Textual Criticism.* Charlottesville: University of Virginia Press, 1992.

Mencken, H. L. *The American Language.* 4th ed. New York: Knopf, 1936.

Miller, Michael V., and Susan Gilmore. *Revolution at Berkeley.* New York: Dial, 1965.

Moore, Marianne. *Collected Poems.* New York: Macmillan, 1951.

Motherwell, Robert, ed. *The Dadaist Painters and Poets: An Anthology.* New York: Wittenborn, 1951.

Nash, Ogden. *Verse from 1929 On.* London: Dent, 1961.

Olson, Charles. *Collected Prose.* Edited by Donald Allen and Benjamin Friedlander. Berkeley: University of California Press, 1997.

———. *The Special View of History.* Berkeley: Oyez, 1970.

Parkinson, Thomas. *W. B. Yeats: The Later Poetry.* Berkeley: University of California Press, 1964.

Pearce, Roy Harvey. *The Savages of America: A Study of the Indian and the Idea of Civilization.* Rev. ed. Baltimore, Md.: Johns Hopkins Press, 1965.

Peterson, Elmer. *Tristan Tzara: Dada and Surrational Theorist.* New Brunswick, N.J.: Rutgers University Press, 1971.

Poe, Edgar Allan. "Maelzel's Chess-Player." 1836. Reprint in *Essays and Reviews,* 1253–76. New York: Library of America, 1984.

Pope, Alexander. *Poetry and Prose of Alexander Pope*. Edited by Aubrey Williams. Boston: Houghton Mifflin, 1969.

Renshaw, Patrick. *The Wobblies: The Story of Syndicalism in the United States*. Garden City, N.Y.: Doubleday, 1967.

Rexroth, Kenneth. "The New American Poets." *Harper's* 230, no. 1381 (June 1965): 65–71.

Rhine, J. B. *New Frontiers of the Mind: The Story of the Duke Experiments*. New York: Farrar & Rinehart, 1937.

Rilke, Rainer Maria. *Duino Elegies*. Translated by J. B. Leishman and Stephen Spender. New York: Norton, 1939.

———. *Sonnets to Orpheus*. Translated by M. D. Herter Norton. New York: Norton, 1942.

Selz, Peter. *Funk*. Exhibition catalog. Berkeley: University Art Museum, University of California, Berkeley, 1967.

Sidney, Sir Philip. *The Countess of Pembroke's Arcadia (The Old Arcadia)*. Edited by Katherine Duncan-Jones. Oxford: Oxford University Press, 1985.

Skelton, John. *The Poetical Works of John Skelton*. 2 vols. London: Thomas Rodd, 1843.

Smith, Hester Travers. *Psychic Messages from Oscar Wilde*. London: Psychic Book Club, [1925].

Solnit, Rebecca. *Secret Exhibition: Six California Artists of the Cold War Era*. San Francisco: City Lights Books, 1990.

Spate, Virginia. *Orphism: The Evolution of Non-Figurative Painting in Paris 1910–1914*. Oxford: Clarendon, 1979.

Stein, Gertrude. "Poetry and Grammar." *Lectures in America*. 1935. Reprint, 209–46. Boston: Beacon Press, 1985.

Stevens, Wallace: *Collected Poems*. New York: Knopf, 1954.

Tallman, Warren. *In the Midst*. Vancouver: Talonbooks, 1992.

Tate, Allen. *Collected Poems 1919–1976*. New York: Farrar Straus Giroux, 1977.

Tedlock, Dennis. *The Spoken Word and the Work of Interpretation*. Philadelphia: University of Pennsylvania Press, 1983.

Valéry, Paul. *The Art of Poetry*. Vol. 7, *The Complete Works of Paul Valéry*. Princeton: Bollingen and Princeton University Press, 1958.

Vriesen, Gustav. *Robert Delaunay: Light and Color*. New York: Abrams, 1969.

Weston, Jessie L. *From Ritual to Romance*. Cambridge: Cambridge University Press, 1920.

———. *The Quest of the Holy Grail*. 1913. Reprint. New York: Haskell House, 1965.

Williams, William Carlos. *Paterson*. New York: New Directions, 1963.

Winn, Marie. *Fireside Book of Children's Songs*. New York: Simon & Schuster, 1966.

Yeats, W. B. *A Vision: A Reissue with the Author's Final Revisions*. New York: Macmillan, 1956.

———. *Collected Poems: Definitive Edition, with the Author's Final Revisions*. New York: Macmillan, 1956.

———. *Memoirs*. Edited by Denis Donoghue. New York: Macmillan, 1972.

INDEX

Lindblad, Paul, 118, 144n.11
Lindsay, Vachel, 230
"Linguistic Atlas of the Pacific Coast" (Spicer), 199
Literary magazines: *El Corneo Emplumado*, 142, 146n.28; *Floating Bear*, 170n.7, 207; *J* magazine, 82, 94n.36; *Poetry*, 98, 108, 157, 217n, 220; *Prism*, xxiii, 91n.2, 97, 102, 143n.1; Spicer's opinion of, 157, 170n.7. See also *Open Space*; *Tish*
Livesay, Dorothy: on baseball as an American game, 122, 123; on "The Book of Gwenivere," 60; on changing the order of serial poems, 70–71; on dream poems, 18; on Eurydice in "A Textbook of Poetry," 19–20; on expectations from the audience, 34; on Lorca's *duende* essay, 139; on the message in Spicer's poetry, 136; on metaphors in "A Textbook of Poetry," 23–24; on method for beginning poets, 75; on Muir, 66; on the poet's preparation, 81; on rhyme, 35, 36, 37; on rhythm in poetic dictation, 14, 108; on rhythm of language in poetry, 85; on serial music, 73; on Spicer's Vancouver Festival poems, 120; at Spicer's Vancouver lectures, xxiii; on voice in poetic rhythm, 113, 114; works of, 46n.25; on writing for the voice in music, 114, 115
"Lives of the French Symbolist Poets, The" (Persky), 91n.3
"Lloyd George Knew My Father" (song), 139
"Local Legends" (Jeffers), 204
Loewinsohn, Ron, xxiii, 28, 46n.32
"London" (Blake), 139
Longinus, 10
"Long March, The" (Mao Tse-tung), 170n.5
Lorca, Federico Garcia: Creeley's "After Lorca," 144n.5; *duende* essay, 139, 142, 146n.25, 179, 212; Rilke contrasted with, 143; Spanish lemon, 200; Spicer as receiving from, 138; Spicer's attraction to, 181, 182; in Spicer's intertextual references, 174n.2. See also *After Lorca* (Spicer)
"Lusiads, The" (Camoëns), 209

Luxemburg, Rosa, 153, 169n.2

MacDiarmid, Hugh, 66
Mackintosh, Graham, xx, 172n.23, 190, 195, 208–9
Magazines, literary. See Literary magazines
Mallory, George Herbert Leigh-, 33, 48n.39, 162
Malory, Sir Thomas: as Grail quest source, 57; and Mallory, 48n.39; *Morte d'Arthur*, 58, 214; and Spicer's *The Holy Grail*, 54; in Spicer's intertextual references, 174n.2
"Man with the Blue Guitar, The" (Stevens), 72, 222
Mao Tse-tung, 153, 155, 156, 170n.5
Marais, Jean, 188
Marlowe, Christopher, 117, 230
Martial, 164
Martians: in film and radio, 189–92; "My Favorite Martian," 48n.40, 192; as source of Spicer's poetry, 2, 3, 43n.3, 133, 189–92; Spicer and Ryan speaking Martian, 12–13
Maximus Poems, The (Olson), 43n.3, 53
Mayakovsky, Vladimir, 162, 163, 171n.18
Mays, Willie, 75, 84, 127, 144n.11
McCarthyism, 159, 189, 191
McCovey, Willie, 28, 46n.32
McDougall, William, 45n.18
McGann, Jerome, 44n.13, 174n.1
Medieval Scenes (Duncan), 52, 55, 91n.6, 143n.3
"Medium, The" (Blaser), 68–69
Mediums (psychic), 7, 10, 17, 42n.3, 43n.8
Meinrad, St., 240–41
Melville, Herman, 180
Mencken, H. L., 196n.23
Mental Radio (Sinclair), 188
Mercer, Johnny, 168, 174n.2
Metaphors, 185–87
Meyerson, Martin, 171n.13
Miles, Josephine, 174n.2
Miller, Henry, 227–28
Mirroring, textual, 218–23
Mondragón, Sergio, 146n.28
Monk, Thelonious, 81, 141
Monroe, Marilyn, 140, 214, 223

Sather Gate, 159, 170n.11; Spicer's lecture at, 149. *See also* Free Speech Movement
"Unvert Manifesto" (Spicer), 151, 217n
Upanishads, 164
Uzbeks, 30, 47n.36

Valéry, Paul, 133, 145n.18, 178, 216
Vancouver Festival (1965), xxiii, 103
Vancouver poetry festival (1963), xxiii, 44n.15
Vietnam War, 149, 153, 215
"Voyages II" (Crane), 83
"Voyages V" (Crane), 83, 95n.39

Wah, Fred, 143n.1
Walker, Jimmy, 32–33, 48n.38
Warren, Robert Penn, 164
Waste Land, The (Eliot), 30, 91n.6, 178
Watts Towers (Los Angeles), 217n
Webster, John, 230
Welch, Lew, xxiii
Welles, Orson, 188
Werner, Marta, 206n
"We Shall Overcome" (song), 163, 168
Weston, Jessie, 57, 92n.12, 174n.2
Whalen, Philip, xxiii
Wheeler, Dennis, xxiii, 75, 90, 96n.47
White Rabbit Press, 199
Whitman, Marcus, 204n.31
Whitman, Walt: in *After Lorca*, 183, 203; on baseball, 192; eastern landscape of, 203; "Facing West from California's Shores," 203; and Ginsberg's "A Supermarket in California," 205; as Grail searcher, 64, 65; "Leaves of Grass," 184; Spicer comparing himself with, 150; in Spicer's intertextual references, 174n.2; Spicer's "Ode for Walt Whitman," 219; Spicer's

"Some Notes on Whitman for Allen Joyce," 93n.21
"Who Is at My Window" (Levertov), 47n.33, 146n.22
Wieners, John, xxiii
Wilde, Oscar, 7, 43n.8
Williams, Ted, 76, 134, 145n.11
Williams, William Carlos: *Desert Music*, 28; and measure, 112; on objectness, 10, 28, 44n.13, 143; *Paterson*, 53; and Spicer's *A Red Wheelbarrow*, 219; in Spicer's genealogy of poetry, 1; in Spicer's intertextual references, 174n.2
Wimpfeling, Jacob, 238–39
Wizard of Oz (Baum), 63, 67, 93nn. 19, 24, 200, 214
Wolf, Leonard, 229
"Wreck of the Deutschland, The" (Hopkins), 108, 143n.4

Yeats, Georgie, 4–5, 40
Yeats, William Butler: "Among School Children," 137; Auden's "In Memory of W. B. Yeats," 160, 171n.14; Crazy Janes, 65; daimon of, 196; in Irish senate, 156; on letters, 210; metaphysical system of, 136–37; "Nineteen Hundred and Nineteen," 136–37, 161, 171n.15; Olson's "This is Yeats Speaking," 44n.12, 208n; poetic dictation in, 4–5, 40, 42n.1, 44n.12, 78; as precursor of Spicer, 1; revising, 78; serial poetry of, 57; in Spicer's intertextual references, 174n.2; stable poetic subject displaced by, 178; on the universe as non-tragic, 126
Young, Geoffrey, 48n.39
Young Goodman Brown (Spicer), 182n.7, 218

Zen Buddhism, 108

ABOUT THE AUTHOR

Peter Gizzi is a poet whose books include *Some Values of Landscape and Weather* (Wesleyan, 2003) and *Artificial Heart* (Burning Deck, 1998). He currently teaches at the University of Massachusetts at Amherst.

Library of Congress Cataloging-in-Publication Data
Spicer, Jack.
    The house that Jack built : the collected lectures of Jack Spicer
/ edited and with an afterword by Peter Gizzi.
        p.   cm.
    Includes bibliographical references (p.   ) and index.
    ISBN 0–8195–6339–0 (cl : alk. paper). — ISBN 0–8195–6340–4 (pa :
alk. paper).
    1. Spicer, Jack—Authorship.   2. Poetry—Authorship.   I. Gizzi,
Peter.   II. Title.
PS3569. P47Z47   1998
811'.54—dc21   97–44231